WE ARE NOT AVATARS

Also by John Barton

POETRY

A Poor Photographer
Hidden Structure
West of Darkness: Emily Carr, a Self-Portrait
Great Men
Notes Toward a Family Tree
Designs from the Interior
Sweet Ellipsis
Hypothesis
Hymn
For the Boy with the Eyes of the Virgin: Selected Poems
Polari

CHAPBOOKS

Destinations, Leaving the Map
Oxygen
Shroud
Runoff
Asymmetries (In the House of the Present and The Strata)
Balletomane: The Program Notes of Lincoln Kirstein
Reframing Paul Cadmus
Visible Not Seen: Queer Expression in the Age of Equity
Windsock

EDITOR

Silences
belles lettres / beautiful letters
We All Begin in a Little Magazine: Arc and the Promise of Canada's Poets, 1978–1998
Seminal: The Anthology of Canada's Gay-Male Poets
The Malahat Review at Fifty: Canada's Iconic Literary Journal
The Essential Douglas LePan

IN TRANSLATION

À l'ouest de l'ombre. Emily Carr, un auto-portrait

WE ARE NOT
AVATARS

— Essays, Memoirs, Manifestos —

JOHN BARTON

PALIMPSEST PRESS

Palimpsest Press
1171 Eastlawn Ave.
Windsor, Ontario. N8S 3J1
www.palimpsestpress.ca

Printed and bound by Webcom in Ontario, Canada.
Edited by Shane Neilson. Series Editor is Jim Johnstone.
Book typography and cover design by Carleton Wilson.

Palimpsest Press would like to thank the Canada Council for the Arts
and the Ontario Arts Council for their support of our publishing
program. We also acknowledge the assistance of the Government of
Ontario through the Ontario Book Publishing Tax Credit.

LIBRARY AND ARCHIVES CANADA CATALOGUING IN PUBLICATION

Title: We are not avatars : essays, memoirs, manifestos / John Barton.
Other titles: Works. Selections.
Names: Barton, John, 1957- author.
Identifiers: Canadiana 20190047712 | ISBN 9781989287217 (softcover)
Classification: LCC PS8553.A78 W4 2019 | DDC C814/.54—dc23

for Derk and Eva

Whether pain is simple as razors edging the fleshy cage,
or whether pain raves with sharks inside the ribs,
it throws a bridge of value to belief
where, towards or away from, moves intense traffic.

—Phyllis Webb

Table of Contents

SNOW ANGELS

INSIDE THE BLIND

How I Came to Lead An Authentic Life:
By Way of Introduction

OVER A RECENT AMERICANO in Discovery Coffee on Oak Bay Avenue in rainy Victoria, I read "The Ballad of Reading Gaol" for the first time. Why I had neglected one of Oscar Wilde's last great works till now eludes excuse. Wilde wrote this long narrative poem about the execution of a fellow prisoner soon after his release from prison on May 19, 1897. His sentence of two years' hard labour for gross indecency, a legal euphemism for sexual activity between men excluding sodomy, had changed him profoundly. Initially published in an edition of 800 copies in 1898, the year my maternal grandmother was born, Wilde's poem would remain a disturbing touchstone for many in the watershed years to come.

Though Reading Goal didn't permit any prisoner to witness the marked man's death, Wilde makes it clear the prison population was aware of his passing the day it took place. The consequential sweep of mortality's anonymous hand couldn't help but touch them all:

> For he has a pall, this wretched man,
>> Such as few men can claim
> Deep down below a prison-yard,
>> Naked for greater shame,
> He lies, with fetters on each foot,
>> Wrapt in a sheet of flame!

Any death makes clocks stop, but it's Wilde's evocations of the annihilating conditions he and the rest of the prison weathered that shall more permanently linger with me:

> The vilest deeds like poison weeds
>> Bloom well in prison-air;
> It is only what is good in Man
>> That wastes and withers there:

Pale Anguish keeps the heavy gate,
And the Warder is despair.

Every stanza in Wilde's poem is as deeply etched a tracing of torment as any print by Goya. By publishing it under the pseudonym c.3.3., the coordinates for his block, landing, and cell, Wilde aimed to deflect attention from himself in order to give his carefully wrought lines a slim chance of fomenting outcry about the penal system's brutalities rather than to risk having his views dismissed because his authorship, if known, would taint them with his own crimes. He had come to feel a solidarity with "the criminal classes"—"a new experience for me"[1]—his conviction having forced him to count himself among them. The agonies Wilde relates are acutely personal:

And the wild regrets, and the bloody sweats
None knew so well as I ....

Maybe Wilde felt he knew shame better than most because, prior to his imprisonment, he could never have guessed he would one day find himself crushed by an unjust conviction. Detention and isolation had shorn him of his naivety and presumption of impunity. "Wild regrets," or "Wilde's regrets," tipped a stoved-in top hat to the poem's autobiographical nature. It invited his coterie of friends, supporters, and later devotees to read in the freedoms he had been deprived of because of his carnal desires, though of these he makes no mention. In comparison, the loss of wealth, status, and reputation, also barely mentioned, seems almost immaterial. The spiritual pain Wilde describes approaches the ecstatic:

Out of his mouth a red, red rose!
Out of his heart a white!
For who can say by what strange way,
Christ brings His will to light ...

Though "The Ballad of Reading Gaol" makes palpable how incarceration broke Wilde physically and psychologically, the Victorian laws that locked Wilde away failed to break him wholly. While the poem betrays few vestiges of his sparkling

---

1   Nicholas Frankel, *Oscar Wilde: The Unrepentant Years*. Boston; Harvard, 2017, 147.

wit, his moral compass and sharp intelligence survive intact. His name eventually appeared in square brackets below c.3.3 on the seventh edition's title page.

It was into Wilde's legacy of brokenness and resilience that I was born in 1957, sixty years after the poem's composition, the year the British government released the Report of the Departmental Committee on Homosexual Offences and Prostitution. Better known as the Wolfenden Report, named after Sir John Wolfenden, the committee's chair who was also rumoured to have had a gay son, it took another decade for the British government to act on Sir John's recommendation to lift the criminal proscriptions against same-sex relations between consenting adults, albeit only in England and Wales once the emending legislation was passed. Apart from chemical sterilization offered to convicted gay men like Alan Turing as an alternative to prison, this repeal stood as the first significant change in our treatment since the laws under which Wilde had been prosecuted came into force in 1885.

In 1967, I wouldn't have understood what such a legal change would mean for people like me, since I was only ten years old. Nor would I have been aware that Canada had then started what turned out to be a two-year-long debate about making similar changes to our own statutes. The many new municipal parks, stadia, arts centres, and eternal flames unveiled as nation-building initiatives during Centennial Year would have more readily caught my imagination. Of course, the liberalizations beginning to see light in the 1960s were decades in the making. As an adult, it took me years of reading to realize I had grown up against a backdrop of change that's made the life I have led and the writing career I have pursued abundantly tenable. The history made around me as a child was never integrated into my junior-high or high-school curriculum. Buggery's virtues were never once debated in Health class.

Nor was an adolescent bedroom in 1970s northwest Calgary, where I hid behind a camouflage of *The Lord of the Rings*, blacklight posters, Melanie LPs, and a portable phonograph, a good place to join the debate. That said, I remember a premonition of self-awareness charge through me when my parents took me to see the film adaptation of *Cabaret* when I was in Grade 10. The fillip of Liza Minnelli's emerald fingernails and Joel Grey's conspiratorial leer signaled to me in a code I did not then attempt to crack that my future could be other than what society kept telling me it should be. I became a lifelong devotee of the novels of Christopher Isherwood, upon whose work the stage play, musical, and film are based, though I'd later learn he disparaged every theatrical and cinematic incarnation of his iconic characters, Sally Bowles and the cipher narrator he'd based on himself. Steady and slow, mine was an ever more literate, literary coming out. It took a while for it to register that the subtext of everything Isherwood wrote pertained to me. When I was a university student, I came across his 1976 memoir, *Christopher and His Kind,* which retells the stories he recounted in *Mr. Norris Changes Trains* and *Goodbye to Berlin,* the two books upon which *Cabaret* is based. This time he does not queer-wash his experiences and instead gives prominence to the not-so-underground gay culture of Germany during the closing libertine years of the Weimar Republic.

The first time I was brave enough to attempt writing a queer poem was in the fall of 1979. I had just moved into a derelict, faux-adobe apartment block on View Street at the periphery of downtown Victoria. The red door into my apartment was discreetly off the building's gateless courtyard; vines of ivy cobwebbed my front window. In "Enfant Terrible" the narrator is haunted by the ghost of Arthur Rimbaud and his decision to forsake renown in favour of running off to live overseas and experience firsthand the illuminations his poems had extolled:

Rimbaud, you look over my shoulder
in white Abyssinian dress
as I attempt to fix you down
each wall, each word

a stress. Though my back is turned
I feel the window behind you
open through your lack of flesh.
You laugh. The notes of your voice

flutter in the wind like the scarves
of Harari women.
                              Arthur, tell me,
how many did you let go

to the highlands to calve your sons?
Or did you have none,
women, I mean, all those years alone
in Aden before you left

to die in France? What of Verlaine,
his bullet in your wrist? Was his
the body you had last? When you gave up
words, did you forfeit love as well?[2]

Rimbaud was twenty-one when he shook off poetry's mantle of gold leaf; I was twenty-two and a student of institutionalized creative writing at the University of Victoria. I definitely couldn't workshop "Enfant Terrible" in class, but I did show it to a friend who immediately observed that it explained *Everything*. It took me another decade to start publishing *Everything* and to formulate an aesthetic of candour and completeness that still animates my work. At the time I wrote the poem's first draft, I didn't know I had put pen to paper ten years after Pierre Elliott Trudeau's government had liberalized Canada's laws pertaining to homosexuality, a clinical word I have never liked. Nor did I know that on June 27, 1969, the day after the bill had received royal assent, the Stonewall Riots occupied the cobbled streets of Greenwich Village in New York for three nights, launching the gay-liberation movement that would shake down attitudes as well as laws. Like so much that has made my life meaningful, I learned about Canada's criminal-code changes and the Big Apple's riots long after they took place, learning also that they had coincided with Judy Garland's death. Unlike Wilde, I was not in Kansas anymore. I've never been vulnerable to being labelled a criminal, at least in the eyes of the law. Accusations of lawlessness in festive and other senses could not be avoided.

Though I had come out to myself years before in poems I had been slow to share, I started coming out fashionably late in the flesh. I was twenty-eight, it was 1985 and by then the AIDS epidemic had gained the force of a juggernaut. The sentence the virus imposed was not two years of hard labour but a death no doctor could commute. There was safe sex, of course, and I found safety in numbers. I had just moved to Ottawa, mecca of librarians; at library school, I'd read David Leavitt's *Family Dancing* and Jane Rule's *Desert of the Heart*. I joined a gay-men's discussion group and later a queer swim team and a gay-men's reading circle that met at After Stonewall, Ottawa's now-defunct LGBT bookstore. For more than a decade, we weighed the merits of books like Alan Hollinghurst's *The Swimming-Pool Library*, Lillian Faderman's *Odd Girls and Twilight Lovers*, Thom Gunn's *The Man with Night Sweats*, Leslie Feinberg's

---

2   John Barton, *Great Men*. Kingston: Quarry, 1990, 70.

Stone Butch Blues, Simon LeVay's *Queer Science,* and Tony Kushner's *Angels in America,* among countless novels, histories, collections of poetry, memoirs, theoretical works, and plays. It was both higher education and basic training. We followed the store as it moved from basement to second-floor to storefront locations and, because of David Rimmer's welcoming smile, it was a social hub for more than just us. In 1990, soon after he opened the store, David hosted what would be his first book-signing when Quarry Press published *Great Men,* my fourth book of poems. We became friends and fell into the habit of having dinner at a nearby Vietnamese restaurant each second Tuesday of the month before going back to the store to set up chairs. Ideas arising from the books the group discussed would take a second breath in my poems.

My writing over four decades has evolved in step with the attainment of equality rights in Canada and with the flowering of an orchidaceous, articulate queer culture. I have written to find a community of like minds and to ensure this community is heard. Many tell me that being so open has involved courage, but does courage pertain when I have had no choice but to map my version of the truth in order to live a life that feels authentic? In the essays, memoirs, and manifestos collected here, I believe my passions are clear. They elucidate a fascination embracing not only queer experience but also poetry and my life's work as an editor. My queerness nonetheless infuses every word and accomplishment, for who we are informs our attitudes, locates our polestars, and filters the light that guides us. I am a gay-male writer, not a writer who happens to be gay and male, and I have many concurrent identities, including those of participant and observer. While I decry the hypocrisies of our liberal, self-congratulatory, often unconsciously homophobic culture, I am in awe of the many from all walks of life whose resolve never fails to stir me. The many may be the queer poets who came before me and upon whose shoulders I find myself standing, or they may be the men who succumbed to or now live with AIDS, men who at their darkest may have wondered if Wilde might have written "And alien tears will fill for him / Pity's long-broken urn" with their sufferings in mind. They may be the men and women who mentored and inspired me as a poet and editor, whose generosity taught me how to mentor. After growing up in a society that has only recently stopped withholding the full pleasures and responsibilities of citizenship from people like me, I have no stake in being critical of others for criticism's and literary discrimination's sake. In essays about queer praxis, the craft of poetry, poets, and the art of editing, I aim to strike a note of affirmation.

It's appropriate *We Are Not Avatars'* publication falls immediately before the fiftieth anniversary in June 2019 of the decriminalization of same-sex relations between consenting adults in Canada. The writing of the book's contents overlaps with the last twenty or so years of this progressively more enlightened half-century. While I have revised these essays for republication and ordered them thematically rather than chronologically, they reflect my thoughts when each was written and I hope, if read together, trace how my thinking's grown and even changed. No longer am I among the outcasts Wilde had so painfully mourned. Maybe I never have been.

Victoria, British Columbia
May 2019

MEN OF HONOUR

Visible but Not Seen: Queer Expression in the Age of Equity

ON NOVEMBER 28, 2017, Justin Trudeau rose in the House of Commons to apologize to members of the LGBTQ2S community.[1] On behalf of the federal government, he expressed remorse that, because of their sexual orientation, thousands of queer people were forced out of the civil service, the RCMP, and the military after the Second World War until the early 1990s. Two months before Bruce McArthur was arrested for preying upon racialized and Caucasian men in Toronto's gay village, I watched the prime minister's apology stream live on my iPhone at my desk at work. While the principal focus of his remarks did not apply to me because I was never stripped of a government job because I am a gay man, I still felt addressed. During my seventeen years as a federal employee in Ottawa from 1986 to 2003, I had known men who had been shown the door, men who constitute not even a meaningful sample of the actual number of people affected. Trudeau also acknowledged that the policies and laws made by postwar governments unquestioningly embraced a societally sanctioned homophobia that had been ruining lives since before the beginning of the last century. Born in Alberta over a decade before New York's Stonewall Riots launched a global struggle for rights in June 1969, I'd enjoyed a degree of schoolyard harassment so corrosive and routine that, looking back, I recognize the consequential self-loathing and fear delayed my coming out by at least ten years.

I watched Trudeau's speech with a friend, a millennial identifying as lesbian. Though she came of age long after the legal instruments protecting our community had become law, she did not feel, based on her own experiences, that

---

1   Remarks by Prime Minister Justin Trudeau in apology to LGBTQ2S Canadians can be read at https://pm.gc.ca/ eng/news/2017/11/28/remarks-prime-minister-justin-trudeau-apologize-lgbtq2-canadians. Retrieved on June 1, 2018. The Just Society Committee of Egale Canada Human Rights Trust (https://egale.ca) and the We Demand an Apology Network (http://p-sec.org/we-demand-an-apology/), a coalition of academics and other stakeholders, led by members of the P-SEC (Psycho-Social Ethnography of the Commonplace) Research Group, successfully lobbied the federal government to have the historic wrongs requiring this apology acknowledged and appropriately addressed.

homophobia had been wholly eliminated from public or private spheres and
agreed that the battle for equitable treatment was far from over. When talking
with my non-queer, albeit queer-positive, friends, I find they often speak of the
struggle for same-sex equality rights as if it were a now-closed historical period. "You guys can marry now." "Can conceive, adopt, and raise children." "We
see you as just folks now." Sometimes it sounds as if our victory is theirs, our
peace in their time. They forget rights may be withdrawn at speeds inverse to
how long they took to enshrine. How many of them know that the legislation
to include freedom from discrimination based on gender identity and/or expression in the Canadian Human Rights Act and to extend protection from
hate propaganda to the trans community in the Criminal Code only attained
royal assent on June 19, 2017? Do they grasp that the amendment is merely a
first step toward other necessary jurisprudence? Many of my non-queer friends
forget—many of my queer friends *also* appear to forget—that though laws can
be enacted, changes of heart aren't as easily legislated. Individual agency is only
as vital as our willingness to honour, enforce, and defend laws.

In April 2017, seven months before Trudeau's apology, the Canada Council
unveiled and began to trumpet the virtues of its revised approach to the administration and awarding of grants. Many privately expressed surprise that the
Council did not identify queer artists as meriting—either as grant recipients or
through opportunities offered by Council-funded arts groups—focused support, recognition, and visibility alongside our Indigenous, racialized, and deaf
and/or disabled peers. This targeted assistance, which is meant to ensure that
space is made for artists who self-identify as members of one or more of these
categories, is very discreetly acknowledged on the Council's website as bringing it into compliance with the Employment Equity Act, which regulates hiring
in federal-government departments and in federally regulated organizations to
ensure that the shards making up the national mosaic more amicably cohere.
In the civil service, if two applicants for a job are determined to have *exactly
the same credentials* after being assessed, it must be offered to the one who falls
into one (or more) of four categories; the Council offers shelter to only three
of them. How it has adapted the federal government's approach to hiring to the
awarding of grants to individuals and arts groups from across the country is not
explained.

The Canada Council's proudly waved conformity to the Employment
Equity Act is not the first instance I've come face to face with the narrowness
with which the latter defines equity. I joined the civil service shortly after the

Act came into force in the mid-1980s and, when browsing job postings in hopes of career advancement, I'd wonder why similar protections were not extended to me as a member of an "invisible minority"—a minority that, as Trudeau's apology shows, long required protection inside and outside federal employ. As the product of an era when rights and who deserves them were differently conceived, an era when little more than a safeguard from criminal prosecution had been extended to members of the queer community, the decades-old Act desperately requires revision. How especially disappointing to me as a writer and a gay man that an institution as proud of being of the zeitgeist as the Canada Council self-presents could embrace outmoded legislation without taking it upon itself to expand the categories meriting protection or even to follow the Act as written. Like the LGBTQ2S community, women, the fourth category named in the Act, are *not* sheltered under the Council's equity's umbrella. Perhaps, safe inside their climate-controlled offices, policy makers took a cafeteria approach to equity by picking and choosing between potential communities of artists to shelter from the rain? How does such grazing and gormandizing jive with the Council's Michelin-star tastes and reputation? Before the new funding strategy was made public, I'd never felt invisible as a queer artist when seeking Council support for my writing. Now I've never felt more. This absurd irony is not lost on many in the present era of greater queer agency.

Does the Council share the opinions of my non-queer friends, comfortably assuming that the queer community's struggle for equal rights is now a fait accompli and that queer artists face no further difficulties in articulating and sharing the particulars of their stories? Or, in its desire not to stand out in all the wrong ways, has the queer community so utterly seduced the non-queer community, which determines policies for all and controls the purse strings at many august institutions like the Council, into believing that, since we are now so like them, no surviving differences merit notice, investigation, or representation? In "The Future of Queer" from the January 2018 issue of *Harper's*, Fenton Johnson, author of the AIDS memoir *Geography of the Heart*, laments that "What we [the queer community] met and worked and marched and wrote and died for was radical transformation. What we settled for was marriage."[2] Encouraged by the assimilationist tendencies of many of my peers, has the Council unthinkingly fallen into a similar mindset? Has the Council forgotten, as Johnson fears that the queer community has itself, that the "embrace of the gift of our essential

---

2   Fenton Johnson, "The Future of Queer," *Harper's Magazine*, 336 (112) 28.

difference was" and *is* "the wellspring of queer creativity"?[3] That sense of difference includes not only our "pride" in our distinctiveness, which is more than
what is celebrated superficially at annual Pride marches nationwide, but also
involves an awareness of the legacy of oppression and resistance from which
we have emerged. The probing of that difference and its history of trauma, endurance, and commemoration, in face of a growing societal complacency as to
what form or forms it takes, strikes me as being what is at stake.

Certainly, there are many well-established queer writers in Canada like
Shyam Selvaduri and Helen Humphreys who enjoy large national and international followings, but anyone familiar with the history of queer publishing
of the last quarter-century knows that many LGBTQ2S authors in North America were dropped by large publishers in the late 1990s and early 2000s when
sales of their books did not realize the commercial hopes placed in them. If
you subscribe, as I do, to Boston's *Gay and Lesbian Literary Review/Worldwide*,
you'd notice that many books discussed or advertised inside its pages are published by obscure or unfamiliar presses. Readers of queer writing should feel
indebted to American academic presses like Minnesota and Wisconsin, which
have taken up the slack by devoting a significant quotient of their lists to LG-
BTQ2S poetry, fiction, and nonfiction. If only their peers north of the border
would do the same. Among English-language publishers in Canada, Arsenal
Pulp deserves praise as our only truly queer-focused press and its list is both
prestigious and diverse. Otherwise LGBTQ2S writers are largely published hel-
ter-skelter by the small presses in this country, and happily so, but we still face
the possibility of being misread by editors, our history misunderstood, and
our candour pushing publishers outside their comfort zones, often to our own
detriment.

Maybe thirty-five years of publishing progressively more open writing
has made me weary. When *Hidden Structure*, my first candidly queer book of
poems was published in 1984, Robin Skelton, with whom I'd studied poetry
for three years, well-meaningly chose the neutral "dual sexuality" to describe
the anguish the book plumbs. In 1994, the marketing department at House of
Anansi, albeit during its Stoddart years, refused to use the word "gay" in the
cover copy of *Designs from the Interior*, my sixth book of poetry, and instead
chose to rely on Timothy Findley's effusive blurb to get the message across in
a voice other than their own, fearing "gay" would limit sales rather than reach

---

3   Ibid, 31.

out to a potentially enthusiastic (and underserved) community of readers. In 1998, a former associate editor of *PRISM international* told me that "Homo-eroticism," a poem I'd submitted the year before, had inspired controversy among her peers on the board. The poem reconfigures Freud's Oedipus complex theory in gay terms, with a young boy projecting his unconscious sexual feelings upon his father instead of upon his mother, yet many at the magazine were shocked and assumed I was endorsing pederasty. In 2002, I chose to alter a poem that ultimately won a CBC Literary Award, downplaying the few obvious queer references because I feared they would over-challenge contest screeners and judges. I presumed they'd been coached to set aside any entry with overt references to "sexually aberrant behaviours" because it mightn't fly with the readers of *enRoute*, Air Canada's inflight magazine, where the CBC Literary Award winners still see print. How justified this fear really was then and may remain, I don't know, but sixteen years ago friends had encouraged me to second-guess myself. In 2007, Zachariah Wells dismissed the significance of the first historically oriented anthology of gay-male poetry published in Canada, *Seminal: The Anthology of Canada's Gay Male Poets*, which I edited with Billeh Nickerson. Its contributors range in time from nineteenth-century Émile Nelligan to twenty-first-century Sean Horlor. "At an earlier date—even twenty years ago, say—this anthology might have made a bold, shockingly defiant, statement," wrote Wells, "but now, with homosexuality not only being 'tolerated' (awful, hateful word) more by an increasingly large percentage of the population, but even enjoying a certain vogue in popular culture, it seems a bit late"[4]—as if defining a tradition or locating a past for it for the first time can ever be a dated idea.

Many will chafe at these examples from the not-so-long-ago, but long-ago-enough "bad-old" days. However, I am sad to say that queer students enrolled in the Department of Writing at the University of Victoria, where I edited *The Malahat Review* until January 2018, have told me often enough that they feel uncomfortable presenting identity-specific work in workshop. Either it's met with silence or the instructors fail to pick up on the homophobia unconsciously articulated by non-queer students.[5] And only recently a friend, a fellow (straight)

---

4   Zachariah Wells, "Seminal," *Career Limiting Moves: Saying Shit I Shouldn't Since 1977* (http://zachariahwells. blogspot.com/search?q=seminal). Retrieved May 28, 2018.

5   According to *The Pink Agenda* (Ottawa: Canadian Centre for Gender and Sexual Diversity, 2017), "51% of LGBTQ2S students reported that they do not feel accepted in school, compared to 19% of non-LGBTQ2S students."

poet, told me that when he asks his (similarly straight) peers if they've read "the latest book by John Barton," they admit that they don't read gay writers, as if there's nothing to learn from or find in common with the likes of me.

Even those who never read queer writing can't help but notice that more of it is published than ever before, which many would suggest throws the legitimacy of my concerns into question. So why am I so bothered? That *The World is a Wound*, a sexually frank first book by Two-Spirit Indigenous poet Billy-Ray Belcourt, recently won the 2018 Griffin Poetry Prize, in addition to being nominated for the Governor General's Literary Award for Poetry and for two other major national literary awards[6], should be a salve to, if not wholly assuage my doubts. Will we look back in five or twenty-five years and recognize Belcourt as the first queer writer to have definitively broken through what R. M. Vaughan has painted as "the lavender ceiling"[7] by winning a prize that's significant not only because it comes with a $65,000 purse? Should we honour him as such now? Zoe Whittall cites Vaughan's epithet in a perplexed review of Anne Marie MacDonald's 2014 novel, *Adult Onset*, recalling that he floated it in remarks made in the mid-2000s on a panel about LGBTQ2S writing to characterize the barriers facing "gay literary authors who, [because they] write honestly about contemporary gay life[,] are rarely published to wide acclaim by mainstream publishers in Canada, and are often relegated to the sidelines and the small presses." The panel member representing "the voice of the young," Whittall remembers being "buoyed to be a part of what might be the generation for which that has shifted." A decade later, in her review of Macdonald, she admits that "Largely, [Vaughan's] observations remain true"[8] despite the fact that *Adult Onset* appeared under the imprint of Knopf Canada. Although Belcourt's book is published by the much-less-known, but still-much-valued Frontenac House (a press more than friendly to queer writing), perhaps the recognition he's received for it thus far is truly a bellwether of change. He is the third Indigenous and first Two-Spirit poet in as many years to win the Griffin Poetry Prize, a streak that nevertheless pales beside the almost uninterrupted

---

6   *The World is a Wound* was also nominated for the Gerald Lampert Memorial Award and the Raymond Souster Award, two prizes given out annually by the League of Canadian Poets.

7   A poet must be considered to have "arrived" after winning a prize that is invariably described as the world's largest financial prize for a single collection of poetry.

8   Zoe Whittall, "Queerer Than Fiction," *The Walrus*, October 21, 2014 [updated September 8, 2017] (https://thewalrus.ca/queerer-than-fiction/). Retrieved June 4, 2018.

number of settler writers to have won it in the years prior.[9] His next book will be more prominently published by the House of Anansi.

Because of the apparently more receptive ear now being turned to queer voices, Rachel Giese recently chided Hollywood in the *Globe and Mail* for continually limiting its queer-focused films like *Love, Simon* (a *Pretty in Pink*-esque rom-com in which a male high-school student falls for another boy) to coming-out stories when so many other queer plotlines and voices deserve mainstream exposure. Hollywood producers need only look, Giese says, to indie films and the diverse new books by queer authors for inspiration.[10] Yet there is a reason why the same kinds of queer stories keep getting told over and over. They're unthreateningly familiar. Non-queer people can still see themselves in plotlines like the coming-out story because they're the ones being come out to. Thus, it becomes their story, entitling them to celebrate their triumph of being "accepting" and "without prejudice." Importantly, the unity of the family, a much-valued and straight-colonized institution, has been preserved. Marriage is another familiar plotline. Being portrayed as grateful, nonthreatening family members who marry against a background of victory is what queer people have allegedly fought for. It allows them to fit in and enjoy their hard-won rights privately—except when everyone queer and non-queer hits the streets to cheer the drag queens and muscle bears flitting by in a corporate-sponsored Pride parade. Though they may have started in the 1970s as marches to advocate for rights in large cities in Western democracies, and though they dangerously continue to do so in countries like Turkey and Russia, Pride parades have more often than not become highly entertaining circuses that gild towns large and small with a colourful, artificial, and *safe* sense of what difference is. The according of rights to excluded communities is one way for governments to exert control over and regulate behaviours once viewed as aberrant and make former pariahs more like the silent majority of voters whose tendency to indifference somehow keeps them in power. It also allows government leaders to more easily apologize after the fact than initiate change at the time of crisis. No doubt, allowing for inflation, it has been cheaper to extend rights (and services) to us now than it was to convict and incarcerate us in the past. But who and what is

---

9   It can't be forgotten that Dionne Brand won the Griffin Poetry Prize for *Ossuaries* seven years earlier in 2011.

10   Rachel Giese, "Lose the plot: why there's more than one queer narrative" (https://www. theglobeandmail.com/opinion/article-lose-the-plot-why-theres-more-than-one-queer-narrative), *Globe and Mail*, April 6, 2018. Retrieved May 27, 2018.

being left out? Has the narrative arc that queer stories trace in popular culture today become unchallenging and has the bandwidth of the mainstream's comfort zone determined that they are the only ones picked up out of the static and heard? Has anyone recently written a play as provocative and ground-breaking as Michel Tremblay's *Hosanna* was in the 1970s? When it premiered, was it embraced more for its commentary on the status of Quebec within Canada than on the plight of non-conforming gay men like the cross-dressing Hosanna and her lover, the leather-clad Cuirette[11]?

Policy makers at the Canada Council should perhaps read *The Pink Agenda*, a report prepared in July 2017 by the Canadian Centre for Gender and Sexual Diversity, whose offices are only a few minutes' walk from their own in downtown Ottawa. The report outlines what the CCGSD has assessed to be the next steps for greater inclusion and recognition of the queer community in the Canadian polis. Alongside greater access to education, improvement in health care, and the rights of LGBTQ2S people to age with dignity,[12] its authors advocate for the provision of material "support [to] artists, performers, and festivals" by "increas[ing] grants and funding for queer and trans artists, activists, and youth."[13] Emphasizing that the redress of colonization would be incomplete if it ignored the Two-Spirit,[14] they give prominence to the urgent need to "rehabilitate and integrate Indigenous Two-Spirit culture in all policies impacting queer and trans people"[15] (an obligation specifically mentioned by Trudeau in his apology). The CCGSD urges politicians and senior civil servants to foster trans and queer rights internationally,[16] pointing out that 69% of Canada's asylum claims involve issues of sexual orientation and gender expression.[17] The stories behind the CCGSD's call to action demand being told and heard. Under what better auspices than the Canada Council and its sensitively articulated and now more robust program criteria? Anyone at the Council who listened to or read a transcript of Trudeau's apology must recall that he affirmed his government "will work with the academic community and stakeholders"—the artists of this country estimate themselves to be stakeholders who'd like to believe that

---

11 "Cuir," similar in pronunciation to "queer," is French for leather.
12 *The Pink Agenda*, Ottawa: Canadian Centre for Gender and Sexual Diversity, 2017, 10.
13 Ibid, 24.
14 Ibid, 21.
15 Ibid, 24.
16 Ibid, 6.
17 Ibid.

the Council has their back—"to ensure that [our LGBTQ2S] history is known and publicly accessible."[18] The prime minister's commitment obliges Council policy makers to establish distinct programs to promote queer artists' creative responses to the specifics of our history and present experience.

For the Council and Canadians in general to take an "the-kids-are-now-all-right" attitude toward the queer community is to negate two interrelated facts: that the struggle to attain rights was difficult and that the circumstances the struggle overcame have left lingering aftereffects. Because queer people are not necessarily related by blood, they are not understood to bear the scars of inter-generational trauma. It is falsely assumed, I would allege, that the legal protections slowly put in place since 1969 have cauterized misfortune's wounds. It's still possible, however, that the consequences Oscar Wilde and Alan Turing had faced may haunt later generations, as they did those who came of age in the twentieth century, especially when lobbies, once they obtain power, can elect to revoke laws or rescind policies that don't mirror their moral taste. The Ford government's cancellation of Ontario's 2015 sex education curricula on July 16, 2018, is an excellent case in point. Many of the queer members of the civil service who were let go in disgrace (suddenly, brutally) from careers that should have lasted them a lifetime bear psychic scars no amount of financial compensation will ever heal.[19] Nor can anyone who lives with the chronic ravages of AIDS or merely copes with the legacy of long-term, routine prejudice truly recover without the public acknowledgement of the cost both have exacted. Who can put aside the stigma of a criminal record for having consensual sex with a member of the same sex?[20] With conscious redress, all these scars will not necessarily fade with the passing of those who originally bore them but may instead surface insidiously in the experiences forming queer identities today and in the future. I have long believed that we will not be able to declare the oppression of same-sex and trans experience as definitively a thing of the regrettable past until the suicide-attempt rate among LGBTQ2S youth falls to the rate among youth in general.[21]

---

18 Trudeau, ibid.

19 The federal government has established a fund of $100 million as part of the settlement of a class action suit under the purview of the Federal Court of Canada and made in the name of the several thousand affected Canadians.

20 To help alleviate the stigma, Bill-66 (The Expungement of Historically Unjust Conviction Act) slowly made its way through the House of Commons and was passed on June 25, 2018. I discuss the weaknesses of the act later in this essay.

21 According to Egale, the suicide-attempt rate among LGB teens was 33% in comparison to

No queer artists working in a western country today should now feel it necessary to censor themselves to the extent that E. M. Forster chose to in his time. He decided that *Maurice*, his only candidly queer novel and a pivotal book for me, should not be published until after his death. Almost sixty years after the first draft was completed in 1914, it was published in 1971. Forster suppressed the novel because of its content, which plumbs the illegalities for which Oscar Wilde had been imprisoned just over fifteen years before. He also felt certain that no one would endorse a story about two male lovers with a happy ending, albeit one occurring off-grid like Robin Hood and his merry men's (a different set of criminals) in a "greenwood" not too unlike Sherwood Forest. By the time he wrote the initial draft of *Maurice*, four years had elapsed in the fourteen-year gap between the publication of his two great books, *Howards End* in 1910 and *A Passage to India*, in 1924, the last novel he published in his lifetime. Over the intervening decade he struggled with the realization he could not write and publish the kind of stories that now compelled him most.[22] *A Passage to India* launched an almost-total, self-imposed literary/imaginative silence that lasted until his death, a silence he broke only with radio addresses, reviews, essays, and lectures later collected and published in books; and volumes of travel writing—activities that allowed him to remain a public figure at the forefront of British letters. According to his biographer, P. N. Furbank, Forster cited a "practical reason for giving up on novel-writing: namely that, being a homosexual, he grew bored with writing about marriage and the relations of men and women."[23] Ever since I first read *Maurice* in the late 1970s, I have wondered what he might have published under different conditions, my sense of his unwritten output deepening with each decade I have gotten older. Had he been alive during our time, and given he was an acute observer of the manners and ills of many classes of people, God knows what kind of comedy Forster might have made of same-sex nuptials in Canada prior to 2005, the year the Civil Marriage Act passed and same-sex marriage became sanctioned nationwide. For just over a year, after the provincial Court of Appeal ruled in June 2003 that

---

7% in the general population in 2007. In 2010, in Ontario, 47% of trans youth in Ontario considered suicide and 19% attempted suicide in the preceding year (https://egale.ca/backgrounder-lgbtq-youth-suicide/). Retrieved April 16, 2018.

22 Damon Galgut's novel, *Arctic Summer* (McClelland & Stewart, 2014), provides fascinating insights into Forster's trajectory as a gay man, a term he'd not have used, during this crucial fourteen years.

23 P. N. Furbank, *E. M. Forster: A Life*. New York: Harcourt Brace Jovanovich, 1978, 132.

queer couples could get hitched in Ontario—over the months to come, the other provinces would start falling like dominoes except for Alberta and Prince Edward Island—it was not possible for them to divorce. Few western writers' circumstances may be as dramatic as Forster's, but Canada has its own examples of queer authors who may not have maximized their creative potential as fully as they might have; and to think that, like them, Forster may not have fully realized his gift is truly an astonishing prospect to entertain, considering his canonical centrality to twentieth-century writing in English. We should not risk having any of our present and future queer writers of substance join the compromised ranks of writers as seminal as Edward Lacey and Scott Symons because of their sexual orientation or gender expression, or even come close to joining them. The Canada Council must guarantee that all queer literary fates are more than likely to be otherwise.

The fiftieth-anniversary revival of *The Boys in the Band* opened in New York at the end of May 2018. Esteemed today as the first canonical "gay play," it premiered off Broadway in 1968 and was still running months later, during the Stonewall riots and beyond. As theatre critic Jesse Green pointed out in the *New York Times* last February, the term "gay play" is crucial to understanding its importance, for unlike, say, Tennessee Williams' *The Glass Menagerie*, *Boys* was authored by an openly gay-male playwright, Mort Crowley, who unapologetically put the lives of gay men on stage for all to see, often to the horror of his gay-male contemporaries.[24] Both controversial and well-attended during its original, history-making run, many now elect to damn it as a period piece about gay-male self-loathing. Others argue it articulates the shame that the queer-rights movement was on the threshold of repudiating and reminds us of the lives gay men felt obliged to lead before destiny turned a contested but necessary corner for the better. As Jim Parsons, star of the situation comedy *The Big Bang Theory* and one of the actors in *Boys'* all-openly-gay-male cast, observes in an interview appearing in *The Advocate*, "It's true how much has changed, and how much hasn't changed. It seems to me that there is not a moment, a reaction, a statement, a feeling, a take on anything, that any of these men have in this play from [fifty] years ago that can't be and

---

24 Jesse Green, "A Brief History of Gay Theatre, in Three Acts: On the Return of Boys in the Band and Why It Matters More Than Ever," *New York Times*, February 26, 2018 (https://www.nytimes.com/2018/02/26/t-magazine/gay-theater-history-boys-in-the-band.html) Retrieved June 4, 2018.

isn't daily replicated in the lives of gay people now—just perhaps not to the same degree."[25]

In other words, fifty years is a very short period of time to enact changes profound enough to render what was arduously overcome suddenly irrelevant to the lives LGBTQ2S people pursue today and will in the future. "[A] lot more people are out," Parson acknowledges, "and…I still think that means there is this struggle at a certain level. It may not be entirely unpleasant—I'm not saying that—but a struggle. You do have, if not an armor that's built up from having to struggle, you do have at least a tiny bit of this ability to wage battle when you need to."[26] We may no longer be legally vulnerable for being caught *in flagrante* with someone of the same sex or face violent opposition in giving voice to a gender expression at variance from the one that birth had arbitrarily assigned us, but all's still not clear sailing either, with RuPaul as the figurehead on our galley ship, waving a hand-sewn rainbow flag. As Jesse Green laments in *The New York Times*, "almost no new [plays] are on the horizon to join"[27] *The Boys in the Band* and other iconic gay plays like *Torch Song* and *Angels in America* that have just stridden, are presently striding, or are scheduled for the boards of Broadway in lucrative revivals.

The prime minister's apology to the LGBTQ2S community is therefore only one more beginning after many previous beginnings, like same-sex marriage, and not, as many non-queer Canadians might assume, a belated pendant to a decades-long struggle for the right to lead fully realized, unpoliced queer lives. As playwright, actor, and journalist Rob Salerno pointed out in *The National Post* the day before Trudeau rose in Parliament, many laws passed years ago to proscribe the rights of queer people to fulfill their lives as they see fit are still in force despite the gradual imposition of a larger rights' framework. "The process of full reconciliation, healing, and inclusion can only be complete," Salerno concludes, "when the government eliminates the [vestigial] legal tools it uses to oppress us."[28] What remains illegal, if thankfully not routinely enforced—adults having consensual relations with more than one person of the same sex at the

---

25 "From *Big Bang* to *Boys* on Broadway," *The Advocate*, May 18, 2017 (https://www.advocate.com/theater/2018/ 5/18/big-bang-boys-broadway). Retrieved May 28, 2018.

26 Ibid.

27 Green, Ibid.

28 Ray Salerno, "Sorry, Justin, Your Apology to LGBTQ people doesn't let you off the hook." *National Post*, November 27, 2017 (http://nationalpost.com/opinion/government-

same time is a sterling example—often runs counter to heteronormative values about what's appropriate social comportment for heterosexuals.

On June 21, 2018, The Expungement of Historically Unjust Convictions Act, which pardons "consensual sexual activity between samesex persons related to the offences of gross indecency, buggery and anal intercourse" received royal assent. The Act also puts in place a mechanism for those affected to apply to the Parole Board of Canada—or their families to apply on their behalf should they be deceased—to have past criminal convictions at long last erased. The queer community's response, though positive, has been mixed because the act omits mention of convictions stemming from bathhouse raids, which though they may not have been specific to sexual orientation, victimized gay men nonetheless. Their omission from the Act is seen as a betrayal. Gary Kinsman,[29] author of *The Regulation of Desire*, an important history of the queer community's relationship to the law in Canada from colonial times forward, commented on this injustice in an interview he gave on the CBC Radio One program, *The Current*, on June 25: "There is a real, major contradiction between [what] Justin Trudeau [said] on November 28, 2017, actually mentioning the bawdy-house laws, and the bathhouse raids [in his apology,] and them not being included in this legislation."[30] He also apprized listeners of a "a whole range of other offences related to trans-people, related to sex workers, related to the criminalization of HIV[,] that are not included." The government argues that "Bill C-66 has been designed in a way that once having this base piece of legislation, we could look at other historical offences."[31] I can only wonder if the government's comfort with queer experience let it go only so far as to erase offences that legislators could imagine having occurred within the sanitized environs of a suburban bedroom, though,

---

oppression-of-lgbtq-community-doesnt-end-with-trudeaus-apology). Retrieved June 1, 2018.

29 Gary Kinsman, a queer-rights activist and professor emeritus of sociology at Laurentian University, in Sudbury, is a member of the We Demand an Apology Network. *The Regulation of Desire: Sexuality in Canada* was first published by Black Rose Books in 1987; a dramatically expanded and revised edition appeared under the same imprint in 1996, with a new subtitle, "homo and hetero sexualities."

30 "There's a 'major contradiction' between Trudeau's apology to LGBTQ Canadians and Bill C-66, prof says," *The Current*, CBC Radio 1, June 25, 2018 (http://www.cbc.ca/radio/thecurrent/there-s-a-major-contradiction-bet...rudeau-s-apology-to-lgbt-canadians-and-bill-c-66-prof-says-1.4720541).

31 Ibid.

in reality they could have been perpetrated in any number of less recognizable places. Let's see how guardedly legislators honour the commitments Trudeau made in their name and in the name of all Canadians, who if they're paying attention at all, are slowly realizing that there's still much to redress before our long-ragged polis can be considered to have been properly darned and hemmed.

Behaviour and partialities that are embraced as queer should be destigma-tized—and left alone, among other opportunities, to inspire great art, art that deserves support not sanction, however potentially eyebrow-raising. Eyebrows sometimes need the exercise. The Canada Council could argue that existing guidelines already advance the production of queer artistic creation, but I'd prefer to see unspoken protections affecting me and my queer peers written out in black and white. The Council should not rely on the unguessed ethics of its jury members to make appropriate decisions about our grant applications, but to have spelled-out policies in place to guide them in the nurturance of queer artistic expression, all in the spirit of that admirable phrase Salerno references in his admonition of Trudeau: truth and reconciliation.

The reversal of such errors and oversights is especially important today. The Toronto Police Service has further broadened what it now describes as the lar-gest murder inquiry in its history. Having called for an investigation to unmask for how long, how often, and how savagely Bruce McArthur's may have preyed with impunity upon his own community, Chief of Police Mark Saunders con-tinues to face questions from LGBTQ2S and straight citizens of Toronto (and of the rest of Canada) as to why he had not launched a probe into McArthur's spree sooner. Some in the queer community have expressed concern that evi-dence to be made public during the accused's trial might potentially jaundice public perception. "[T]he case also reminds [gay men] about our more-tenu-ous-than-we'd-like-to-admit position in Canadian society," Paul Gallant points out in The Walrus, "and how any salacious details to emerge during the mur-der trial—promiscuous, perhaps kinky sex—could stigmatize us anew."[32] In other words, should the curtain be pulled open to reveal that some gay men don't restrict themselves to the gay-male equivalent of the missionary position, however that position might be expressed in same-sex terms, it could enflame

---

32 Paul Gallant, "Why Bruce McArthur's Murder Trial Could Stigmatize Gay Men," *The Walrus*, February 9, 2018 [updated February 16, 2018] (https://thewalrus.ca/why-bruce-mcarthurs-murder-trial-could-stigmatize-gay-men/). Retrieved March 12, 2018.

non-queer heteronormative scruples.[33] There is a reason why Trudeau *père* had admonished Canadians to get out of the bedrooms of the nation: so they'd not have to look or, horror of horrors, learn. Not enough time has transpired for the LGBTQ2S community to forget that powerful elements of the conservative movement in this country lobbied to enshrine marriage as the exclusive prerogative of straight men and women because they could not live with what went on in the post-nuptial same-sex bed. It is censures of this ilk that can slip subconsciously and not so subconsciously into the psyches of even the most apparently open-minded of people, including artists, when exposed to how the other half—or two to ten percent—live. It is why minorities, even the most seemingly accepted of minorities, argue for protections to be enacted in advance of any circumstance turning unexpectedly and coercively sour.

Properly conceived and administered equity guarantees are key. The Canada Council, for it to remain the forward-thinking institution it purports to be and not the laggard camp follower that I fear it is becoming, must reconceptualize its own guidelines and not rely upon an out-of-date statute to give it backbone, a statute it may take present and future governments years to amend, in order to assure queer artists that their applications for support will enjoy equal consideration stripped of bias, intentional or otherwise. If the necessary changes are not made soon, its grant officers may look down from their office windows and notice to their chagrin that yet another bank-sponsored parade—the one in Ottawa in 2017 was led by the prime minister—has passed them by, drag and shirtless muscle queens having distributed the condoms and lube previously reserved for them to more suitably kitted-out recipients.

2018

---

33 On January 29, 2019, a few months after Anstruther Press published this essay as a chapbook in its Manifesto Series, Bruce McArthur surprised Canadians by pleading guilty to all charges against him, avoiding a trial during which his crimes could have been aired in full and thus saving the eight victims' families and the queer community from being traumatized further (https://www.cbc.ca/news/canada/toronto/bruce-mcarthur-murder-plea-guilty-closure-1.4997242). Retrieved March 27, 2019. On February 8, 2019, he was sentenced in Ontario Superior Court to eight concurrent life sentences and will not be eligible for parole until he is 91 in 2033 (https://www.cbc.ca/news/canada/toronto/bruce-mcarthur-sentence-parole-eligibility-1.5009291 3). Retrieved March 27, 2019.

Introduction to *Seminal*

"THE HOMOSEXUAL POET," ACCORDING to Robert K. Martin, "often seeks poetic 'fathers' who in some sense offer a validation of his sexual nature. Whatever he may learn poetically from the great tradition, he cannot fail to notice that this tradition is, at least on the surface, almost exclusively heterosexual."[1] It is out of such a desire for affirmation, for exemplars and mentors, that the impulse to compile *Seminal*, the first historically comprehensive compendium of gay-male poetry written by Canadians, first arose. Even today, after the hard-won battles in the political arena to enshrine the equal rights of gay men and lesbians in Canada as legitimate have been won, the desire to make gay experience a more traceable plotline in the "central" Canadian story is difficult to realize. The reader—and writer—of gay poetry in this country still has a hard time finding it easily, as if it were composed just outside the spotlight of mainstream literary success.

In the almost forty years since May 1969, when the Trudeau government decriminalized homosexual acts between consenting adults, one would think that an anthology like *Seminal* would have already been published and already be familiarly dog-eared in the hands of the aspiring and the curious. Most express surprise that no previous compilation is to be superseded by this present effort. Such a long-standing gap in the published record does not fit with Canadians' sense of themselves as well-informed and living within an enlightened community of ideas. Yet librarians still do not routinely provide apposite access points in their catalogues; publishers may not always choose to highlight the gay content in a forthcoming book for fear it would compromise sales; and poets themselves may sometimes continue to hesitate in characterizing their work as homoerotic—or themselves as gay—anxious that the appreciation of their accomplishment could potentially be narrowed to this single trait of their humanity or, worse, be dismissed as ghettoized.

In the past, for anyone interested in how a gay tradition in poetry might actually read in Canada, the search for it could yield to feelings of creative

---

1   Robert K. Martin, *The Homosexual Tradition in American Poetry* Austin: University of Texas Press, 1979, 148.

frustration, even isolation. *Seminal*, therefore, is an attempt, in Canadian terms and in a single comprehensive volume, to prevent our gay poets of present and future generations from being obliged to approach the literary "past" as something that must be "repeatedly reinvented anew, [as a] tradition [to be] created afresh."[2] Readers and writers may wish to do so nonetheless, but now they have a clearly defined point of previous departure to revisit, revise, or even repudiate.

This first anthology of Canadian gay male poetry takes its place in a line of similar anthologies published elsewhere in the English-speaking world, including Edward Carpenter's *Ioläus* (1902),[3] Patrick Anderson and Alistair Sutherland's *Eros: An Anthology of Friendship* (1961),[4] Ian Young's *The Male Muse* (1973) and *The Son of the Male Muse* (1983),[5] and Stephen Coote's *The Penguin Book of Homosexual Verse* (1983).[6] Carpenter, Anderson and Sutherland, and Coote all start with ancient times and work their way up. In the case of the first two, they do not focus on poetry exclusively while, in the third instance, Coote also includes work by women. Only living poets appear in Young's anthologies, with mutually exclusive sets of contributors published in each. In 1995, Michael Holmes and Lynn Crosbie, two straight Toronto writers, published the much smaller *Plush*,[7] Canada's first contemporary anthology of gay male poetry, featuring three Canadian and two American poets. Five years later, Timothy Liu published *Word of Mouth*,[8] collecting into a single volume fifty-eight American poets born in the twentieth century (he did not have to deal with Whitman or

---

2   Ibid, 161.

3   Edward Carpenter, ed., *Ioläus: An Anthology of Friendship*. The online version found at http://www.fordham.edu/halsall/pwh/iolaus.html#pref is the edition that was published in New York by Mitchell Kennerly in 1917.

4   Patrick Anderson and Alistair Sutherland, *Eros: An Anthology of Friendship*. London: Anthony Blond, 1961.

5   Ian Young, ed., *The Male Muse*. Trumansburg, N.Y.: Crossing Press, 1973. Young tried to interest Canadian publishers in *The Male Muse* without success, so instead went south of the border where it was accepted without reservation by John Gill, publisher of The Crossing Press and also one of the contributors (letter of August 25, 2004, from Young to author). *The Son of the Male Muse* was also published by The Crossing Press in 1983.

6   Stephen Coote, ed., *The Penguin Book of Homosexual Verse*. London: Penguin, 1983.

7   Lynn Crosbie and Michael Holmes, eds., Plush: Selected Poems of Sky Gilbert, Courtnay McFarlane, Jeffrey Conway, R. M. Vaughan, and David Trinidad. Toronto: Coach House Press, 1995.

8   Timothy Liu, ed., *Word of Mouth: An Anthology of Gay American Poetry*. Jersey City: Talisman House, 2000.

Crane, as a consequence), an anthology he affirms in the introduction was conceived in light of the many gay-male poetry anthologies that had already been
published in the United States; Liu's efforts to map American gay-male poetry
have served as a model for *Seminal*.

Unsurprisingly, few Canadians appear in any of the anthologies of international scope. In either of the *Male Muse* anthologies, Young includes only two
Canadian poets of note, Edward A. Lacey and bill bissett, besides himself. Edward A. Lacey does appear in Coote's Penguin anthology, though he seems to
have been a last-minute addition, along with a handful of other contemporary
poets who are tacked on at the end and not interfiled by date of birth among the
majority of the contributors. Coote also leaves out Patrick Anderson—an important figure in the Montreal poetry community of the 1940s, a fellow Briton
who returned to England in the 1950s, and who died in 1979, four years before
the anthology was published—or at least Anderson is left out by name, for his
poem, "Spiv Song," is attributed to Royston Ellis. Anderson happened to have
represented himself with the same poem in his earlier *Eros* (Coote must have
been conversant with this trailblazing anthology, one would think, and should
have caught his mistake).

Just how much the approach to gay writing has and has not changed over the
course of the twentieth century is revealed by what each editor has to say about
how and what they chose. In 1902, Carpenter reflects that while *Ioläus* "is only
incomplete, and a small contribution, at best, towards a large subject,"[9] he feels
he has succeeded in making visible what was previously hidden, noting that
"I have been much struck by the remarkable manner in which the customs of
various races and times illustrate each other, and the way in which they point to
a solid and enduring body of human sentiment on the subject."[10] Almost sixty
years later, after acknowledging that the contents of *Eros* has "teased [him since]
adolescence" and has revealed itself to be "less of the smell of sulphur than [he]
had imagined," Anderson describes his subject as "any friendship between men
strong enough to deserve one of the more serious senses of the word 'love'" and
goes on to say—remember that he was writing at the height of the Cold War between the release of the Wolfenden Report in 1957 and the decriminalization of
homosexuality in the United Kingdom in 1967[11]—that "this limiting extremism

9   Carpenter, (http://www.fordham.edu/halsall/pwh/iolaus.html#pref).
10 Ibid.
11 For a good synopsis of the Wolfenden Report, which influenced social change on

is far from most people's taste. Against the background of our society, whether conceived in terms of Christian ethics or of the 'natural' self-realization implicit in scientific humanism, to accept it for oneself is pretty obviously to invite moral and psychological disaster."[12] Young in contrast claims *The Male Muse* is "not an anthology of 'gay poets' (a difficult and useless category), but rather a collection of poems by contemporary writers on themes relating to male homosexuality, gay love, romantic friendships, what Walt Whitman called 'the dear love of comrades, the attraction of friend to friend.'" He further contextualizes his work by maintaining that "until 1972, the project [of anthology-making] seemed impossible to carry out ... because the aura of taboo was still strong enough to prevent all but a few writers from contributing. But quite suddenly ... the growing impetus of the homophile/gay liberation movement began to be felt by the rest of society—both gay and straight—and 'Gay Pride' became not just a slogan but a reality."[13] A decade later, Coote articulates his own rationale for his Penguin anthology, contending that "a gay poem is one that either deals with explicitly gay matters or describes an intense and loving relationship between two people of the same sex."[14] For Crosbie and Holmes, compiling *Plush* still another decade on, their "conviction grew that the poems—words and work all too often neglected by the mainstream—spoke to one another and to a much wider audience than any notion of an anthology of gay poets could possibly suggest"[15] while, for Liu, his millennial *Word of Mouth* was "a gathering of poets whose poems represent a plurality of forms, poems that may or may not directly traffic in 'gay experience,'" acknowledging that he "still question[s] the notion of gay sensibility."[16]

As a consequence, it is very difficult not to be affected by, respond to, or work against the assumptions of anyone previously, or even currently, working in the area or not to be influenced by the attitudes of the poets under consideration. The fifty-seven writers in *Seminal* were born between 1878 and 1981 and represent over a century of writing. They each reflect the beliefs and aesthetic concerns of their own time and, depending on when they were born, have been

---

both sides of the Atlantic, see Hugh David's *On Queer Street: A Social History of British Homosexuality, 1895–1995*. London: HarperCollins, 1997.

12 Anderson and Sutherland, 8–9.

13 Young, *The Male Muse*, 7.

14 Coote, 48–49.

15 Crosbie and Holmes, 8

16 Liu, xv, xviii.

more or less open about their erotic lives in and outside of their work. It seems less interesting nowadays to specify what legitimately constitutes a gay poem or whether someone is a "gay poet" versus a "poet who happens to be gay." The time to feel diminished or emboldened by labels—or to feel one should trumpet, duck, whistle around, or deny them (strategies that all imply hubris, anxiety, or discomfort)—should be long over. Any of the poets in *Seminal* could as validly fit into an anthology organized around an entirely different point of commonality, for all poets are both one and many, but, at the same time, the placement of universal truth and universal experience above all else risks homogenization through a denial of specificity. A simple recognition of fact—that a poet is homosexual / gay / queer / same-sex / bi / transgender / poly-amorous or not—should be sufficient and demands a reading of his/their work (and what it took him/them to write it) that goes as far as possible into its depths in order to see what it reveals about *his/their* human condition— and about his/their sense of the human condition *itself*.

What the human condition really is persists as yet another conundrum, and appropriately enough, like so many things pertaining to gay experience, *Seminal* begins on a speculative note, a gaydar moment, if you like. The earliest poems are by Émile Nelligan, the second poet by chronological arrangement, and they date from the late 1890s. Born in 1879, Nelligan was at the beginning of what should have been a long and celebrated career when, after a mental collapse, he was committed to an asylum in 1899 until his death in 1941. Robert K. Martin suggests that his "incarceration is widely taken to indicate his homosexuality and he can still function as an icon of the gay man in Quebec, destroyed by his culture and his assimilation into English."[17] Whether or not Martin's supposition is accurate and whether or not every cause needs a martyr to whatever rallying cry—culture, sexuality—as a kind of tragic inspiration, when it comes to Canadian gay-male poetry, this is where *Seminal* draws the line in time's very unsettled sands. Frank Oliver Call, another Quebec-based poet born one year before Nelligan, is in comparison forgotten, though he is credited with being among the first poets in Canada to have experimented, however tentatively,

---

17   Robert K. Martin, "Gay Literature" in *The Oxford Companion to Canadian Literature*, 2nd edition. Eugene Benson and William Toye, general editors. Toronto: Oxford University Press, 1997, 453.

with modernism.[18] Call's pamphlet with Ryerson, *Sonnets for Youth* (1944), is said to be the first collection of homoerotic verse published in Canada, however coded and oblique it happens to be in its references.[19]

The poets born in the two decades after Nelligan's confinement could not be forthright about their sexuality in their work for obvious reasons. John Glassco, notorious for *Memoirs of Montparnasse* (1973), a "nonfiction" account of his years in Paris now more often characterized as fictional revisionism, even as a kind of in-joke send-up of the reader in its twisting of the author's personal gay history,[20] did not start publishing poetry in book form until later in life (interestingly, he did not include "Noyade 1942," a poem dating from 1958, in his Governor General's Award-winning *Selected Poems* of 1971). The fact that he had two marriages to women in the last half of his life after an earlier fifteen-year live-in relationship of some description with a man, and also had a reputation as something of a squire and gentleman farmer active in horse-racing circles in Quebec's Eastern Townships, may have influenced how he negotiated the writing and publication of his work. Douglas LePan "came out" as a gay poet memorably at the age of seventy-six, when he published *Far Voyages* in 1990, a passionate extended elegy for a recently deceased male lover many years his junior (though anyone who carefully reads the new autobiographical poems in the earlier *Weathering It*[21]—LePan's new and collected poems published in 1987—can see how he was consciously working up to his great moment of openness). Brion Gysin, raised in Edmonton in the 1920s by his Canadian-born mother after his British-Swiss father died on the battlefield during the First World War, was perhaps an exception. He pursued a more open homosexual lifestyle in the Isherwoodian sense from young adulthood onwards. However, except for a stint in the Canadian Army on the home front during the Second World War, he cut his links with Canada and instead moved, as a poet, artist, and novelist,

---

18 Louis Dudek and Michael Gnarowski, "The Precursors: 1910–1925," *The Making of Modern Poetry in Canada*, Toronto: Ryerson, 1967, 3, and Ken Norris, *The Little Magazine in Canada 1925–1980*. Toronto: ECW Press, 1984, 10–11.

19 Letter of August 11, 2004, from Ian Young to the author.

20 See Richard Dellamora's "Queering Modernism: A Canadian in Paris," *Essays in Canadian Writing* 60 (1996): 265–273 and Andrew Lesk's "Having a Gay Old Time in Paris: John Glassco's Not-So-Queer Adventures" in *In a Queer Country: Gay and Lesbian Studies in the Canadian Context*, Terry Goldie, ed. Vancouver: Arsenal Pulp, 2001, 175-187.

21 Douglas LePan, *Weathering It: Complete Poems, 1948–1987*. Toronto: McClelland & Stewart, 1987.

in the circles of Paul Bowles, William Burroughs, Gregory Corso, and Harold
Norse in London, New York, Paris, and Tangiers. Still, his experiments with
form brought him to the heart of the innovations in sound poetry and performance at a world level, which in turn informed so much of what came to pass of
a similar nature here.

The sexuality of a gay-male poet was seldom, if ever, impugned publicly in Canada until the poetry of Patrick Anderson was reviewed by John Sutherland in
1943. While the import of Sutherland's remarks is still raised in the debate over
the origins of Canadian modernism, little is ever made of them beyond their
characterization as part of the persistent "disagreements" between *Preview*, the
little mimeographed magazine that Anderson edited, and Sutherland's equally
modest *First Statement*. While it is true that queer scholars have recently "reread" Sutherland's "outing" of Anderson,[22] I suspect that a deeper understanding of what transpired between these two men could go a long way to explaining why Canadian gay-male poets have had to work in isolation, with barely a
sense of community or wider recognition, in the decades since, even the decades after Stonewall.

In "The Writing of Patrick Anderson,"[23] Sutherland asserts that something is
not quite right in Anderson's poem "Montreal," commenting that

> Now I am willing to take Anderson at his word that the boy [in
> the poem] is "a substitute for poetry." As I interpret it, in his
> case the boy adds an impetus to poetic creation, and is even the
> source of his present poetry. At the same time, while I have no
> desire to make an exposé of Anderson's personal life, I surmise
> that the distinction between the "frightened boy" and "the hero
> who sings of joy" could be traced back to some period in the

22 See the following chapters and articles: "Critical Homophobia and Canadian Canon-
   Formation, 1943–1967: The 'Haunted Journeys' of Patrick Anderson and Scott Symons"
   in Peter Dickinson, *Here is Queer: Nationalisms, Sexualities, and the Literatures of Canada.*
   Toronto: University of Toronto Press, 1997, 69–100; Justin D. Edwards, "Engendering
   Modern Canadian Poetry: *Preview, First Statement* and the Disclosure of Patrick Anderson's
   Homosexuality," *Essays on Canadian Writing* 62 (1997): 65–84; Robert K. Martin, "Sex and
   Politics in Wartime Canada: The Attack on Patrick Anderson," *Essays on Canadian Writing*
   44 (1991): 10–25.
23 John Sutherland, "The Writing of Patrick Anderson," *First Statement* 1.19 (1943): 3–6.

writer's childhood, when there occurred a sexual experience involving two boys, one of whom was frightened and the other
demonstrated his joy. Whether or not this deduction is completely correct, I do know that something of the kind occurred
in Anderson's childhood. The point that I wish to make is that,
in the lines quoted from "Montreal," some sexual experience
of a kind not quite normal has been twisted and forced into its
present shape in the poem, where it wears the false aspect of
some universal fact, or has to be accepted as a general mood in
which people today participate. Surely, these lines alone would
signify the falsity of the poet's medium and his habitual distor-
tion of content. His message is not wrong in itself, but his method of arriving at it, and his manner of stating it, make his poem
appear like a wholesale falsification.

We can only imagine the impact such a review would have had on any poet.
Anderson was then married and taught school-age boys during a time when
homosexual crimes were punished with prison sentences. Though the circulation of *First Statement* was miniscule, Anderson threatened to sue. To placate
him as well as to protect his own reputation, Sutherland printed a brief retraction in a subsequent issue.[24] Though the "crisis" passed, it was very likely not
forgotten, especially by Anderson who was by then no doubt aware of his own
homoerotic desires[25] and may have felt that Sutherland, in his blundering and
bombastic way, had intuited something essential.

   This apparent defamation has to be read in context of the larger ongoing disagreements and rivalries between *Preview* and *First Statement*—and especially in
context of how they have been conceptualized and distorted by later critics[26]—
in order to understand how it might have affected the gay-male poets to come.
Quite simply put, the poets of *Preview*—P. K. Page, A. M. Klein, and F. R. Scott,
being the best remembered today—were perceived as older, upper-class, cosmopolitan, artificial, and too influenced by the "foreign" or "imported" British

24 John Sutherland, "Retraction," *First Statement* I.20 (1943), cover.
25 See p. 91 in Patricia Whitney's "First Person Feminine: Margaret Day Surrey" in *Canadian Poetry* 31 (1992): 86–91.
26 For an excellent overview of the battles between *Preview* and *First Statement*, see Brian Trehearne's "Critical Episodes in Montreal Poetry in the 1940s," *Canadian Poetry* 41 (1997): 21–52.

modernism of T. S. Eliot (formerly an American), W. H. Auden (a Briton then living in the United States), and Dylan Thomas (a Welshman). The poets of *First Statement*—Irving Layton, Louis Dudek, Raymond Souster—were esteemed to be young, native, and natural, connected to the robust (albeit American) modernism of Ezra Pound and William Carlos Williams. A. J. M. Smith inadvertently first coined and enshrined the distinction between "cosmopolitan" and "native" in *Book of Canadian Poetry* (1943),[27] with the poets of each "tradition" grouped together. Because many of the *First Statement* poets were left out entirely, unlike those of *Preview*, this canonizing anthology provoked immediate anger (the small world of poetry does like its dustups).

It is not hard to see how the terms "cosmopolitan" and "artificial" could become further tainted with queer inflections, particularly when "native" became allied with "masculine." Sutherland further stirred the pot in 1947, when he harshly reviewed Robert Finch's Governor General's Award-winning book, *Poems* (1946)[28] in *Northern Review*, the successor to both *First Statement* and *Preview*, when the two editorial boards merged. Sutherland refers to Finch as a "dandified versifier."[29] An unsigned editorial in the next issue gave notice that several board members (or what amounted to all remaining members formerly associated with *Preview*) had resigned en masse over "a difference of opinion about editorial policy, particularly concerning criticism and reviews."[30] Thirty-five years later, in a review of Finch's *Variations and Theme* (1980), Susan Gingell-Beckman noted that "Ever since John Sutherland's virulent attack on the bestowing of the Governor General's Award on Finch's *Poems*, Finch's critical reputation has dwindled to the point where he has been excluded from virtually all the contemporary major anthologies of Canadian poetry...."[31]

27 A. J. M. Smith, *The Book of Canadian Poetry*. Toronto: W. J. Gage, 1943.

28 John Sutherland, Review of *Poems* by Robert Finch, *Northern Review* I.6 (1947): 38–40. It is interesting to note that Louis Dudek and Michael Gnarowski reprint this review in *The Making of Modern Poetry in Canada: Essential Articles on Contemporary Canadian Poetry in English* (Toronto: Ryerson, 1967) but not Sutherland's attack on Patrick Anderson of three years before.

29 For an in-depth discussion of how Finch's poetry fits into the aesthetic tradition, see Brian Trehearne's article "Finch's Early Poetry and the Dandy Manner" in *Canadian Poetry* 18 (1986): 11–34.

30 Editors of *Northern Review*, Notices of Resignation, Northern Review, II.1 (1947): 40. Reprinted in *The Making of Modern Poetry in Canada*.

31 Susan Gingell-Beckman, "Against an Anabasis of Grace: A Retrospective Review of the

In the criticism that started to appear in the 1950s and 1960s and became the texts to which later critics would in turn invariably refer, the opposition of "cosmopolitan" and "native," with its echo of "artificial" and "masculine," attained the status of received wisdom. The poets associated with *First Statement* wrote the story of Canadian modernism in part because key *Preview* poets had left the country by the early 1950s—Page as the wife of a Canadian ambassador and Anderson to England (after two years in Malaysia), where he continued to teach and wrote travel books. He did not get a chance to address the distortions of his legacy until the 1970s, when he renewed his ties to Canada and also again began to write poetry. Yet, by then, the position advanced by the *First Statement* diaspora had inveigled itself firmly into the chronology of Canadian poetry rehearsed almost to this day. The very heterosexual dramatis personae of poets like Irving Layton, arguably the preeminent poet of the 1950s and early 1960s, and the critical assessments of Louis Dudek and those who trained under him raked the stage sharply in their favour, a stage upon which they have had enormous, long-lasting, and influential careers. When considering the straight-male poets who have held sway in Canada for the last sixty years and while acknowledging the growing diversity of their aesthetics, it is striking how much of a boy's club Canadian poetry has remained (just ask the girls). Their articulations of self recall the goings-on of a club or a locker room, a locker room from which, ironically if typically, many straight-male poets also have felt excluded. Even in today's climate, which is nuanced by multiple perspectives and subject positions, it feels inevitable that a Gen-X frat pack will assert itself, assume the mantle of their elders, and attempt to hold sway.

Wanting to be on an equal footing in society, to "belong," to be one of the boys, has proved complicated for many gay-male poets, who may well write from a slightly different point of reference, but with the same sense of engagement as all poets do. In 1944, American poet Robert Duncan, then a young man in his mid-twenties, published his essay, "The Homosexual in Society,"[32] in which he declares his homosexuality, and goes into detail about the predicament in which he finds himself as a poet who wants to be honest:

Poems of Robert Finch," *Essays on Canadian Writing* 23 (1982), 157–62.

32   Robert Duncan, "The Homosexual in Society," *Politics* 1 (August 1944); it is included in his *Selected Prose*. New York: New Directions, 38–50.

> In the face of the hostility of society which I risk in making even the acknowledgement explicit in this statement, in the face of the "crime" of my own feelings, in the past I publicized those feelings as private and made no stand for their recognition, but tried to sell them as disguised, for instance, as conflicts arising from mystical sources.

While Duncan comes across as unwilling to identify himself too closely with "the homosexual cult," he does make a case "for a group whose only salvation is in the struggle of all humanity for freedom and individual integrity," making a plea for homosexual themes to be written and read as human themes, not written and consequently corrupted (which he defines as "the rehearsal of unfeeling") for a coterie of sympathetic readers, but for the most widespread audience. However Duncan's public declaration of sexual orientation might now be read (in 1959 he characterized it as more of a "confession"), it is impossible to imagine that Patrick Anderson could have met his accuser's allegations in a like statement in Canada the year before. Nor is it imaginable that any Canadian publisher or poet could have won a case like the obscenity trial that City Lights Books and Lawrence Ferlinghetti fought successfully over Alan Ginsberg's *Howl*.

Instead, in 1965, Edward A. Lacey privately published *The Forms of Loss*. In 1963, Lacey, who would spend most of his adult life in the South America and Asia teaching English and working as a translator, had been teaching for a year at the University of Alberta, in Edmonton, when he became reacquainted with Dennis Lee, whom he had known as a student at the University of Toronto (Lacey studied languages with Robert Finch at University College). Lee encouraged him in his project to compile a first book of poems, and two years later, with Margaret Atwood's and Dennis Lee's financial help,[33] the book was printed.[34] This slim volume of twenty-six poems is thought to be the first openly gay-male poetry published in book form in Canada.[35]

---

33 In an email to the author, Ian Young indicates that both Atwood and Lee underwrote the cost of publishing *The Forms of Loss*, not just Lee, as Fraser Sutherland indicates in his introduction to Lacey's *Collected Poems*.

34 Coincidentally, *The Forms of Loss* did not include "Quintallas," which dates back to the 1950s and was, according to Sutherland, Lacey's first openly gay poem.

35 Fraser Sutherland, "Introduction," The *Collected Poems and Translations of Edward A. Lacey*.

While the importance of Lacey's book cannot be overestimated, he was not the lone Canadian to write on homoerotic themes in 1965. The consideration of *The Forms of Loss* as our first openly gay book of poetry must first be tempered with the recognition that, in the same year, Jean Basile's *Journal poétique*, published by Les Editions du Jour, featured several homoerotic poems. Phyllis Webb's landmark *Naked Poems*[36] also appeared that year; it is felt to be "an early example of Canadian literature with lesbian content."[37] Webb may not have been as open in her book as Lacey—she "reveals that the object of her love is a woman while deflecting attention from this fact by avoiding pronouns and using codes...she withholds as much she tells"[38]—but the book attracted immediate interest and is still remembered because of its formal finesse and because it was written by an already admired poet.

John Herbert was also then refining his play, *Fortune and Men's Eyes*,[39] which examines the violence and homosexuality at a reformatory. After rejections elsewhere, Herbert submitted it to the Stratford Festival, which accepted it for the 1965 Young Actors Workshop. Yet because of the content, "the Stratford Board of Directors forbade the single planned public performance, and it was performed privately for the Stratford actors."[40] It eventually premiered in New York in 1967, one year before *The Boys in the Band*, running to acclaim for nearly a year, followed by a tour to Chicago and San Francisco, new productions in Toronto, Montreal, and Los Angeles, and a return engagement in New York under the aegis of Sal Mineo. It is also the most widely published and most anthologized play by a Canadian.

Daryl Hine, a Vancouver-born poet on faculty at the University of Chicago who would later hold the position of editor at *Poetry* from 1968 to 1978, had already published four books, the first two in Canada, the third in England, and the fourth in America. From the beginning, his work was homoerotically allusive,[41] with openly gay-male poems like "The Visit" published in *Minutes*

Toronto: Colombo & Company, 2000, vi–vii.

36 Phyllis Webb, *Naked Poems*. Vancouver: Periwinkle Press, 1965.

37 Catherine Lake and Nairne Holtz, eds., *No Margins: Writing Canadian Fiction in Lesbian*. Toronto: Insomniac Press, 2006, 310.

38 Ibid.

39 John Herbert, Fortune and Men's Eyes. New York: Grove Press, 1967.

40 See entry on *Fortune and Men's Eyes* in *The Canadian Theatre Encyclopedia* (Athabasca, Alberta: Athabasca University) at www.canadiantheatre.com.

41 In an email to the author, Hine described some of the poems he published as early as 1955

(1968). From 1965 onwards, he published almost exclusively with Atheneum, then one of the most respected literary houses in the United States, and built an enviable reputation as part of America's literary establishment. In contrast, Scott Symons' novel, *Place d'Armes*,[42] was published by McClelland & Stewart in 1967 to almost universally bad notices that seemed motivated by an intolerance that was "as much a political response as it was a reaction against Symons' exploration of homosexuality."[43] Not only did the book foment critical outrage, it emboldened the parents of Symons' underage lover to have authorities chase after the couple all the way to Mexico.[44] Symons has enjoyed an outlaw or anti-establishmentarian reputation ever since, though, in 2005, the *Literary Review of Canada* placed his novel among the 100 most important books written by Canadians.

Lacey may not have fared as well in reputation as Webb, Herbert, Hine, or even Symons, but he was very much part of a trend toward more openly gay-male writing by Canadians. Out of the social and political changes wrought by the 1960s, a more confident gay-male poetry emerged. Dennis Lee, Lacey's benefactor, having read Ian Young's work in *Acta Victoriana*, the Victoria College literary journal at the University of Toronto, featured several of Young's poems in the anthology, *T.O. Poetry Now*, which he published in 1967 through his new press, House of Anansi. In 1969, Anansi released Young's *Year of the Quiet Sun*,[45] making it the first book of openly gay-male poetry to have appeared under the imprint of a recognizable English-Canadian publisher. Lee's support of Young and Lacey could be said to be the planting of a seed from which many roots spread—disoriented, far-ranging roots whose awareness of one another seldom intertwined, but from which, however distantly, so much else that has grown up since may choose to trace its origins.

By the early 1970s, the poets born between 1939 and 1950—whom I judge to be the Stonewall generation, for they were the first to benefit as young men from

---

(in *Five Poems*) as "explicit," an opinion he says was shared by others.

42 Scott Symons, *Combat Journal for Place d'Armes*. Toronto: McClelland & Stewart, 1967.

43 Peter Buitenhuis, from his introduction to the paperback edition of Symons' book published by McClelland & Stewart in 1968.

44 *Place d'Armes* went on to win the Beta Sigma Phi Best First Canadian Novel Award for that year.

45 Ian Young, *Year of the Quiet Sun*. Toronto: Anansi, 1969. In 1968, Anansi had published an edition of Allen Ginsberg's *Airplane Dreams*.

the liberalizations by then well underway in Canada, Britain, and the United States—were able to write more directly about their erotic lives, should they choose to, without real fear of legal consequence. Along with a proliferation of gay liberation groups on and off university campuses and the founding of community-based gay newsletters, newspapers, and magazines, the most famous of which is Toronto's *The Body Politic*, attempts were made to establish gay-centered literary presses. In 1970, Young founded Catalyst, which he describes as the first queer press anywhere in the world, and published thirty gay and lesbian titles in diverse genres, including Edward A. Lacey's *Later* (he also distributed Lacey's self-published *Path of Snow*) and his own book, *Common-or-Garden Gods*, before ceasing operations in 1979.[46] A more modest attempt at gay publishing was made by Doug Wilson when he founded Stubblejumper Press in Saskatoon in 1977, publishing only a handful of titles, with his own single book of poems as its first. bill bissett's legendary blewointmentpress, established in Vancouver in the 1960s, was not exclusively gay in its mandate, but bissett did publish several gay-male poets, including himself and Bertrand Lachance. From the first, gay publishing has only ever been an ephemeral grassroots activity in Canada, with no viable and independent, solely gay literary press or magazine of any consequence able to survive for long. After bissett sold blewointment, its new owners rechristened the press as Nightwood Editions, now an imprint of Harbour Publishing and the home of Andy Quan's and Norm Sacuta's first books of poetry, which appeared in 2001. Also, since the mid-1970s, several other mainstream literary presses have laudably fostered the careers of many gay-male poets, most notably Anansi, Arsenal Pulp, Coach House, Écrits des Forges, ECW, Guernica, Les Herbes Rouges, New Star, Noroît, Polestar, Talonbooks, and TSAR.

bill bissett, as an icon of the 1960s and 1970s counterculture, is as beloved today as he was reviled by members of the House of Commons who denounced him as much for the "extremity" of his work as its manner, which did not conform to their limited understanding of literary forms. bissett is almost a "trickster" figure, due in part to his memorable sound-poetry performances complete with rattles and to early poems like "eet me alive" or "a warm place to shit," that manifest an ecstatic awareness of the body. A colleague of bpNichol, who published his first book, bissett expresses his dissidence—a dissidence that cannot be defined as queer—through a highly personalized,

---

46 Ian Young, "Memoirs of a Catalyst," unpublished memoir, dated April 2003.

decades-consistent, morphologically, and orthographically aberrant approach to the transcription of text to the page and through his virtuosic concrete poetry. His work demands that the reader ascribe to the principles under which it has been written, a demand that is in no way aggressive, for once the challenge of breaking his "code" has been met, his world of subtle insights, candour, and fine simplicities opens beautifully.

Immediately before and after 1970, Robin Blaser, Stan Persky (both in 1966), and George Stanley (in 1971) arrived from San Francisco. Protégés of Jack Spicer and Robert Duncan and, except for Persky, older than the gay-liberation-inspired poets of Stonewall, they brought with them a core of aesthetic principles that have had an enormous impact on the writing of the West Coast. Blaser in particular, with his cosmic sense of language and the public interconnectedness of texts, traditions, philosophies, and politics, is today a poet of international standing perhaps better recognized outside the country than within. Blaser and Stanley retained their links with the writing communities they were attached to in the United States and continued to publish there, perhaps initially to the detriment of their Canadian reputations, where their "foreign" books and pamphlets would not necessarily have been available. Stanley, however did issue several books of new and previously published poetry with New Star, Oolichan, and Talonbooks, and in the 1980s, Blaser began to publish regularly with Coach House. Persky only published one book of poems, but has made his reputation on such pioneering works of creative nonfiction as *Buddy's: Meditations on Desire.*

Blaser has described himself as "cosmopolitan," a loaded concept that is recognizable, from Anderson's experiences, as difficult for Canadians to metabolize.[47] In 2000, when asked if he had a queer poetics, Blaser replied, "No, I would not. I am queer and I concern myself with a poetics, and queer would not describe everything I attempt in my poetics. I'm hoping that the world of queer poetics is included and that gay people will be interested in what I am doing, because they are very much a part of my community."[48] Known for his great "Image-Nation" poems as well for the ongoing project, *The Holy Forest*, that contains them, Blaser voices an eloquent queer poetics in "In Remembrance of Matthew Shepard."

---

47 R. W. Gray, "'…we have to think in communities now…': An Interview with Robin Blaser," *Arc* 44 (2000): 34.
48 Ibid.

It is an understatement to say that gay writing in Canada, like everywhere else, was profoundly changed by AIDS in the 1980s. Michael Lynch, Michael Estok, and Ian Stephens all succumbed to the disease, leaving behind moving records of its effects in their collections of poetry, *These Waves of Dying Friends* (1989), *A Plague Year Journal* (1989), and *Diary of a Trademark* (1994) respectively, the first two being posthumous. Doug Wilson also died from AIDS-related complications, but lived long enough to complete the last novel by his lover, Peter McGehee, who predeceased him. Estok's *A Plague Year Journal* is a particularly remarkable document for the bite of its anger and passionate, even vehement, use of language, almost as if, ironically, the experience of the disease itself matured him as a writer.

AIDS, of course, became one of the great themes of the age, with its "treatment" poetically evolving almost as rapidly as medical understanding. Even a cursory perusal of the books by any of the contemporaneous poets in this anthology will locate individual poems that respond to the social and physical challenges that the disease has posed for gay men, excellent examples being Gregory Scofield's *Native Canadiana* (particularly his poem, "Queenie"), André Roy's *On sait que cela a* été écrit *avant et après la grande maladie*, or Richard Teleky's allegorical "The Hermit's Kiss." Sadly and strangely, with the turn of the millennium, it appears that, for some, the urgency to address AIDS has fallen off. Is it because of its transformation from an automatic "death sentence" into something "chronic" and "treatable"? Or because of its widening sweep into straight communities in the Western democracies and through the Third Word—almost as if it were no longer "ours"? Or maybe gay-male poets have exhausted it as a theme or have simply become exhausted? Still, AIDS has had a profound effect on the psyche of any "active" poet. Self-consciousness must be at play during the composition of an erotic love poem since we have all had to become, even in the performance of the most casual acts of love, more self-aware. As Robin Blaser says, "Any poem is close to the body."[49]

The number of gay-male poets writing in Canada has continued to grow, with nearly half of the poets in *Seminal* publishing their first book that contains openly gay-themed poems after the late 1980s. In her foreword to the 1991 issue of *The Church-Wellesley Review*, Jane Rule begins "In the olden days, we had few choices of tone, either the tragic self-pity of Radclyffe Hall in *The Well of Loneliness* or

---

49 Ibid, 28.

the flippant disguise of Oscar Wilde and Noël Coward. Now, as is evident in this second literary supplement to *XTRA*, we have claimed the full range of attitudes toward our experience." After summarizing the strengths of the writing to be found within the supplement, Rule cautions readers and writers alike that "content still too often overpowers form because we are new at being able to speak the range of our experiences, and urgency overcomes us. Critical of styles used to disguise, we must not make the mistake of discarding eloquence now that it can serve the truth."[50] While Rule was no doubt responding to the grassroots or amateur ambitions of many of the featured authors, her call to action has certainly been answered in the collections of poetry published by writers as diverse in style, attitude, and background as David Bateman, Todd Bruce, Clint Burnham, Brian Day, Gilles Devault, Dennis Denisoff, Sky Gilbert, Blaine Marchand, Daniel David Moses, Jim Nason, Billeh Nickerson, Brian Rigg, Ian Iqbal Rashid, Stephen Schecter, and R. M. Vaughn. They have broadened and enriched Canada's gay-male poetry, bringing into play issues of race, ethnicity, and post-colonialism that have leavened the narcissism, stridency, and technical infelicity of some of their peers, lessers, and forgettable antecedents.

Jean-Paul Daoust's remarkable *Les cendres bleues*, which won the Governor General's Award for Poetry in French in 1990 (Nicole Brossard was on the jury), is one of the period's masterworks. Narrated by a middle-aged man who exposes, mourns, and celebrates the adult lover of his preteens who, after initiating him to the joy and complexity of physical and emotional intimacy, commits suicide. Subverting the paradigm that it is only the recipients of 'abuse' who are the victims, this book-length poem is audacious as well in its technique. Structured as a single unpunctuated sentence, it proceeds for over fifty pages without pause or stanza break, relying only on line breaks to calibrate the unfolding of its bold and compelling story. Walter Borden's verse play, *Tightrope Time: Ain't Nuthin' More Than Some Itty Bitty Madness Between Twilight & Dawn*, a one-man show (performed by Borden) that George Elliott Clarke has described as "a contemporary Africadian drama,"[51] is equally important. Though not primarily gay in focus, it features a "*bizarrerie*" of twelve characters

---

50 *The Church-Wellesley Review* was a literary annual published in the late 1980s and early 1990s as a supplement to the Pride issue of *XTRA*, Toronto's bimonthly gay and lesbian newspaper.

51 George Elliott Clarke, "Must All Blackness Be American? Locating Canada in Borden's 'Tightrope Time,' or Nationalizing Gilroy's *The Black Atlantic*" in *Odyssey's Home*. Toronto: University of Toronto Press: 2002, 74.

who in cabaret-style monologues articulate a Canadian perspective on black experience as distinct from its American counterpart and "rescue[s] the devalued black body" and, through Ethiopia, a drag queen, and Chuck, a rent boy, "redeems that of the homosexual."[52]

A new generation of gay-male poets—poets born in the 1970s and 1980s and who are publishing their first books today—is beginning to make its presence felt. They express a more fluid sexual orientation than the one voiced by the poets of Stonewall and AIDS, a sexuality that may often be secondary to other preoccupations. Without deflecting the marginalization or anger that are among their elders' traditional themes, they take their sexuality in stride and do not automatically let it trouble the surface of their poems or draw attention to itself. Seldom do they attempt to state a case for tolerance or solicit empathy for themselves as gay men but, when they are motivated to address issues of sexuality (as does Michael V. Smith in "Salvation"), they often do so in order to shed light on a transgressive complexity, which might have daunted past generations of poets, or in order to connect their sexuality to issues like masculinity, as Michael Knox does in his book, *Play Out the Match*. These poets do not inhabit a "subculture," do not see themselves as outside the "canonical" traditions of poetry, and do not perceive their stories as excluded from it or something to slip in subversively because in broad strokes, if not in the details, they feel more confident that these stories are now recognized as part of an inclusive human narrative.

These poets are perhaps the natural inheritors of Robin Blaser, if not in style or ability (for how they mature as poets is yet to be seen), then in an emphasis on a queer poetics felt as a *part* of a larger poetics that embraces the plenitude of experience in the public realm. The stridencies of the past forty years may not necessarily interest them, but their sense of themselves is not in any way a reversion back to the straight-acting and polarizing rubric of not being a "gay poet" but being a poet "who happens to be gay." Rather, their attitude is one of synthesis, a confidence that moves beyond identity politics because identity itself is no longer questionable, but a fact to be parsed and questioned. Compare Sean Horlor's "In Praise of Beauty" or "For St. Jude, or What Gets Him Where He Is" to Blaser's "In Remembrance of Matthew Shepard." Both see experience on a higher metaphysical plane that neither denies its grittiness nor excludes queerness.

---

52 Ibid, 79.

Seminal, with its self-confident, even arrogant, subtitle, "*the* anthology," is a representation of the gay-male poets writing in this country past and present as well as a sampling of the poetry written by its fifty-seven contributors. Billeh Nickerson and I have attempted to broaden its scope by locating and including poets writing from other subjectivities besides our own—black, Indigenous, Jewish, South Asian, Chinese, Québécois—those poets whose points of reference are different from the blandishing defaults of the "English" language and "white" culture. We hope our efforts provide the basis for a more nuanced understanding of what it has meant to write "queer" poetry in Canada for just over one hundred years.

Of course, there are inevitable omissions. Several poets or their estates declined our invitation because they felt discomfort at the idea of being included in an anthology circumscribed by the word "gay," believing this filter "narrowed" possible readings of their work by de-universalizing and devaluing it in some diminishing way. In its diversity this is a fear that *Seminal* entirely refutes. More worrying are those writers whom we might have left out simply because we could not find them. We did not widely circulate a call for submissions, concerned that only those poets who did not heed Jane Rule's call for technical rigour would respond and overwhelm us. Instead we solicited recommendations from as many quarters as possible. Still, who knows what questions we failed to ask, what leads we did not pursue diligently enough? That a poet might not have been found after such an exhaustive search as ours suggests Canada may still have a long way to go as an inclusive literary culture.

During the assembly of any anthology like *Seminal*, the question of greatness inevitably comes up—raised immediately after the question as to why such an anthology is needed at all (a question usually raised by straight middle-aged men who hate to be excluded from any club that's going, even if they do truly grasp what the method of initiation is) has been ignored as defying credulity. Who is Canada's great gay-male poet? Is there more than one? Why haven't we produced a Walt Whitman? Where is our Hart Crane? Our W. H. Auden, our Robert Duncan, our John Ashbery? Why do we not see one or more among us, or is it only that we don't know where to look? Each of *Seminal*'s readers will decide on his (or *her*) own, but I hope critical judgement will not be clouded by typically Canadian myopias not too different from the ones I raised when discussing the long shadow that I believe the fate of Patrick Anderson's work has cast over Canadian gay-male poetry in general.

As Canadians, we have a hard time keeping track of our expatriates while at the same time appreciating the "strangers" among us, and English Canadians have a particularly hard time developing an awareness of anything written or experienced in the "other" official language. Would not permanent expatriate Edward A. Lacey (whose published works have never moved beyond a base-ment-press milieu) or Illinois-resident Daryl Hine (whose *Recollected Poems* will be published in 2007 by Fitzhenry & Whiteside, making his work avail-able in a Canadian edition for the first time since his *Selected Poems* of 1980) or Idaho-born Robin Blaser (whose revised and expanded collected poems, *The Holy Forest*, was published by the University of California Press in 2006) or Jean-Paul Daoust (who has published two limited *Selected Poems* in English translation with Guernica in 1991 and 1999) all be worthy of consideration as equals among Canada's other canonical figures? To be fair, Blaser is revered in many quarters and Gary Geddes did represent his work in *15 Canadian Poets* × *Three*,[53] but when an anthology of contemporary Canadian poetry was re-cently published in the United States, its Canadian-born editor admitted that the name of no living Canadian gay-male poet came to mind when drawing together its contents.

However, the merits of gay-male poetry and its potential to grasp Parnassus have been placed into perspective for me by John D'Emilio in an article recently published by *The Gay and Lesbian Review*. This respected University of Illinois historian makes the following salient observation:

> *Since the early 1960s, the lives of many, many heterosexuals have become much like the imagined lives of homosexuals.* Being hetero-sexual no longer means settling as a young adult into a lifelong coupled relationship sanctioned by the state and characterized by the presence of children and sharply gendered spousal roles. Instead, there may be a number of intimate relationships over the course of a lifetime. A marriage certificate may or may not accompany these relationships. Males and females alike expect to earn their way. Children figure less importantly in the lifespan of adults, and some heterosexuals, for the first time in history, choose not to have children at all. [The italics are D'Emilio's.][54]

---

53 Gary Geddes, ed. *15 Canadian Poets* × 3. Don Mills, Ont.: Oxford University Press, 2001.
54 John D'Emilio, "The Marriage Fight is Setting Us Back," *Gay and Lesbian Review* 13 (November-December 2006) 10–11.

Who knew that the Joneses were trying to keep up with us homosexualists and not the other way around? Though D'Emilio happens to be talking about social change in context with the Gordian knot that same-sex marriage has sadly proven itself to be in the United States, a knot that certain conservatives[55] in our own country have attempted to retie without any judicial or legislative success, he affirms and reminds us that the social standing we have built for ourselves is the definitive "new normal," to appropriate—and hopefully debase—another politically loaded term.

In decades past, we have viewed, even valorized ourselves as aberrant and have been treated as such. We have decried and praised ourselves for our innate and accursed "otherness." Though some in the queer community truly do mourn the loss of our fabled outlaw status in exchange for the attainment of our rights, as if we should have our cake and still be able to eat it, too, on the sly, this new normal we have called into being opens up our possibilities substantially today—especially if we continue to *drag* the rest of society forward with us.

For the gay-male poet, the range, parameters, and depth of potential themes at last are limitless. Still, simply to imagine that the societal changes improving our queer lives might have been triggered more by heterosexuals following our subliminal cues and less by our persistent demand for an equal (poetic) voice could turn any understanding of a century's progress on its pink-lined ear.

Who knew our poets had been queering the world so beautifully and productively all along?

2007

---

55 The social conservatives have their apologists in surprising quarters. Even respected McGill University ethicist Margaret Somerville, while first arguing discrimination based on sexual orientation is morally repugnant, attempts to develop a convincing argument against same-sex marriage in the 2006 Massey Lectures (see *The Ethical Imagination* [Toronto: House of Anansi, 2006]: 101–104).

Men of Honour: Prototypes of the Heroic in the Poetry of Douglas LePan

IN OCTOBER 1941, DOUGLAS LePan, twenty-seven years old and a former Harvard lecturer anxious to join the fight against Germany, sailed for Europe. Refused by every branch of the Canadian military for being shortsighted, he decided nonetheless to throw his hat into the war effort. Within months of his arrival in England, LePan was a civilian advisor to General Andrew McNaughton on army education, charged with developing non-combat training courses for Canadian Army troops stationed in England while awaiting deployment. He came to know "the General" well, remembering him in *Bright Glass of Memory*, a memoir he published in 1979, in worshipful terms as "a great man, one of the greatest I have ever known, and certainly the greatest Canadian" and as "a man in whom the heroic spirit breathed more constantly" than in any he had encountered before or since.

By comparing McNaughton to Headley Court, the stately seat of the Canadian Army in Europe, LePan uses his regard for the General to draft a blueprint of sorts in "Two Views of Army Headquarters," one of fifty sonnets that constitute the third-person "autobiography"-in-verse opening *Weathering It* (1987):

> It was like a Renaissance palace, he would tell his London
> friends. And by that he meant that its corridors and conference-
> rooms, even its gables and clustered chimneys, were informed
> by the presence and virtue of a single man, as they might
> have been by the presence of the prince at Urbino or Ferrara;
> that his authority invested it; that its secrets were made darker,
> its decisions more final because of his passionate intelligence.

With distance, LePan also admits to his hero's faults: "But now, compared with what followed, it seems rather flimsier, / more like a castle that a child might have cut out of paper." History was unkind to McNaughton; he is forever linked with Canada's losses in the failed attempt to retake Dieppe in 1942. LePan's regard, therefore, was never blind, and it is crucial to realize that, for him, failure does not necessarily compromise greatness.

LePan's belief in greatness—in the heroic—runs through his writing. His heroes are thrown into focus through diverse lenses. He may pick up his field glasses and, depending on which end he looks through, try to see from up close or afar what it is that makes a man; nearly all of his protagonists are men—admirable as explorers, soldiers, or lovers. Achilles, the Green Man, and others provide him with useful metaphoric washes.

What so disposed LePan towards prototypes of the heroic? Like many of his generation, the imperative to defeat Nazism fired him, for, after finally succeeding to enlist, he saw action in Italy. Yet, he recalls, "there was nothing in my [previous] experience, or almost nothing, that might have led me to honour the military virtues as I was to come to later. In spite of my growing unbelief, the specifically Christian virtues still shone far more brightly in my personal pantheon of values than the military virtues of courage, patience, and loyalty." Still, despite having steeped himself in Marx and the left-wing politics fashionable among his peers in face of the Depression and the growing "menace" of fascism, LePan admits any apparent consensus he shared with them "impinged...less as experience than in the realm of the intellect." Even before Hitler invaded Poland in September 1939, he knew that he "could never be a pacifist or a communist"; war was "inevitable and Canada would be involved, and I would be involved too."

Born on May 25, 1914, in Toronto, his father responsible for buildings and grounds at the University of Toronto, Douglas Valentine LePan grew up conventionally and comfortably middle-class. He did well in school, and went on to study at the University of Toronto and Oxford. In "Arthurian Enchantments," he describes the engaged nature of his childhood reading:

> Start with a boy engrossed in "King Arthur and his Knights"
> and let that sink in until he is hardly aware of the residue
> lost in his bloodstream. Now he has left knights in armour far
> behind, their crests, plumes, mantlings, streaming in the wind;
> but he still likes a style of military dash and crispness,
> with hints of heraldry, of tapestry, or ancient music.

"Hints of heraldry" provide LePan with a treasury of images to gild his protagonists, as does the residue of what once was considered an essential "classical" education. The master in his poem "Reading the *Iliad*" guides his pupil through the difficult ancient text, having "heard of no dispensation" from death and defeat and

> who accepted it, welcomed it, rejoiced in it, but believed
> that it still mattered enormously to try to make something of it
> and that all ages could be, should be heroic ages—
> ah, there was something to stick to your ribs....

That all ages, even LePan's own, should be "heroic," and that all men (and women) should strive to be "heroic," is what pumps hot blood through every vein of his poetry outwards from its noble heart to the extremities.

The explorer, a figure cutting a path through the wilderness of all of LePan's books and his first prototype of the hero, is sighted in "*Coureurs de bois*" from *The Wounded Prince* (1948). He identifies his hero with the Precambrian shield to give him rugged, weathered, and monumental substance, a standard against which other men—even the unidentified "you" of the first line—are measured:

> Thinking of you, I think of the *coureurs de bois*,
> Swarthy men grown almost to savage size
> Who put their brown wrists through the arras of the woods
> And were lost—sometimes for months.

However, he is not a Longfellowesque hero bushed in the romantic torpor of the nineteenth century, but is caught up in the compromising logjams of the twentieth:

>   ...But now
> That the forests are cut down, the rivers charted,
> Where can you turn, where can you travel? Unless
> Through the desperate wilderness behind your eyes,
> So full of falls and glooms and desolations,
> Disasters I have glimpsed but few would dream of.

Though the journey into the mind's *terra incognita* may well present LePan's explorer with challenges any Canadian reader would expect a hero to face, it is seen in the poet's signature heraldic terms:

You seek new Easts. The coats of difficult honour,
Bright with brocaded birds and curious flowers,
Stowed so long with the vile packs of pemmican,
Futile, weighing down on slippery portages,
Would flutter at last in the courts of a clement country,
Where the air is silken, the manners easy,
Under a guiltless and reconciling sun.

It is as if Paul Kane had adopted Dante Gabriel Rosetti's palette when he canoed west to paint the Indigenous peoples of the central plains. Though LePan's use of Indigenous imagery is in danger of causing most contemporary readers significant discomfort, he may have at first improvidently seen them as part of his patrimony as a Canadian writer. Were he alive today, how well would he have understood an Indigenous reading of his work? I would like to think that he could see some justice in their anger.

In "The Green Man," from 1982's *Something Still to Find*, LePan's explorer reappears, still robust, almost forty years later, but he moves through a darker, grittier, late-twentieth-century landscape:

But I have glimpsed him almost everywhere.
In pool-rooms and bargain-basements. In the glance of the dark
prisoner in the dock, not knowing how to plead,
passionate the criss-cross light that sifts through leaves.
In pale changing-rooms at the atomic energy plant
the young technician is changed into a sylvan man,
shadowed with mystery, and suffering from the sap
like a young green tree, quick thrall of earth and frenzy.

By nature, he is still a sensuous creature at liberty in "the carnal wood" shaping human psyches ("dreams flow into the woods, woods flow / into dreams,"), but the forest remains real, where "Champlain, green traveller, trader, / debauchee…. was cooked and eaten."

It seems inevitable that LePan, by sensing the wilderness in the Canadian soldiers he fought beside up the boot of Italy, would feel immediate kinship. Without diminishing the horrors they faced together, he puts a romantic spin on his comrades in arms. His second prototype of the hero, met in *The Net and the Sword* (winner of the 1953 Governor General's Award for Poetry), is the explorer in khaki:

> Arrange the scene with only a shade of difference
> And he would be a boy of his own native
> And fern-fronded providence,
> With a map in his hand, searching for a portage overgrown
> With brush.

Though the boy in "An Incident" is shot by chance against the ruins of a once-civilized Italian landscape ("A stray round has caught him at the nape of the neck / And splayed him flat on the earth, / His blood flung wide as a sunburst."), as a type the soldier, whose integrity is forged through his connection to the land, is stalwart. In "A Man of Honour," redemption resides in preparedness and strength:

> Silently as an Arctic convoy steers
> He must be stern and lonely, from the raked wings
> Of his patrolling vices hide his fears.
> At action stations always. One false move brings
> A pack of submarines, one whimper tears
> The tissued pallor where salvation sings.

The soldier-hero archetype finds its apotheosis in LePan's last book, *Macalister, or Dying in the Dark* (1995), a verse drama about John Kenneth Macalister. A Canadian born in the same year as LePan was, Macalister parachuted into occupied France as a secret agent and was almost immediately captured, imprisoned, tortured, and later executed at Buchenwald. Like T. S. Eliot's *Murder in the Cathedral*, the book's climax is a foregone conclusion, tragedy lying in the destruction of an ethical man. A ghost with whom LePan engages in a series of dialogues (with asides from a historian and the hero's wife and mother), Macalister knew the risks:

> Somehow I saw our civic polity stripped of its sophistications,
> stripped to a beating heart, a single courage, that pumped
> its lifeblood through our puny efforts at comity and justice.
> And saw myself stripped of my ambitions and aspirations,
> stripped to something much more simple and afraid, wondering

what I would be willing to die for, and in that wonder
somehow forgetting fear and gaining a strange new sense of being…

That one can be remade through a willingness to die is central to LePan's concep-
tualization of the heroic: those cognizant of risk establish a new praxis. Yet LePan
also does not glamorize or whitewash how brutally Macalister met his end:

Don't close your eyes. Don't turn away. I'll help you.

Being beaten up by the SS. His face swollen, his eyes almost shut.

Then a coil of piano wire noosed round his neck

and that looped round a meat-hook cemented into the wall.

Then being hoisted up and being dropped softly, softly,

so that his neck wouldn't mercifully be broken.

Then turnings, twistings, twitchings, twitterings.

And then the iron maw of the ovens.

Macalister is LePan's greatest hero, embodying virtues he places above all
others:

　　　　　　　—And without a core of courage
how can anything ever be achieved, can anything be built?
And courage shadowed by weakness may be the most precious
of all, since it carries sweetness into the heart of the building,
carries it like honey into the hollows of the honey-comb.

However much LePan may cloak his soldiers in heraldic vestments—"Archaic
creature, I would wear you chevroned / On my arm as emblem of a naked
heart" (from "The Lost Crusader" in *The Net and The Sword*)—he sees them as
vulnerable yet brave. They overcome human frailty through sacrifice and attain
honour.

In 1990, five years before the publication of *Macalister*, LePan made manifest another "new" sense of being with the release of *Far Voyages*. A collection of ecstatic, elegiac poems, it stands as a lasting tribute to Patrick Fabbri, a younger man he'd loved, whose death five years earlier at the age of thirty-seven brought their fifteen-year affair to an end. These autobiographical love poems encourage a subtle reappraisal, not a repudiation, of LePan's previous work. In "Coureurs de bois," the enigmatic "you" is now potentially scrutable as a lover: in *Bright Glass of Memory*, he alludes to an affair that was still wounding him when he arrived in England in 1941; he later acknowledged it was closely connected to this poem.[1] LePan's one novel, *The Deserter* (winner of the 1964 Governor General's Award for Fiction), recounts the story of a soldier, who, despite decorated acts of bravery, abandons his post at war's end, eluding capture by hiding out with his own kind until he finally, ironically, turns himself in. LePan further encourages such reappraisals by republishing in *Far Voyages* "A Cluster of Love Poems," a sequence that had appeared in *Something Still to Find* eight years earlier. The poet's object of desire was now clarified.

In "A Stream of Images," LePan celebrates the lover, his third heroic prototype, and he clothes him in recognizable trappings:

It's because of you these images return,
images of clay, or watery bronze, or gold,
images of athletes, gods, and heroes,
images of wounds, or wounds transcended,
images emerging from green wilderness
but then opening like the flowering lotus,
like water-lilies at the margins of our lakes,
into pure radiance as at the world's
first morning, fresh, vivid, undismayed,
instinct with love and vision that make
them flow, yet hold them in a flowing
timeless river. Because of you this stream of
                     Images returning
                     Images of the hero and the river

---

1   This connection that was explained to me via email by his son, Don LePan.

In "Lords and Commons," he compares his lover to chivalrous Richard the Lionheart, "whose attributes in war and peace, so the chroniclers / say, were a rare courage and liberality and constancy; / and those gifts are yours, too— whether in the traffic / of your daytime occasions or in the dark play of *jouissance*." In "Dread," after his lover is struck with terminal illness, LePan perceives medical treatment as a "battle with insurgent cells, that grim / guerrilla war" which they face the prospect of losing together: "Down into dread, now we go down into dread together." LePan describes the end in terms that anticipate those he would employ to describe Macalister's far more horrific death, by using metaphors of being bound:

> It's a strange kind of sundance, a harsh leathery sundance,
> as the subtleties of referred pain bind us together, the thongs
> looped under my chest, the pain round my heart, circling
> your pain, as if hoping to restore a clouded brightness,
> as if to restore a young sun-king to his youthful vigour.

Ultimately, in "According to La Rochefoucauld," LePan approaches love as an arena for ethics, where intimacy is governed by conscious choice as well as desire:

> Constancy in love is of two kinds
>   wrote terse La Rochefoucauld.
> One is like an inexhaustible spring and comes from constantly finding
> new things to love in the one you love. The other comes from
> making it a point of honour to be constant. (And you might want
> to remember that he was a soldier before turning aphorist.)

In "Bravado of Spring," he characterizes what he shares with his lover as having "the weight and breathing of bulls," eschewing the genteel refinements of the love shared by so many other pairs of lovers ("Leaves falling, snowflakes falling, tears falling"), believing "There'll be time enough for that when we're both in our graves."

Douglas LePan lived another eight years after the publication of *Far Voyages*, dying on November 27, 1998, at age eighty-four. He had been a soldier, a diplomat, an academic, a husband, a father, and a lover. He left behind eight volumes of poetry, fiction, and nonfiction and was recognized by numerous awards, including the Order of Canada just prior to his death. In 1956, Northrop Frye described him as a "genuine poet" (*The Bush Garden*, 1971), yet little mention is made of him today. In *Bright Glass of Memory*, he laments that he did not write and publish more, wondering if he had too closely adhered to Eliot's rarified standards of excellence; indeed, almost thirty years of silence separates the publication of *The Net and The Sword* in 1953 from *Something Still to Find* in 1982. Would we still remember him had he been more prolific?

Or do deeper reasons exist? Are LePan's heroic prototypes too idealized for current taste? Though he created opportunities for fashionable new interest in his work by writing openly about his homosexuality in his last years, are today's readers—including the baby boomers who protested against Vietnam and the GenXers who entered adulthood in the Cold War's aftermath—put off by the noble soldier figures that predominate throughout his poetry?

Maybe LePan fought the wrong war. Despite the recent marking of the sixtieth anniversaries of the D-Day landings and of V-E and V-J Days, Canadians seem more engaged with the First World War, entranced by its anointed place as crucible of our nationhood in celebrated novels from Timothy Findley's *The Wars* of 1977 to Joseph Boyden's *Three Day Road* of 2006 (books such as Anne Michaels' *Fugitive Pieces* are less about Canadians in the Second World War than the Holocaust). However, now that the parents of the baby boom—the generation that defeated the fascists in Germany, Italy, and Japan—are dying off with greater dispatch, perhaps our nostalgic literary interest in LePan's war might be more thoroughly aroused. The time for Douglas LePan's poetry could still be ahead.[2]

2007

---

2   Twelve years after *Arc* published this essay in its theme issue, *Canada's Forgotten and Neglected Poets* (Summer 2007), Dundurn and Porcupine's Quill republished LePan's novel, *The Deserter*, and *The Essential Douglas LePan*, a selected poems that I edited, in the spring of 2019.

We Are Not Avatars: How the Universal Disembodies Us

"To discover the truth in anything that is alien, first dispense
with the indispensable in your own vision."

—Leonard Cohen

HOW OFTEN HAVE WE heard critics pronounce a book good because they feel that its author has succeeded in saying something universal about the human condition? Is it because the author has managed to rub their classic-in-waiting free of inessential detail to such a degree that anyone who turns its pages is able without trouble to see reflected in it a recognizable, comprehensive meaning? Over the years, I have become suspicious of the universal, even though I may have once been consciously or unconsciously susceptible to the eye-catching allure of its patina myself. I have come to wonder what my peers and I had attempted to accomplish when we hoped to make what we wrote shine with a profundity that was commonly held. I now question those who revere universality and who presume such an accolade entitles them to exert influence.

The Canadian edition of the *Collins English Dictionary* cites the following meanings for the adjective "universal" (there are nine more):

> 1 of or typical of the whole of mankind or of nature 2 common to or proceeding from all in a particular group 3 applicable to or affecting many individuals, conditions, or cases 4 existing or prevailing everywhere.

Definitions 2 and 4 are revealing. The latter affirms that the universal embraces everything and everyone and, therefore, everything and everyone must exude it. The former qualifies universality somewhat, intimating that it applies to a subset of humanity or, to reiterate, is "common to… a particular group." The use of "all" in definition 2, which *Collins* describes as a "determiner," calls attention to itself. Does "all" mean that no deviation is allowed?

As a queer writer of emphatically homoerotic texts, I have often felt marginalized and made to feel that what I write about is not the common ground most readers expect to find beneath their feet. Some publishers once shied away from the G word in the materials they prepared to promote my books, worried that use of it would compromise sales even more in the already small poetry market. Some among us, queer writers like Larry Kramer and Colm Tóibín, have enjoyed wide readerships despite what they write about and have helped to create an audience for lesser known writers like myself. How can authors of such calibre be considered tangential? Even though, as a poet, I will never match them for reach, why should I be perceived as ghettoizing myself because of what I choose to write about? Is there even a gay ghetto anymore? In literary contexts, some, it seems, would say yes. The ungenerous might even insist that I wear my ghetto sensibility as a medal pinned to my chest.

Coming of age in the mid-1970s, I was formed by the after-effects of a gay-liberation movement that fostered open articulations of a once-stigmatized otherness. From the early 1980s onwards, I witnessed and supported the fight to secure effective AIDS treatment, especially when the disease, in the western democracies at least, appeared mostly to affect gay men. Many saw the slow response of certain governments as purposeful erasure. The political correctness of the 1990s that called for the restraint of inappropriate speech and determined who had the right to speak for anyone about anything shaped me profoundly. While these forces did not exert influence upon everyone who lived through the same years, it should surprise no one that I take umbrage with often self-appointed tastemakers who argue for universality while simultaneously contending that what I have to say does not pertain to or interest them. Why should I pay heed to the promulgation of any universal that does not give much credence to my queer experience?

Over the course of my career as a poet, I developed my craft, discovered my subject, and found my voice. Glancing over my writing, however, I can see that it took me a while to disabuse myself of the universal, which I view as an automatic default that displaces a broad range of thoughts and feelings, including my own, in favour of those that are understood as *a priori*. In my poems of the late 1970s and early 1980s, I remember being determined to describe and speak for a figure whom I called "Representative Man," though I did not then recognize the sexism that he embodied. I hoped to populate my poems with a pathos bracing enough for readers to respond with fellow feeling. In "Saint Francis of the Passmore," a poem I wrote in 1981 or 1982, my goal was to create a portrait of another tenant in the building that was my home in downtown Victoria for two years, an eon for anyone in their twenties:

> Being reticent he is easy
> with stray cats and Karl Marx.
> Slipping through the creaking
> red door into the shadowed
> chaos of the courtyard,
> the dialectic mewing
> greedily at his feet,
> two bowls of milk balanced
> in one hand, he smiles,
> certain of small things.
>
> Just home from the grave
> yard shift, the Saturday
> sun catches him unprepared.
> Out of habit he shields
> his eyes. Years of want
> nourish the irony ripening
> inside the cage that ribs
> slowly knit; the heart an apple
> condensing on the tree of blood—
> his mother, his father dead;
> one brother drowned,
> the rest—windblown seeds.
> Silently he laughs.
> Deep eyes follow each twist
> of ivy snaking over white
> tenement walls into light
> and warmth. He has read
> nothing stills the heart.

The poem's narrator exhorts readers to feel empathy for my friend by presenting him as a gentle-hearted shift worker of perceptible depth: this soft-hearted man feeds neighbourhood strays (he views them as some sort of underclass); he is alone (the members of his family are either dead or distant); and he is resilient (he knows nothing in this world compromises the possibility of compassion). Basically, he's "representative" of all neo-sensitive everymen of the time period, but we don't know much else about him. Despite how nice he is, he's a cutout, a skeleton without flesh.

"Saint Francis of the Passmore" later appeared in my 1993 collection, *Notes Toward a Family Tree*, which offered sanctuary to a few vestigial heterosexual love poems that three years earlier I had purposely not gathered into *Great Men*, my first substantial book of gay-themed poems. Emerging out of a persistent confusion about the direction in which my attractions lay, my fourth and fifth books were published in an order incompatible with any gay man's stage-managed coming out. I had originally intended to publish their combined contents gathered as a single volume with the working title of *Comedians in the Same Desire*. Other writers convinced me that publishing gay- and straight-themed poems together would confuse readers so, like a vaudeville magician, I sawed *Comedians* in two and began submitting the cauterized halves to publishers simultaneously. The gay book was accepted first. Today such compartmentalizing stagecraft likely would not be necessary.

Narcissist that I was, when the *Notes Toward a Family Tree* was at last published, I feared the love poems addressed to women that it contained would expose me to prurient scrutiny. Would the readers of *Great Men* think I was recanting or had been the willing subject of conversion therapy? I felt I had to make it clear that in these poems I was tying up the loose ends of what for me was a literary vasectomy. No progeny of this ilk shall henceforth be heard. The collection ends with an afterword I called a "Social Note":

> Some readers may be curious to know how a gay writer can write about straight experience. Some gay writers would respond that gay men and lesbians have a detached position in society, one which anthropologists seem to value so much: that of the participant observer. However, that sense of detachment is not one of which gay people are always initially aware, especially early in life.
>
> Consequently, some of us pursue values and love objects in harmony with those of our straight brothers and sisters, friends and relatives, under the hopeful if not always perceptive eyes of our parents. Our experience is first hand and not just because

we were raised to be straight and to live in a straight world. We remain literate in its culture, even after the acknowledgement of our true nature.

My use of the word "literate" is significant. Through it I asserted my familiarity with what I would have at the time called the heteronormative mainstream. Maybe I had planned (hoped) to keep tabs on the universal as something to define myself as *not* being. When it came to sexual orientation, I saw, and continue to see, heterosexuality as society's default for universality, even while I willingly hung a toe over the abyss of "otherness." As the inevitability of my fall loosened my grip, I trusted my voice—or the echo of my voice—would still be heard by the mainstream after I hit bottom. The poems in *Notes Toward a Family Tree* resonated loudly enough with jurors that it won an Ottawa Book Award while *Great Men*, albeit nominated for the same award, did not. Of the two collections, the latter has exerted more consequence in my career.

In the poems that became *Great Men*, Representative Man began to evolve, to take on less universal attributes. The book's first and last sections house more politically strident poems ("Those like us / refuse like us / to live as if we have never been.") while the section sandwiched in between is a refuge for love poems grounded in the private and the intimate ("I take your hand in the dark, / the car lights off, transmission in neutral"). Though the direction of my gaze had shifted, I still wanted the narrator of and the person addressed in my love poems to remain empathetic and accessible to all readers, whatever their own objects of desire might happen to be. Like the great Greek poet C. P. Cavafy, I chose to use pronouns—"you," "I," "we," and "us," but never "he" or "him"—that wouldn't impolitely betray my narrator's and [his] lovers' genders. Readers instead had to infer the nature of their intimacy and the slant of their sexual obsessions through the frame that *Great Men*'s first and third sections provides.

It was in "Sustenance," the last love poem in the middle section, that I most overtly tipped my hand to show what my previously dealt cards had more subversively played out:

I tuck my hand under your bath robe
where your heart is, stubbled
chin resting on your shoulder as I suck
on your ear, your testes
at rest in my palm

> while you test the omelet's texture,
> ease the whole in two,
> the wedges light and fragile,
> the wedges risen half moons.

The reviews of *Great Men* broke into two distinct camps. Critics for mainstream publications like the *Ottawa Citizen* preferred the less-obvious love poems more and the apparently more attention-seeking gay political poems less. Reviewers writing for gay media like *The James White Review* felt exactly the opposite. This mixed response was my first true glimpse of how conflicted my readership would become. For some straight readers, I am overly explicit; for some of their gay peers, I am too evasive, even prim. One person's chastity belt is another's fetish. I began to understand the ideal of the universal to be a construct determined by a "particular group," to echo the *Collins English Dictionary*, that happened to constitute the majority. I came to feel that Representative Man's DNA had no valid standing in the world I had chosen to write about more candidly. I hope an anthropologist will someday exhume Representative Man's bones and wire them up for display between our disinherited Neanderthal ancestors and the recovered skeleton of his 1980s contemporary, the feminist male.

How love poems are read is based on the assumptions we make about their authors and who their protagonists should be. In a love poem by a straight author, the gender of the beloved is automatically set, accepted, and understood to be the opposite, not the other—i.e., the same—sex. Even if the reader's gender is different from the author's, he (or she) nevertheless knows which figure in the poem to identify with. Take, as an example, Eavan Boland's poem, "First Year"[1]:

> At night
> when we settled down
> in the big bed by the window,
> over the streetlight
> and the first crackle of spring
>
> eased the iron at
> the base of the railings

---

1   Eavan Boland, "First Year," *Against Love Poetry*. New York: Norton, 2001, 12–13.

unpacking crocuses
it was
the awkward corners of your snowy town

which filled
the rooms we made
and stayed there all year with
the burnt-orange lampshade,
the wasps in the attic.

Where is the soul of a marriage?

The gender of the author—unless a persona has clearly been adopted—is invariably a marker of the nature of the relationship that the narrator shares with the poem's addressee. Here, another marker is "your boyhood," which occurs later in the poem; it unambiguously confirms the addressee's gender. Readers now literally know the lay—and not the lie—of the land in that big bed. They may identify with the gender of whichever protagonist most closely matching theirs or with the role that best suits them and/or their own sexual orientation. As a gay reader of Boland's poem, I can identify with either protagonist. I can imagine my beloved's boyhood and I can imagine my beloved contemplating my own. Or I can decide not to identify with either protagonist, but appreciate the poem as an opportunity to get an inside view of what a heterosexual marriage is like in its initial (dis)orienting year.

Imagine of how differently "First Year" would be understood if Eavan Boland were a gay man, the love's queerness signaled to readers the moment we encountered "your boyhood," our experience of [his] poem taking us in an entirely different direction. The present debate about same-sex marriage in the Unites States could not fail to impinge upon the line, *"Where is the soul of a marriage?,"* which would elicit an interpretation that no heterosexual reading of it need contemplate, especially in California, where Boland teaches at Stanford and where, in a ballot question, voters overturned the legality of marriages between two people of the same sex.[2] Because "First Year" is the eighth

2   This essay was written in the aftermath of the November 2008 election that made Barak Obama president. In California, voters cast ballots in favour of Proposition 8 and repealed gay-marriage, which had been legal in that state since 2004. California Supreme Court

in an eleven-part suite of love poems in Boland's ironically titled 2001 collection, *Against Love Poetry*, its placement in relation to what precedes and follows it further determines how readers are meant to interpret a line that italics additionally freight, and how they are intended to apprehend the intimacy to which the sequence makes them privy at this stage of its unfolding. Once the poet signals that this marriage was "solemnized" over thirty years ago, savvy readers would immediately realize that no church of any denomination in the 1970s would have agreed to host, let alone sanction, a union between two men; nor would it have been legal. The couple would have instead appropriated the idea of marriage for their own purposes, with the poet intending the poem to read as a testament to the resolve of "forbidden" love to rise above societal prohibition, its resilience equal to heterosexual love's putative stability. The celebrants attending this unrecognized marriage of alike bodies and two minds might even tender its candidacy to be declared universal—but only in a subcultural way, to affirm *Collins'* second definition of universal ("common to or proceeding from all in a particular group"). Depending on each reader's capacity for tolerance, such a union would be viewed wrong or right. Either conclusion would allow them to feel morally superior. The poem's decorous tone might let it fly under the radar, much like the love poems in *Great Men* did, for not once does Boland violate the shibboleths against sexual explicitness. There's nothing juicy in this poem no matter how you read or misread it, as I willfully just have.

I can't help but wonder how straight readers navigate gay-authored poems. Where do their identifications settle? Do they feel or not feel alienated? How would they read "He Is"[3] by Métis poet Gregory Scofield:

> earthworm, caterpillar
> parting my lips, he is
>
> slug slipping between my teeth
> and down, beating

---

declared Prop 8 to be unconstitutional in June 26 2013, almost exactly two years before the U.S. Supreme Court made same-sex marriage legal nationwide in the United States. More complete details about Proposition 8 are found at https://en.wikipedia.org/wiki/California_Proposition_8_(2008). Retrieved September 10, 2018.

3   Gregory Scofield, "He Is," *Love Medicine and One Song*. Vancouver: Polestar, 1997, 21–22.

moth wings, a flutter
inside my mouth

he is snail kissing dew
from the shell of my ears,

spider crawling breath tracks
down my neck and weaving

watersnake, he is
swamp frog croaking my chest

hopping from nipple to nipple,
he is mouse

on my belly running circles
and circles, he is

grouse building his nest
from marsh grass and scent

This adroit, elliptical poem celebrates sexual intimacy between the narrator and his male lover. Readers establish the orientation of their relationship in exactly the same they do in the Boland's poem by equating the narrator's gender with the author's and by noting the stated gender of the beloved, which is established, at the earliest moment possible, in the poem's title. By layering his poem in lush imagery, Scofield might deflect the gaze of some readers: dazzle them in order to blind them to what is really going on. If they pay close attention, most will come to appreciate his skill at deploying images to evoke beautifully and candidly the sexual intimacy between two men. The insects, reptile, amphibian, and rodent that find safe harbour in this poem evoke how two entwined male bodies touch, kiss, and perform oral and anal sex. The images he draws from the natural world bond the two men and in their sensuality affirm that bond. The tenderness they give expression to through touch and taste confers a luminous dignity upon the love these two men share. This is not some meaningless casual encounter, but one through which sustaining emotions are felt in concert with intense physical sensation. Those feelings are further elevated by the pleasure Scofield takes in his playful use of language. The couple could even be marriage material.

Experience has taught me that heterosexual readers are sometimes intimidated by such poems because the queer physicality they body forth, once it is recognized behind its lustrous, mesmerizing, even anaesthetizing metaphorical artifice, is *frankly* unfamiliar. Even when this obstacle is overcome and the poem is *embraced*, to use another charged term, a fence is placed about it nonetheless. How often have I noted how the poems and stories that gay men write about sexual intimacy are characterized as "courageous"? In 1990, the publisher of *Great Men* used this word in the back-cover copy, *coupled* with "outrageous."[4]

Sometimes, whatever the gender or sexual orientation of a love poem's protagonists, they are figures stripped of flesh. They are each deployed as an avatar, which *Collins* defines as:

> **1** Hinduism the manifestation of a deity in human or animal form **2** a visible manifestation of an abstract concept.

Crucial words for me here are "manifestation," "visible," and "abstract." *Encarta* goes further:

> **3** online image of somebody in virtual reality: a movable three-dimensional image used to represent somebody in cyberspace. **4** computer game persona: a character or persona of a player with a graphical representation.

In literature, avatars can represent us, though they need not fully replicate or express us. They can even be consciously created to misrepresent us. They somehow become disconnected from the writers who breathe life into them by giving readers only those characteristics that allow them (the readers) to identify—and identify with—them (the avatars, the projections of their creators). This duel act of apparent empathy is based upon often fragmentary, if mutually recognizable terms of reference and is, I believe, the problematic heart of the universal's ills.

---

4   Twenty-five years after the publication of *Great Men*, Ben Ladouceur, in an interview with Jan Zwicky in *Contemporary Verse 2*, reveals that his 2015 book, *Otter*, elicited like responses: "I've only written the one book, and like me, the book is openly gay. I was surprised to see it characterized, in a few reviews and event listings and the like, as a brave or political book." Plus ça change, plus c'est la même chose. Jan Zwicky, "A Conversation with Ben Ladouceur," *Contemporary Verse 2*, 40.3 (Winter 2018), 8.

Sadly, when only some characteristics in the visual dictionary of human experience are limned, the so-called universality a poem or story claims to evince becomes questionable. Perhaps a better word for what we should aim for when we write is totality. While we work toward such an ideal of completeness, we must recognize that each of us can contribute only one puzzle piece in the completed picture. Did Shakespeare say everything about the world that needs to be said? I am sure Li Po would have an opinion.

The assumption that universality drops its anchor in mutuality flies in the face of what I maintain are the two reasons why any of us read: to see ourselves by having our experience of the world elucidated for us, and to learn something new by having our experience of the world broadened, if only vicariously. No writer should feel compelled to sacrifice the latter in order to guarantee the former. A friend once rebranded jetlag as "location shock." Unlike many travellers, he does not dismiss this sensory experience as something negative, but welcomes it as the new experience it is. I encourage readers who feel destabilized upon arriving somewhere unexpectedly exotic in what they read to literally relax and take in the scenery.

As a writer, I feel that it is appropriate to have expectations of my readers. To write may be an effort of the imagination, but to read is one also. Each act of identification through reading confirms what the word "act" implies: to be active. Reading is therefore not a passive experience of seeing only oneself. Readers must engage and enter into the experience of what is written. No longer am I willing to people my poems with figures I trust shall mirror back who readers think they are to themselves and others. To do so is to reduce my readers to avatars as well. Some may immediately acknowledge the agency of my protagonists; some will not. I encourage the former to plumb the nuances of my poems more deeply; I challenge the latter to push forward the frontiers of their empathy. My obligation in return is to write well and to ensure that the reading experience is enriching, even pleasurable, intellectually, spiritually, and emotionally. Neither author nor reader should feel disembodied. In place of universality, I propose and pursue *specificity*, which allows for the elucidation of my shard of a complex totality, and by this, I mean the clear and frank expression of all markers of its individuality.

I can think of nothing more specific, individual, or achingly tender than these lines from "Naked in New York,"[5] a poem by George Stanley:

---

5   George Stanley, "Naked in New York," *At Andy's*. Vancouver: New Star, 2000, 6–7.

A boy being kissed by another boy could tip over the applecart,
all the shiny red apples in the stacks, pyramids, buffed up for sale,
that were once in the dark of the barrel, homophobia, high school,
hoping none of us was rotten, no bad apple, no queer,

certain we were all unwanted, none wanted by any of the others—
tipped over, apples rolling, bumping, bouncing in the street, in the mud,
bruises, kisses (like pool balls), bites,
desire all over the place.

Stanley's long lines, barely contained in a single sentence, roll as sensuously as his apples tumble and shine. His is a patently queer Eros, the pain of stigma felt and, through desire, overcome. In "Divertissement," a poem from my forthcoming book, *Hymn*,[6] neither protagonist has anything to do with my long-lost avatar, "Representative Man," or with default universality:

Sex without kissing is all
about form, lips opened

for breath only, the unnamed
torso heraldic, the pierced

right nipple a medal of valour
untarnished by the tongue

face turned away as hands
work past hips, tattooed

skin of parted inner
thighs and buttocks a raised

map without relief of whose
sensate territory no one

---

6   I delivered this talk at the Sage Hill Writing Experience in Saskatchewan six months before Brick Books published *Hymn* in the fall of 2009.

can liberate, scrotum fanned
out above the perineum under

the about-to-flare lightning
head of a cobra, with no

lines to withdraw
behind, no matter how

deeply any are
hilted, pale

conscripts, eyes
closed or blank.

Gender and sexual orientation light up the forum where I argue against the falsehoods of the universal because they are what I know most about. Similar arguments can be waged from other vantages, including race, belief, and dis/ability, among the countless many. Whenever they are, I am committed to going where I have not read before. Whatever is at stake, the challenge is to find ourselves not only in what we know, but also in what we don't, and in every particularity to recognize what was once unfamiliar as innately human.

2009

"It Will Be Me": Stayin' Alive, AIDS as Part of Life, and Life Writing

As BOOKENDS, TO OPEN and close *Still Here*, an anthology of memoirs, short stories, and poems by people living with HIV/AIDS who joined writing groups offered by Mount Sinai Hospital in Toronto, editors Allan Peterkin and Julie Hann collage feedback received from participants.[1] Shared anonymously, the comments show how writing for these groups has affected, and even changed, lives. One participant "found that I gain insight into myself when I write. Specifically, this time, I learned about grief and HIV."[2] Another acknowledged that this "experience…has helped me to deal with a lot of disturbing issues that have haunted me for years. I have begun resolving a number of family issues relating to childhood, being gay, and having AIDS. My self-confidence and self-esteem are improving and my anxiety has decreased."[3] Therapeutically, such comments point to how putting sometimes inchoate, often challenging and isolating personal experiences into words and sharing them with others can make a substantial, affirming difference to people's lives. I wonder how many "professional writers"[4] would be as forthcoming about how their own work has influenced the way that they cope?

The sixty-six pieces collected in *Still Here*, which Peterkin and Hann published in 2008, were "submitted generously and voluntarily" by thirty-one Torontonians living with HIV/AIDS who had attended one or more of the fourteen groups they had led over the previous seven years. Most contribute one or two pieces to one or more of the anthology's five sections: "Change" (usually about the disorienting impact of becoming infected), "Hope" (poignantly, the section with the least number of contributions), "Severance" (the impact of AIDS on personal and professional relationships), "Treatment" (the most harrowing section), and "Loss" (the longest). A handful contribute three or more pieces—one

---

1   Allan Peterkin and Julie Hann, eds. *Still Here: A Post-Cocktail AIDS Anthology.* Toronto: Little Rattle, 2008, 327 pp.
2   Peterkin and Hann, 295.
3   Ibid.
4   Ibid.

participant clocks in at ten. Contributions range in length from half a page to thirteen. Whatever genre chosen by the authors as the most apt mode of expression, they're all autobiographical in focus and can be considered to be examples of what many call life-writing, which the Oxford Centre for Life-Writing defines as "encompassing everything from the complete life to the day-in-the-life, from the fictional to the factional. It embraces the lives of objects and institutions as well as the lives of individuals, families and groups."[5] While technique of course is important in order to achieve candour engaging enough to move readers, what is said matters more. And because all of the contributions to *Still Here* were written to be read and discussed in a therapeutic workshop environment, the impact on the author perhaps matters most. In fact, the anthology's publication might be considered an affirming, perhaps not final, stage in treatment.

Nine years after *Still Here*'s publication, Peterkin, a psychiatrist and founding editor of *Medica: A Journal of Medicine, the Arts and Humanities*, and Hann, a registered occupational therapist, both still work for the Clinic for HIV-Related Concerns, a division of the Department of Psychiatry at Mount Sinai. According to the anthology's introduction, it is "Canada's oldest psychiatric and psychotherapy clinic for men and women living with HIV/AIDS, their partners and family members."[6] As more effective treatments became available in the mid-1990s, the clinic must have seen less need to provide urgent palliative care to patients facing a deadly virus and a growing requirement to offer new psychotherapeutic approaches to support clients who were suddenly not facing the certainty of imminent death, but instead "an uncertain future."[7] Hann and Peterkin, having reviewed the medical literature about art and writing therapies established for other patient groups, obtained approval to offer a sixteen-week-long writing group for Torontonians who "had to be HIV-positive; [who] had to have an interest in writing, whether they had done much before or not; [and who] had to be able to attend regularly (barring any new illnesses)."[8] That men respond more robustly to writing therapies than women do was a further incentive because ninety percent of the clinic's clients were male[9]—and all the contributors to *Still Here* are gay men.

---

5   https://oxlifewriting.wordpress.com/about/what-is-life-writing/. Retrieved November 14, 2016.

6   Peterkin and Hann, 1.

7   Ibid.

8   Ibid, 303.

9   Ibid, 301.

The Narrative Competence Psychotherapy Group is now into its second decade. Peterkin and Hann offer "a creative opportunity for individuals living with HIV who share an interest in writing and the discussion of writing. Learning how to write your own stories and sharing them with others in a confidential setting may foster creative problem-solving and allow you to find a greater sense of meaning as you navigate your illness and its impact on your life."[10] Participants are asked to write each week for forty-five minutes, either at home or in a room designated for this purpose at Mount Sinai. The poetry or prose brought to the group must evince "narrative competence"—a term I am sure could be transferrable, with great potential positive effect, to both undergraduate and graduate-level creative writing—with a beginning, middle, and an end that are comprehensible to "a listener or reader, and [revealing of] the author's feelings or stance about the incident described." Unlike in other writing-therapy programs elsewhere, group members are invited to suggest ways to improve their peers' stories or to share something equivalent from their own life experience. This two-fold approach combines the strengths of group therapy with those of the writing workshop. Peterkin and Hann even solicited advice from the University of Toronto's creative-writing program. The longevity of the narrative-competence-group program is a measure of its usefulness, but more objective-assessment tools have been used elsewhere to determine the effectiveness of expressive-writing techniques. At the University of Auckland in New Zealand, for example, CD4 cell counts—an indicator of the health of the immune system and of HIV progression[11]—were found to rise among HIV-positive participants in a therapeutic writing program.[12] Peterkin and Hann offer no indication that similar testing was administered at Mount Sinai to see if expressive writing ameliorated the physical as well as the psychological health of group members. Perhaps they have embarked upon such studies in the years since Still Here's publication.

Statistics are certainly one way to come to grips with AIDS. In 1985, four years after the first documented cases of AIDS in the United States among gay men in Los Angeles were reported by the Centers for Disease Control, Ottawa began

---

10 https://www.mountsinai.on.ca/care/psych/patient-programs/hiv-clinic/narrative-competence-psychotherapy-group. Retrieved November 13, 2016.

11 https://www.aids.gov/hiv-aids-basics/just-diagnosed-with-hiv-aids/understand-your-test-results/cd4-count/. Retrieved November 6, 2016.

12 Peterkin and Hann, 300.

collecting data about the incidence of HIV in Canada. In the years since, 80,469 people have or have had HIV in this country; of these, 23,535 cases developed into "full-blown" AIDS—a descriptor I remember from the height of the AIDS crisis in the mid-1980s to the mid-1990s. At the end of 2014, the most recent year for which statistics are available, the estimated number of Canadians living with HIV/AIDS was 75,500, and it is believed that 16,020 of them are unaware of their status. The number of new diagnoses per year ranges from 1940 to 3200 (with an average of 2570 new diagnoses), and of these, 54% are gay men, many of whom are in their thirties, which is not surprising, I suppose, since most of them would theoretically have more than a decade's worth of sexual activity under their belts. According to the most recent data reported, 303 people died of AIDS in Canada in 2011.[13] At the height of the crisis in 1993, over 1800 Canadians succumbed to the virus[14]; it is estimated 26,400 men and women have died from AIDS or HIV complications in Canada since the epidemic began[15] (in comparison, 1.2 million have died in the United States[16]). Before effective treatments became available, the most optimistic estimate for life expectancy after being diagnosed was ten years.[17] Anyone who's lived in the shadow of the epidemic for as long as I have knows from experience that many lived only two.

Everything changed when, in 1996, the highly active antiretroviral therapy (HAART)—or drug cocktails, as they are more commonly known—started to be administered to AIDS/HIV patients in Canada. In what is often termed the Lazarus effect, these antiretroviral medications allowed patients whose symptoms had brought them perilously close to death literally to pull back almost overnight from succumbing to any of the opportunistic illnesses to which AIDS had made them vulnerable. Many of us can't forget watching friends and family whom we had feared losing begin to put back on weight, have colour return to their faces, and light brighten their eyes. At the time, I swam with the Rideau

13   Government of Canada. "Report to the Executive Director, UNAIDS, January 2014–2015," *Global AIDS Response Progress Report,* 2016, 3.

14   Government of Canada. *Public Health Agency of Canada. HIV and AIDS in Canada: Surveillance Report to December 31, 2014,* 11.

15   CATIE, "The Epidemiology of AIDS in Canada," *Fact Sheet,* 2016 (http://www.catie.ca/en/fact-sheets/epidemiology/epidemiology-hiv-canada). Retrieved November 12, 2016.

16   Bromberger, Brian. "HIV Survivors and the '16 Election, *The Gay & Lesbian Review Worldwide,* September-October 2016, 13.

17   CATIE, "Growing Old Gracefully, "*The Pos+ive Side,* Summer 2007. Retrieved October 26, 2016.

Speedeaux, a gay-and-lesbian masters swim team in Ottawa, and two men in my lane went back to work after years of being on long-term disability, the Kaposi's sarcomas that had once spread like inkblots all over their skin disappearing. They resumed active lives with once fast-approaching end dates no longer on the horizon. Their deaths became almost as abstract and theoretical as my own was—and still is—to me.

If the cocktails have pushed the possibility of, and the reality of, an AIDS death from front of mind for the well and the sick alike, they have not wholly erased the fear of premature death through the pursuit of sexual pleasures among gay men of my generation. AIDS has cast too long and dark a shadow for it not to persist in shadowing our lives. For some, such fear has been a more constant companion than many lovers. Had I come out when I turned eighteen in 1975, I may well have become any one of the above-cited statistics. Or I might now have been living with AIDS for two or three decades and contributed to this anthology. Instead I learned to protect myself, as did the friends I made after 1985—the year that Rock Hudson's highly publicized death pushed AIDS into mainstream consciousness—and I was also very lucky. We followed the safer-sex guidelines that began to circulate in Canada that year. Taking a sex-positive approach to guard against potential infection, they nevertheless emphasized that any partner could have the virus and unknowingly or knowingly pass it on and kill: Russian roulette one ejaculation and/or possibly defective condom at a time. We could not take anyone at their word, and still can't. Caution, if not outright suspicion, has become a reflex response, without doubt compromising the possibilities for emotional as well as physical intimacy. To our shame, many of us still avoid getting close to and loving any man we know is or may be HIV-positive. In a recent issue of *The Gay & Lesbian Review*, Brian Bromberger intuits the headspace of many AIDS survivors—and by "survivors" he means those who are infected and those who are witnesses: "despite advances today in treatment and prevention, '[they] are still reacting to AIDS emotionally as was done in the 1980s.'"[18]

However, for many who became sexually active since the late 1990s, AIDS is apparently less Grim Reaper than irresponsible uncle who happily leads them to believe that any breach resulting from failures in sexual hygiene can nevertheless be washed back with a cocktail of drugs mixed to match as exactly as possible their particular ill-gotten symptoms, thereby blunting infection's

---

18 Bromberger, 13.

once annoying and deadly embrace. The dodging of potential death became same-old, same-old. I find this difficult to countenance, as if many now see AIDS in the same way gay men once saw gonorrhoea in 1970s—as a one-stop-shopping inconvenience treatable with a script from the doctor. For me and many of my peers, HIV/AIDS will always be nothing less than fatal, however forestalled, however many pills popped or sensation-dulling layers slipped into. Though it might well be apt to now describe the disease as "chronic," this is not a term I can comfortably adopt—a term Peterkin and Hann use in their front and back matter, albeit I am sure in a purely clinical sense, freighting it with qualifications I can't or may not wish to appreciate—to characterize its impact on those now living with it daily. As Bromberger points out, "[m]any survivors must contend with a number of chronic and sometimes debilitating conditions as a consequence of living with AIDS, or as a side effect of the drugs themselves…. Survivors may age faster after long-term use of antiretrovirals, which can accelerate the onset of cancer, diabetes, and heart disease. Additional health risks can include neuropathy, viral hepatitis (as high as one-third of all survivors), kidney failure, bone degeneration, mobility problems, and cognitive impairment…. Various psychological problems are common…including depression, anxiety, nightmares, survivor guilt, social withdrawal, loneliness, emotional numbness, alcohol and drug addiction, sexual risk-taking, insomnia, low self-esteem, suicidal ideation, and so on."[19] The anguish that a word like "chronic" belies is incalculable. The editors of *Still Here* must know this better than I do, after their long and admirable years of clinical practice supporting patients living with AIDS/HIV in the "post-cocktail" era.

For the men contributing to *Still Here*, all of whom are living with HIV, I can only imagine just how much of a *deus ex machina* the arrival of the cocktail must have been. No background details are provided for any of the contributors to allow me to construct a narrative arc of their lives: when they fell ill, the extent to which they have suffered, how they support themselves, and their worldly accomplishments and disappointments. Many are identified only by their first names, their first names and their initials, or by their initials only, and no biographical notes are tucked into *Still Here*'s concluding pages as they would be in most "literary" anthologies. Many of them must have become very sick by the time the cocktails came on stream; lived in constant fear and suffered the stigma

---

19 Bromberger, 12.

of being ill. They were perhaps shunned by family, colleagues, and friends, including other gay men; gave up their homes and often well-paying, fulfilling jobs; had already lost too many friends and lovers to the disease; and were stoically or not so stoically resigned to shortly follow. The new drug therapies may have addressed and even reversed physical symptoms, but not necessarily their emotional and spiritual consequences. For many, being "diagnosed with HIV [as early as] the 1980s, celebrating a birthday in 2007 [would be] something of a miracle."[20] While reprieve was and must continue to be a welcome near-miss, euphoria must also wear off since, as with most other "chronic" conditions, life must somehow be lived. *Still Here* provides eloquent testimony.

In "The Stranger," a brief page-and-a-half-long story collected in the anthology's first section, "Changes," D. W. describes the impact of sero-conversion in starkly existential, even pragmatic terms. His newly HIV-positive protagonist has "at some point [...] lost touch with who he was." The third-person point of view is aptly estranging as the business of being "ill" takes hold: "Health, appointments, eating, sleeping, pace, pills, exercise, relaxation, worry, and anxiety and often depression appeared to be what this new person was all about." The infected "new" person is distinct from the narrator, underscoring a duality that illness has caused to exist in the self. He longs for agency: "to have the strength and flexibility to take on a variety of tasks…"—especially those activities that reminded him of his pre-infection self—and as a result, the protagonist "decided he must help this stranger. He resolved to be the overseer of tasks…. This was the trinity: the stranger, himself, the tasks."[21]

The role of "overseer" also comes into play in David King's "Changes," the section's title story: "This change seems to have a life of its own and I must constantly cultivate it, prune it and feed it to get it to grow in the manner I want it to. It is also the largest and thorniest change I have ever had to deal with…." For King, the change—or more precisely, the HIV—walks with him: "The HIV companion that haunts the dark places of my body, feeding on both my flesh and soul, gradually changed, taking on less the role of feared marauder to become more a part of me." King reaches for a positive slant on his predicament, extending the gardening metaphor that holds together what he has to say: "The roots of these orchids become invaded by a fungus, but in some way, the orchids

---

20 Ibid, 12.
21 Peterkin and Hann, 55–56.

can respond to control the spread of this 'infection' and the two live together in a state of constant battle in which neither triumphs over the other." What better way to describe the impasse that AIDS has become for many? Use of the ever-adjustable, constantly changing cocktail is a balancing act: acceptance of the reality of being irreversibly infected must be juggled with the resolve not to let this deadly virus steal one's life. "The orchid is the source of food the fungus needs…. the fungus collects scant water from the rocky soil to sustain the orchid and even produces vitamins which the orchid uses."[22] I can't imagine there is anything to gain physiologically from being HIV-positive—in this sense King's metaphor falls short—unless he intends another meaning. The strength of character that being positive demands in order to manage symptoms more than tips the scales in his favour and in favour of staying healthy. The writing of this short and moving piece must have occasioned many epiphanies both dark and uplifting for the author. It reads like synthesis.

Philip Fotheringham opens the anthology's second section, "Hope," with "Fortuitous Tsunami,"[23] the first of his four offerings that are found in three of the anthology's four other sections. Fotheringham recounts a stroke of luck that led to his securing a subsidized housing unit on Parliament Street in central Toronto. "Well my biggest problem really is that I need an apartment," he tells two men screening him as a potential member of an HIV and depression support group offered by the AIDS Committee of Toronto. "I'm currently in a room, temporarily. The people and ambience are friendly and comforting, but I have tons of furniture and belongings in a storage basement and it's costing me every month." He had recently been hospitalized to recover from a "manic period." Psychological instability and reduced circumstances, in comparison to those he had perhaps enjoyed in a more stable pre-infection period of his life, had made him vulnerable. One of the men interviewing him however "had a friend who owed him a favour." Within three months Fotheringham ends up with an apartment, one "not in a top choice neighbourhood, nor in a top choice building," nor looking over "thousands of others living in similar apartments," but with a view: "a second tsunami flows over me after I open the door and see my second home, the lake where I have enjoyed sailing for two decades. And the place is relatively decent"—the first tsunami being his good luck to "jump ten years ahead on the list for subsidized housing." Anyone

---

22 Ibid, 9–11.
23 Ibid, 61–64.

familiar with how bureaucracies work realizes that having an advocate almost always leads to a better outcome. I find myself dwelling upon the impact that "Fortuitous Tsunami" must have had on the other members of Fothering-ham's writing group. Had many of the men also experienced a loss of their "first" home and a life style that permitted such luxuries as sailing? How many of them were uplifted by his humour and expression of joy? Among many other responses, the most effective writing inspires identification. Each of the five stories gathered in "Hope" describes similar triumphs over adversity and of faith or self-worth restored through another's act of kindness—in other words, hope hard come by.

With Steven B, in "Goodbye, Traitor,"[24] AIDS enters the workplace, ushering in one of the most memorable stories in the third section, "Severance," if not in the anthology. Steven had been a senior manager in a foreign-owned affiliate whose head "was the first Canadian to be appointed president of the company's Canadian division, and he wanted to show his bosses in the U.S.A. that he could do a better job than any of the American presidents before him had done." Because Steven's division brought "in about two-thirds of the company's revenues and profits, and now Gordon [the president] is worried that those profits may be in jeopardy because [I] won't be here to manage [my] department." A few weeks before, Steven had been diagnosed with anal cancer and, after a brief period of sick leave, had decided to go on short-term disability "partly because my doctors wanted to switch my meds and put me on strong new antivirals and protease inhibitors"—the incident he's recounting took place in late 1997, early 1998, a year or two after the new and more effective options to treat HIV/AIDS were introduced—"they expected me to feel too sick and too stressed to continue working effectively." Steven had come back to work for a week to clean up his desk, advise his staff, and make sure his responsibilities would be seen to during the indefinite period of his absence. Yet Gordon felt "betrayed" and wouldn't meet with him, even to say goodbye, his secretary rationalizing that he was too busy "after a two-week Christmas ski weekend with his family" to do so, although in the past "he could squeeze a quick meeting with me into his day no matter how packed his schedule might be." As he embarks on an "uncertain future" that would eventually bring him to the Clinic for HIV-Related Concerns, Steven looked up from the parking lot and saw:

---

24 Ibid, 97–105.

Gordon standing in his office window, his face frozen in a sullen, bitter mask, watching me through a gap in the blinds. When our eyes locked he frowned and stepped back from the window. I could only see his dark silhouette as the blinds swayed from side to side against the glass.

At that moment, I realized exactly why Gordon was so furious with me. If the company didn't reach its profit target, he wouldn't collect his enormous annual executive performance bonus. This was about money—money he wanted in his pocket, not the company's bank account.

"Fuck you, asshole," I muttered and drove off.

I can't let go of the symbolism of the closed blinds in Gordon's office, richly telegraphing his blinkered capacity for empathy. Nor can I shake a sense of the bitterness that Steven must have felt, as he turned the key in his ignition, to be so ill-treated, after years of loyal, effective service to the company and its bottom line.

Edward Berger's "The Mustang Pill,"[25] drawn from "Treatment," the anthology's fourth section, exemplifies the impact that the approach to care has on people living with HIV/AIDS: "Normally, my anxiety level increases with every doctor's visit I have. Will there be med changes? Will there be any anomalies in my blood tests[?]" In the incident that he's narrating, it had turned out that "[m]y viral load had doubled and my T4 count was down by half. 'Don't worry,' said the doctor. 'These things happen. Your numbers aren't at a point where you should worry.' Easy for you to say!" As a result, it's recommended that he try a "new combination"—or "Witches brew you mean, I thought. I could just picture it. Me standing at the kitchen sink. Dressed in black. Crushing my pills and then mixing them with a dash of water and poof. When the foam rises, drink…drink it as fast as you can and try not to vomit." And so began Edward's marathon to adjust to the new drugs, which only caused "the usual possible side effects" and perhaps some initial "mild anxiety." He filled the script and "the next morning I was fine, but the morning after that I felt the changes. I couldn't sit still. I caught myself, on numerous occasions, wringing my hands. Give it a week, I thought." Twenty-two days later, he couldn't take it anymore:

25 Ibid, 178–181.

I ran all the way to the hospital. To the emergency ward. I had no idea what I was going to say to them. "Help me. I think I'm losing my mind?" I had to. I had no choice. So, through clenched teeth, I explained to the nurse that I was on a new HIV drug that was giving me extreme anxiety attacks but that I had stopped taking it three days ago and knew that it would all go away. "I wanted you to know that it won't be a crazed lunatic pacing outside the hospital doors. It will be me. I just wanted to be close to the hospital so that I would feel safe. I will be fine. I will just be outside."

He was told that there was a pill that would:

"…make it all go away," but he had to "come inside, fill out some forms and they would give it to me. I looked at [the nurse] through my water fogged eyes and said "NO MORE PILLS. Thank you anyway."

She went back in. My breathing started to return to normal and my crying stopped. I sat on the wall: knees to my chest rocking back and forth until around five-thirty in the morning. Finally, I went home, changed my sheets and got back into bed.

When I woke up the next afternoon I went to the doctor and asked him for some of those pills. "I give in!" I said.

Berger's narrative achingly speaks for itself and puts paid to the foolhardy idea held by far too many that HIV, once caught, is easily managed by medication. If anything, *Still Here* makes soberingly palpable the consequences of HIV infection two decades after HAART came on the market and seemed to change everything pertaining to the disease, including our respect for the implications of falling ill.

Better than anyone, Berger knew exactly what he needed in this temporary crisis within his "chronic" existential crisis and, he makes it the theme of his memoir: to feel safe. Other contributors whose pieces are grouped with his in "Treatment" also speak to the bewildering labyrinth that medicine is in this country and its complicated and complicating relationship with HIV/AIDS. However, sometimes the experience of being healed *is* positive. In "My Brush with OHIP,"[26] Peter Scott describes the care that he received, after an attack of pancreatitis, at a Toronto hospital, where he patiently interacts with doctors, nurses, dieticians, and candy stripers, one of whom "was about seventy and wore an AIDS ribbon" and is happy to debate about the nuances in Carol Shields' *The Stone Diaries*, which he was reading while convalescing. After his release he reflected:

> I don't know what to make of this brush with death [....] AIDS is an accumulation of small indignities. An ignominious end awaits anyone who hasn't realized this by now, like Ray Cohn in *Angels in America*.
>
> Speaking of Americans, it still appals me that fifty miles south of here, in Buffalo, this little trip to the hospital would have cost twenty-five thousand U.S. dollars.
>
> I'd be utterly bankrupted.
>
> So I'd say my brush with OHIP went the right way.

Before concluding *Still Here* with a clinical history of the Mount Sinai program and a starter kit on how best to establish therapeutic expressive-writing treatment elsewhere, Peterkin and Hann gather together accounts in "Loss," the anthology's fifth and final section, that members of their groups had written in honour of friends and lovers they had lost to the disease afflicting them. In them, participants narrate first meetings ("GWM, 43, HIV-positive, 5'8"; 142 lbs, uncut, seeking casual encounters and possible relationship with same. Into oral sex and fun times. Live downtown"[27] or "Then you and I met through Brian and Scott."[28]), final moments ("I was standing at Jim's shoulder when his breathing stopped and after a respectful few seconds of quiet and tears, I slipped my hand over his eyes and closed them"[29] or "Then his breathing seemed to settle down into a nice normal rate. I could feel myself start to get comfortable and about to doze off. Then it stopped. He had left."[30]), blocked or missed farewells ("Then he was gone, pirated away by his parents, back to his birth city, his haven. Six

---

26 Ibid, 182–186.
27 R.T., "Jacques and I: The Relationship," Peterkin and Hann, 267.
28 Edward Berger, "Dear John," Peterkin and Hann, 252.
29 Kenn Chaplin, "A Sense of Peace After Thirteen Years," Peterkin and Hann, 214.
30 William Stewart, "Parting Breath" Peterkin and Hann, 241.

months later, he waved good-bye to me from the other side and I waved back"[31] or "I was out of town when he suffered from a sudden fever. He walked into the local ER at noon and was dead by midnight"[32]), legacy ("My understanding of what type of person he was became even more apparent through the grieving of many hundreds of people who came to pay their last respects"[33]), enduring loss ("My first thought, indeed intuitive, would be that not only was she still in grief, but that I would also be, after so many years"[34] or "I cried for my lover this morning. He's been dead nine years"[35]) and a sense of one's own mortality ("I lost my life today. I am now a corpse"[36]). Quite simply, death complicates life.

Among the most eloquent of many heartfelt accounts of men who died before the cocktail could have helped them is Ellington Brown's "Sweet Bitter,"[37] about a lover he'd "stolen" from another man. A theft perpetrated before the clientele of Chestnut Lounge, a gay bar in west Philadelphia, the relationship lasted only eleven months:

> I remember the night when Charles told me that our relation-ship was over. He was so nice about it. I didn't realize what had happened until days later, that's how inexperienced I was.
>
> I didn't cry for Charles until years later, when I found out that he had died of AIDS. I talked to his brother, who told me that Charles never stopped loving me and was hoping somewhere, in the future, we would get back together when I was a little more mature. As he delivered the horrible news it was like someone taking a razor and cutting every major artery going to my heart.

So many young gay men who became adults at the same time that AIDS asserted itself watched it fell their friends, acquaintances, and strangers whose eyes they'd met across a smoke-filled dance floor. It deprived the dead of the opportunity to share what they might have learned as years they never saw squared off their arrogant, naïve rough corners. And because their voices are

---

31 R.T., Ibid, 268.

32 Paul Smith, "Good-byes," Peterkin and Hann, 273.

33 D. W., "My Friend," Peterkin and Hann, 250.

34 Philip Fotheringham, "Grief's Grip, Peterkin and Hann, 222.

35 Peter Scott, "An Illness," Peterkin and Hann, 277.

36 Peter Scott, "Loss II," Peterkin and Hann, 289.

37 Peterkin and Hann, 257–261.

lost, they cannot speak of their experience of the disease that took them, stories offered to the young as cautionary tales. Cleve Jones, founder of the Names Project AIDS Memorial Quilt, acknowledges to Bromberger that "I feel sad for young people because their experience of the pandemic is different from my generation. They don't have the solidarity we had. Even if they get tested, they are reluctant to talk about their status with their friends or sexual partners. They feel isolated." Bromberger goes on to say that "[y]ounger survivors report being subjected to shaming on dating and hookup sites such as Grindr where coded language such as 'DDF' ('drug-/disease free') or 'clean' are used as filters to screen out the HIV-positive, creating in effect a separate category of users who are to be avoided."[38] Clearly, therapists like Peterkin and Hann have their future work cut out for them.

The life-writing in *Still Here* brings to mind the AIDS literature that once dominated queer letters from the mid-1980s to the early 2000s, a literature that faded from sales shelves faster than the disappearance of gay and lesbian bookstores, once a commonplace in many North American cities. Literary responses to the disease helped those of us traumatized by its arm lock on our imaginations, as well as on our ill friends, and allowed us to recognize and comprehend our own experience. Landmarks of this literature include Paul Monette's *Borrowed Time* (memoir), Thom Gunn's *The Man with Night Sweats* (poetry), Tony Kushner's *Angels in America* (drama) and Michael Cunningham's *The Hours* (fiction), great works embraced by straight readers and critics almost as rapturously as they were by queer readers and critics. The two plays that make up Kushner's diptych have enjoyed recent revivals by theatre companies across the continent, as if we are collectively ready to look back to a time whose concerns are mercifully remote from our own and thus merit the cool commemorative re-examination that is occasioned by distance.

On Netflix I recently watched *Holding the Man*, a feature film based on a memoir of the same name by Australian actor Timothy Conigrave, in which he documented his sixteen-year relationship with John, a chiropractor and Australian-rules footballer whom he'd met in secondary school in 1976 and who died of AIDS in 1992. Conigrave followed him in 1994, ten days after he had finished the manuscript of his memoir. Upon publication, it became an Australian bestseller and won a U.N. Humanitarian Book Award. While watching the

38 Ibid, 14.

film, it occurred to me that the impact of AIDS has fallen so far from mainstream consciousness that it is now safe to revisit it creatively, not with new works about the contemporary situation, but through new treatments and re-mountings of AIDS "classics"—that much devalued word.

In 2014, HBO aired a subsequently Golden Globe and Emmy Award-winning mini-series based on Larry Kramer's angry and iconic play, *The Normal Heart*, which dramatizes the fight to secure government-funded care for AIDS patients and support for AIDS research and AIDS education in the United States (the lack of the latter may explain in part why so many more men per capita died of HIV/AIDS in that country than did in ours), starring Mark Ruffalo, Alfred Molina, and Julia Roberts. There is a key difference between the play's premiere in 1985 and the series HBO broadcast almost thirty years later. The former urgently raised the curtain on an agitprop call to action in face of the Reagan administration's indifference to a scorned, if tolerated minority; the latter merely invokes us to remember. While I confess I enjoyed both *The Normal Heart* and *Holding the Man*, I can't help feeling that this kind of nostalgia is an anaesthetizing prophylactic against mainstream recognition of the real-action dramas that men like those contributing to *Still Here* live daily. I fear they help seduce people into thinking AIDS is a "chronic" condition and therefore not a dangerous disease that threatens to kill many, not only in Africa, but on First Nations reserves and in suburban neighbourhoods across our own country.

It is a telling coincidence that *Rent*, Jonathan Larson's musical about a group of musicians, performance and street artists, and actors residing in New York's Lower East Side whose bohemian lives are endangered not only by gentrification but by AIDS, arrived on Broadway in 1996, the year the antiretroviral cocktail changed the direction of the disease. Mimi, an exotic dancer, and Roger, the former lead guitarist and singer for an East Village indie band, both wear pagers to remind them to take their doses of AZT, which, when it was introduced in 1986, was the first AIDS drug therapy approved for use in the United States. The only cocktails either imbibe would be those they'd drink at the Cat Scratch Club, where Mimi dances. The moment *Rent* opened, and even before it won a Pulitzer Prize, it became what I would describe as a history play, turning AIDS into a set piece no more challenging than a Noel Coward comedy of manners. However often I might find myself humming any of the musical's redemptive, show-stopping pop songs, I can't help but feel it obscures the real depth of suffering that many continue to experience while it renders AIDS palatable to audiences who are otherwise untouched by it. After all, Roger and Mimi keep on singing. I doubt many audiences leave theatres worrying about how the disease continues to mutate and spread. AIDS, in works like *Rent*, has become an artefact, safely sealed under climate-controlled conditions so that anything more troubling about it—such as an awareness of the present-day predicament of long-term AIDS patients—cannot spread.

It is therefore heartening recently to discover "HIV Here and Now," a web-based initiative of Brooklyn-based Indolent Books, a website where from June 5, 2015, to June 5, 2016, poets were able to post poems about HIV. The ultimate objective was to attract enough material to publish a contemporary anthology of HIV/AIDS poetry. The modest writings of the contributors to *Still Here*, like these poems, are much more immediate and affecting than the re-stagings of Broadway hits or the filming of AIDS literature landmarks. *Still Here*'s mostly anonymous contributors are not writing to establish reputations or achieve immortality. They have committed words to the page in order to connect with themselves and others, to *stay* alive. As I close *Still Here* for the umpteenth time, I find myself thinking how strange it is to be asked to review a book eight years after publication. I wonder how these men are all managing. I trust that they are still responding well to the drugs they are prescribed and continue to rise to the challenges facing them each day. I presume they are all still with us. I have no way of knowing, but I wish them well.

2017

WORKS CITED OR MENTIONED

Brian Bromberger, "HIV Survivors and the '16 Election, *The Gay & Lesbian Review*, September-October 2016, 12-14.

CATIE, "The Epidemiology of AIDS in Canada," *Fact Sheet*, 2016.

CATIE, "Growing Old Gracefully, "*The Pos+ive Side*, Summer 2007. Retrieved October 26, 2016.

Timothy Conigrave, *Holding the Man*. Ringwood, Vic., Australia : McPhee Gribble, 1995.

Michael Cunningham, *The Hours*. New York: Farrar Straus Giroux, 1998.

Government of Canada. "Report to the Executive Director, UNAIDS, January 2014–2015," *Global*

AIDS Response Progress Report, 2016.

Government of Canada. *Public Health Agency of Canada. HIV and AIDS in Canada: Surveillance Report to December 31, 2014.*

Thom Gunn, *The Man with Night Sweats*. New York: Farrar Straus Giroux, 1992.

Holding the Man (film). Sydney: Screen Australia, 2015.

Larry Kramer, *The Normal Heart*. New York: Dutton, 1985.

Tony Kushner, *Angels in America* (Parts I and II). New York: Theatre Communications Group, 1993.

Jonathan Larson, *Rent*. New York: William Morrow, 1997.

Paul Monette, *Borrowed Time: An AIDS Memoir*. San Diego: Harcourt Brace Jovanovich, 1988.

The Normal Heart (two-part mini-series). Los Angeles: HBO Films, 2014.

Approaching Utopia: The Poetries of Billy-Ray Belcourt and Ben Ladouceur

"NO FILTERS"

Last spring, before Chapters closed its storefront in downtown Victoria, a sign with this sales slogan hung above a display of books by Instapoets near the Douglas Street entrance. My curiosity was piqued. While thumbing through Rupi Kaur's best-selling collections, *Milk and Honey* and *The Sun and Her Flowers*, both prominently positioned among other best-selling titles by Amanda Lovelace, Atticus, and D. M. Drake, I began pondering the implications of poetries that are unfiltered. Does the simplicity of Kaur's often brief poems, which she illustrates with her own line drawings, mean they don't need to be interpreted? Do her aesthetics guide her to hold nothing back from her nation of 2.7 million Instagram followers? Is her interiority theirs? A Punjabi-Sikh poet born in India and raised outside Toronto, Kaur told the *New York Times* her style "grew in part out of her struggles when she was learning English after moving to Canada, wanting her work to be accessible."[1] Her directness presents anyone reading it online and off with an oasis as unequivocal as a mirror. They're permitted to see themselves while enjoying a private moment of connection:

> this is the recipe of life
> said my mother
> as she held me in her arms as i wept
> think of those flowers you plant
> in the garden each year
> they will teach you
> that people too
> must wilt

---

1   Carl Wilson, "Why Rupi Kaur and Her Peers Are the Most Popular Poets in the World," *New York Times*, December 15, 2017 (https://www.nytimes.com/2017/12/15/books/review/rupi-kaur-instapoets.html. Retrieved December 3, 2018).

fall
root
rise
in order to bloom[2]

Technically, there's nothing to argue with here. Kaur's line lengths and line breaks parse her syntax with such straightforward poise, it makes sense why her family-centric observations about how tragedy feeds growth go right to the heart for many. Indeed, for millions.

Writing for the *Poets & Writers* website, Maggie Millner characterizes Kaur's poetry as exemplifying "the prevailing Instapoetic style, with its epigrammatic brevity, plain language, and empowering messages."[3] According to Sara Sargent, an editor at HarperCollins, the genre "is the height of feeling that your lived experience is shared... [and] part of the growing cultural trend around self-care and self-discovery. Journaling, coloring books, self-help: it all has to do with our commitment to figuring out who we are."[4]

But, doesn't "figuring out who we are" sound like poetry's centuries-old purpose? "NO FILTERS," I thought while standing beneath Chapters' banner, may be a useful rubric to apply when attempting to compare the poetries of Billy-Ray Belcourt and Ben Ladouceur, Canada's two most successful new gay-male voices. Factoring out their shared attraction to men, I can't think of two more different poets. Belcourt writes poems with an impact so immediate they need only to be read once to grasp they are transcripts of near-uncontainable affect. In contrast, a single reading of any Ladouceur poem encourages readers to bring to it more than their expectation to be moved. Belcourt and Ladouceur's having emerged at almost the same time turns a spotlight on what makes their unalike poetries equally compelling. The answer may have everything to do with filters, even if, in Belcourt's case, he appears to have thrown them aside. While many readers of standard-issue Canadian poetry, despite its emphasis on benign eloquence, may cringe to have Kaur placed in the same company as Belcourt and Ladouceur, they need to admit that all three poets are skillful enough to make their poems meaningful to their audiences. Internationally known B.C.

---

2   Rupi Kaur, "the sun and her flowers" (rupikaur.com/books. Retrieved December 4, 2018).

3   Maggie Milner, "Instapoets Prove Powerful in Print," Poets & Writers, June 13, 2018 (https://www.pw.org/ content/instapoets_prove_powerful_in_print. Retrieved June 17, 2018).

4   Ibid.

Instapoet Atticus uses the word "classical" to distinguish Instapoetry from other canonical and contemporary poetries.[5] But is there really such a genre as a poetry without filters? Even in Instapoetry, every word must be filtering something.

Ladouceur and Belcourt, were born respectively in Ottawa in 1987 and Driftpile Cree Nation in northern Alberta in 1995. Even before Coach House and Frontenac House published their first books, *Otter* (2015) and *This Wound is a World* (2017), each had been awarded an important contributor prize from a literary magazine known to launch significant literary careers. Ladouceur won the Earle Birney Prize for Poetry from *Prism international* in 2013; Belcourt, the P. K. Page Founders' Award for Poetry from *The Malahat Review* in 2017. Even greater recognition was to follow. *Otter* attracted Lambda Literary Award and Gerald Lampert Memorial Award nominations, winning the latter in 2016. Ladouceur next won the 2018 Dayne Ogilvy Prize for LGBTQ Emerging Writers from the Writers' Trust of Canada; the jury citation states "one gets the sense of an artist who long ago absorbed and synthesized his influences, who is incapable of the derivative or the repetitive," and who is "bent on risk."[6] Belcourt received equally robust accolades. In 2018, *This Wound is a World* earned an Indigenous Voices Award, the Robert Kroetsch City of Edmonton Book Award, and the Griffin Poetry Prize, and also attracted three additional national award nominations, including one for the Governor General's Literary Award. The Griffin Poetry Prize citation reads, "Belcourt pursues original forms with which to chart the constellations of queerness and indigeneity, rebellion and survival, desire and embodiedness these poems so fearlessly explore."[7] Despite how different their books are, this amount of attention makes it only natural to consider them together.

In *This Wound is a World*, Billy-Ray Belcourt lays his cards on the table so readers may turn them over easily. He's given his collection of poems an intriguing, straightforward title, includes an epilogue, notes to the poems, and a list

5   Lauren Lambert, "An Interview with Atticus, The Masked Poet and Bard of Instagram." *Study Break*, November 10, 2017 (https://studybreaks.com/culture/atticus-masked-poet/. Retrieved December 4, 2018).

6   https://www.writerstrust.com/awards/dayne-ogilvie-prize/. Retrieved November 13, 2018.

7   http://www.griffinpoetryprize.com/awards-and-poets/shortlists/2018-shortlist/billy-ray-belcourt/. Retrieved November 13, 2018.

of bibliographic references, as if he were documenting academic research. With the exception of Michi Saagiig Nishnaabeg scholar, writer, and artist Leanne Betasamosake Simpson's 2014 book of songs and stories, *Islands of Decolonial Love*, the three monographs, journal article, and YouTube video Belcourt cites are theory-driven works published or posted since 2011, all with compelling titles like *Ethical Loneliness: The Injustice of Not Being Heard* by Jill Stauffer, *Depression: A Public Feeling* by Ann Cvetkovich, and *The Black Outdoors: Fred Moten & Saidiya Hartman at Duke University*. Belcourt also prefaces his book with "When I go extemporaneously, I lose myself," an epigraph quoted from the work of José Estaban Muñoz, a New York-based Cuban-American academic who died suddenly of heart failure in December 2013. Munoz's interests centred on queer theory; race and affect, culture, and performance studies; visual culture and ephemera; and queer utopia. While readers don't need to be conversant with Belcourt's source material to appreciate his poems, they're welcome to look them up before (or after) plunging into the intense, eruditely limned chasm where his Indigeneity and queerness face-off with colonialism and patriarchy.

Before the 2018 Griffin Poetry Prize winners were announced, Jonah Brunet observed in *The Walrus* that "Belcourt doesn't write the way he speaks"[8] or, I might add, the way he thinks. His poems instead attest to his ability to express in uncomplicated terms the complex ideas he absorbed to make sense of his experience. "There are a lot of poets who take up the call to be opaque or indecipherable," Belcourt argues. "Then there are others who nest in simplicity, where it's more about this raw sense of connectivity,"[9] or to "only connect," to riff on the trope E. M. Forster coined in *Howard's End* in 1910, when he was only a few years older than Belcourt is now. If the novelist were alive today, would he post an initial draft of his book on a website as the poet did a draft of *This Wound is a World*? Brunet describes this early website of Belcourt's as "the kind of DIY project many of us born in the mid-nineties attempted."[10] I am particularly struck by Belcourt's use of the word "nest" to suggest the compensations of "simplicity." His conscious adoption of simpler means perhaps spurred me to compare him to Instapoets like Rupi Kaur. The opening lines of "Notes from a Public Washroom" evince Instapoetry's plainspokenness:

---

8   Jonah Brunet, "Billy-Ray Belcourt's Radical Poetry," *The Walrus* (https://thewalrus.ca/billy-ray-belcourts-radical-poetry). Retrieved August 29, 2018.

9   Ibid.

10 Ibid.

i never dream about myself anymore.
i chose a favorite memory
and named it after every boy
i have broken up with
grief is easier that way.
i need to cut a hole in the sky
to world inside.
is the earth round,
or is it in the shape of a broken heart?

This extract could even be mistaken for a complete Instapoem. The first paragraph of *This Wound is a World*'s epilogue, however, provides the frame through which to read it and the rest of his poems:

> Love, says cultural theorist Laurent Berlant, "always means non-sovereignty," but only if we think of love as what opens us up to that which feels like it can rupture the ground beneath our feet. Berlant insists that love requires that we violate our own attachments, that we give into instability, that we accept that turbulence is the condition of relationality as such. We might agree, then, that love is a process of becoming unbodied; at its wildest, it works up a poetics of the unbodied.

Thus, contrary to appearances, Belcourt's poems don't eschew filters. They lend his poems lucidity and allow them to flow purely, as if his ideas were a carbon drinking-water filter. They allow him to create vivid pictures of the toxic situations history has forced him, as an Indigenous person, to witness, without poisoning the stream of his poetry or passing on the ill-effects to others. He instead expresses and inspires empathy.

The disjuncture between Belcourt's often plainspoken poems and the recondite ideas that inform them most reminds me of Erín Moure's paradigm-shifting collection of poems, *Furious*, which won the Governor General's Literary Award for Poetry in 1988. Unlike *This Wound is a World*, *Furious* enacts its bifocal nature by literally dividing in two. "Pure Reason," a sequence of emotionally charged, polemical poems, is followed by "The Acts," a manifesto elaborating the aesthetics that shaped the poems' composition. "The Acts" releases any compositional energy the poems couldn't accommodate themselves, making clear to readers how the poetics Moure formulated should be applied while they experience the full force of her gorgeous and focused fury. In comparison, Belcourt's ideas are reasoned out off-stage and referred to tangentially. The lingering heat of debate is felt through his bibliography and notes: the ideas to which they lead the reader are ghosts hugging every vulnerability his poems make visible without haunting them too overbearingly. Resolving Belcourt's cerebrality with his easily understood poetic voice, Brunet concludes that his "poetry is remarkable not for how it elevates him above his peers, but how it allows him to speak directly to them."[11] Brunet's use of the word "peers" needs further interpretation. They are not the anonymous readers who lurk like silent literary-chatroom zombies behind the countless copies of *This Wound is a World* that they purchased in reputable bookstores but other queer First Nations youth who, like him, are looking for a way to turn their "wounds" into "a world." The rest of us are welcome to listen. As with the Moure of *Furious*, *This Wound is a World* is not primarily our show. But pay attention and learn.

Complementing the thinkers Belcourt cites are the elders, and in particular his grandmother, whom we meet in "Sexual History," who stand at the heart of several circles of community support:

> i call my kookum to tell her i have a boyfriend and that she will
> meet him in ten minutes. i piece together a world inside the
> quiet before her next breath and name it earth."

Family and culture provide Belcourt with the fundament he needs, without which his academically gained intellectual apparatus would be mere theoretical badinage. As "Sacred" makes clear, however, his queerness is not universally embraced by the Indigenous people he encounters:

> a native man looks me in the eyes as he refuses to hold my hand
> during a round dance. his pupils are like bullets and i wonder
> what kind of pain he's been through to not want me in this world
> with him any longer. I wince a little because the earth hasn't held
> all of me for quite some time now and i am lonely in a way that
> doesn't hurt anymore.

---

11 Ibid.

The narrator's discomfort continues to build:

> and I think about the time an elder told me to be a man and
> to decolonize in the same breath. there are days when i want
> to wear nail polish more than i want to protest. but then i re-
> member that i wasn't meant to live life here and i paint my nails
> because 1) it looks cute and 2) it is a protest. and even though i
> know i am too queer to be sacred anymore, i dance that broken
> circle dance because I am still waiting for hands that want to
> hold mine too.

The man's pain appears to make him homophobic and makes the narrator self-conscious, causing him both to believe he doesn't belong and to want to assert his non-conforming identity by applying gender-inappropriate nail polish. The narrator finds himself thinking about

> native boys who couldn't be warriors because their bodies were
> too fragile to carry all of that anger, the ones who loved in that
> reckless kind of way. you know, when you surrender your body
> to him.

Surrender is essential to who the narrator is as a queer person, yet the Indigenous body can be incapable of letting go because, as Belcourt acknowledges, colonialism "turn[s] bodies into cages that no one has the keys for" ("Colonialism: A Love Story"), making them "a catch-22" ("The Oxford Journal") since you're made to know "your body is both too much and not enough for this world" ("Love and Other Experiments").

In *This Wound is a World*, the lovers are frequently settlers: "he told me he was into natives, but he couldn't love the traumas hidden in my breathing" ("Love and Other Experiments"). For Belcourt, to live with colonialism's aftermath, as he explains in "Okcupid,"

> is to say that to be native and queer
> is to sometimes forget how to love yourself
> because no one else wants to
> is to bandage the wounds with strangers
> you met an hour ago

> and count the number of times
> they baptize you with words like
> beautiful and handsome and sexy
> because sex is the only ceremony
> you have time for
> these days

These days such trysts, as the title of the poem (a popular dating app) implies, are more often than not arranged electronically. The bar scene has largely been supplanted by contemporary online-hookup culture, which, as long as there's access to cell service and the Internet, can be accessed anywhere, from downtown Edmonton to the southern shores of Lesser Slave Lake, where Belcourt grew up 259 km farther north. In "Love and Heartbreak are Fuck Buddies," time and space are cut through by texting and GPS:

> love and heartbreak are fuck buddies who sometimes text each other at 10 in the morning. today, love asks: *is this what the living do?* as he tries to shit but can't because he doesn't eat enough fibre or exercise regularly. *it's the little things that'll kill you,* he adds. heartbreak responds, ignoring the first message: *you emptied your body into the floorboards of me. they creak when I am lonely. if I am a haunted house, then let's make up a theory of negativity that notices the utopian pulse of sad stories like ours.* well fuck, love types out. he deletes it.

Heartbreak and love are literally Belcourt's male protagonists throughout *This World is a Wound*. Here, love is so preoccupied by emptying his bowels, he's incapable of hearing how emotionally empty heartbreak feels. Depending on the poem, the protagonists switch identities, with Belcourt's narrator sometimes the lover, sometimes the heartbroken. In "Wihtikowak Means 'Men Who Can't Survive Love,'" heartbreak is a man shattered by colonialism:

> if you must know more, know that the thin white man blindfolded himself and fucked the *wihtikow.* that he put his mouth to its ear and whispered, *i will learn to love a monster. wihtikowak* means "men who can't survive love," so each time the thin white man kissed his *wihtikow* it would ache and groan and flinch but

still ask for more until it stopped breathing and melted into the
mattress. i think it felt something like freedom.

Such freedom is brusque, as short-lived as an orgasm, that uncomfortably annihilating little death. The anguish passion briefly blots out resurfaces fast. In
"The Rubble of Heartbreak":

> when love looks
> into the rubble
> of heartbreak
> he sees his
> kookum
> standing there
> and he thinks
> about how
> she made
> old worlds
> feel livable
> again
> and about
> how those
> who died
> already
> never forget
> what it is
> to become
> and unbecome
> a body

The comfort his kookum offers by reminding him of the traditions from which
he's sprung is tempered by the loss of those who couldn't be saved: the mur-
dered and missing, the teen suicides (" what is suicide / but the act of opening
up / to the sky?" from "Wapekeka"), and willful indifference and neglect of settler society ("remind them / that canada is / four hundred / afghanistans / —
call it colonialism," from "God's River"). Short-lined poems like "The Burden
of Heartbreak," with the line breaks falling with and against the syntax, recall
Métis poet Katherena Vermette's Governor General's Literary Award-winning

first collection of poetry, *North End Love Songs*. Seeing an affinity between Belcourt's poems and hers is perhaps more apt than comparing them to Rupi Kaur's (though I recently noticed Indigo included Vermette's most recent book, *River Woman*, in a Christmas display of titles by Instapoets). Vermette's poem, "Found," is indicative of her style:

> they find him
> they say
> dental records
> no need to see
>
> she imagines
> her brother's body
> swelled
>
> like hers
> pushed all the way
> to the edge
> unidentifiable
>
> they think
> he tried
> to walk across the river
> in a cold november when
> it was almost frozen
> just not
> all the way.[12]

This Wound is A World also recalls Métis poet Gregory Scofield's 1996 collection, *Native Canadiana: Songs of the Urban Rez*, which evokes the challenges First Nations people—and queer First Nations people in particular—face in settler cities like Vancouver.[13]

---

12 Katherena Vermette, *North End Love Songs*. Winnipeg: Muses' Company, 2012, 88.

13 Vermette's second book, *River Woman*, was published by House of Anansi in the fall of 2018; Scofield's *Native Canadiana* was published by Polestar in 1996; it won the Dorothy Livesay Poetry Prize at the B.C. Book Awards in 1997.

The struggle to free the body from colonialism's grip and the insinuation of inimical mind-sets like homophobia into Indigenous concepts of relatability are central themes for Belcourt. In "Towards a Theory of Decolonization," Belcourt instructs himself to "forget everything you've learned about love." Yet unlearning is something done on the fly: "investment is social practice whereby one risks losing it all to be a part of something that feels like release. lose everything with me." Every attempt to find release could in hindsight be reappraised as having led risktakers (i.e., lovers) toward complications or, alternatively, it causes them to strike a path whose terminus, as "The Oxford Journal" suggests, is the attainment of equipoise:

> you want to capture the sense of a present that is not quite *the* present, a present that thickens in the underbelly of social reality, you want the prefix un-, hoping that it will let you see glitches, that it will unearth a hole in the ground, something of a gateway to a world you are spotting any- and everywhere, a world you are spotting nowhere. you are sad, so at first you believe that an un- can be found in the body of men. you begin looking for doors, not enclosures. doors without locks. doors that swing open. soon, you decide that doors are a transference of cacophonous feeling; they are ecological, unseen. leanne simpson: "she is the only doorway to this world." the un- is a woman like your kookum who rips open time.

Sometimes, as in "Native Too," the narrator's lovers are other Indigenous men like himself:

> he was native too
> so I slept with him.
> i wanted to taste
> a history of violence
> caught in the roof of his mouth.
> i wanted our saliva to mix
> and create new bacterial ecologies:
> contagious that could infect
> the trauma away.
> i wanted to smell his ancestors

in his armpits...
i wanted him to fuck me,
so I could finally begin
to heal.

In his epilogue, Belcourt quotes Leanne Betasamosake Simpson's *Islands of Decolonial Love*: "I think we fucked, and maybe I should say make love, but maybe not because we didn't actually make love. it was sadder than that. we were sadder than that. but it wasn't bad and it wasn't wrong. it wasn't desperate. I think it was salvation." He goes onto say:

> To be unbodied is the "sadder than that" of love, but it is also love's first condition of possibility. That indigeneity births us into a relation of non-sovereignty is not solely coloniality's dirty work. No, it is also what emerges from a commitment to the notion that the body is an assemblage, a mass of everyone who's ever moved us, for better or worse.

The "mass of everyone who's ever moved us" embraces his family members, friends, and lovers, even the inevitable Indigenous and non-Indigenous strangers met online. To be moved by the possibilities in others may not displace the sadness but with time it may supplant non-sovereignty. Self-determination starts with one, then two, then many twos, until its attainment spreads exponentially and is irreversible.

Ben Ladouceur is likewise preoccupied with the friends, lovers, and occasional family members who move him. Unlike Belcourt, he provides the reader with scant infrastructure on how to read *Otter*. With the exception of giving each of its three sections a heading—"The Honeyman Festival" (the title of a 1970 novel by the late Marian Engel), "The Rites of Spring" (the title of Modris Ekstein's cultural history of the First World War and more famously the title of the early twentieth-century Stravinsky/Nijinsky ballet), and "Dead Dreams of Monochrome Men" (the title of "a dance conceived and directed by Lloyd Newson")—Ladouceur has not corseted his poems inside a contour-defining set of references and therefore does not point his readers in any direction he may wish them to go. Nor does he provide any sort of infrastructure to substantiate the conclusions his poems may have caused him to draw from his own experience. He does not open *Otter* with an epigraph; nor do any of his individual poems start with one. The collection's title can potentially be read as an equally unyielding gesture, for no four-footed, river-flowing or ocean-going mammals poke their heads up through the surface of his poems. They may well be as mythical as sasquatch. While *This Wound is a World* may read as if unfiltered despite the intellectual infrastructure Belcourt goes to great lengths to make clear, Ladouceur foregrounds his filters unexplained. It's up to his readers to find and crack his codes.

In response to a question Jan Zwicky poses to him in an interview published in *Contemporary Verse 2*, Ladouceur tips his cards somewhat: "Kissing the person you love goodbye at a train, for instance, is not an automatically political gesture, but when you and the person you love are the same gender, it is. Even, if to you, it's just an expression of a very human emotion.... When I write about my own experience, the poems get politicized, they get drawn into the world beyond."[14] Zwicky probes deeper: "Are you saying for gays—or for all who identify as LGBTQ2[S]—the slogan [the personal is political] needs to be altered: the personal isn't always political? That heteronormative culture is oppressive because it won't let anything LGBTQ2[S] be straightforwardly personal?"[15] Ladouceur replies: "Part of me would encourage altering the old slogan, as you suggest. If the world let the personal stay personal, I'd learn so much about how it is most commonly experienced. I'd also feel safer and less interesting. But this must be a very small part of me—I just have to look at my own choices, my own writing, to determine that."[16] Perhaps by making *Otter* hermetic, his filters demanding careful interpretation or insider-slash-subcultural information, so to speak, in order to be understood, Ladouceur attempts to retain a modicum of the personal for himself despite how frankly queer his poems nonetheless are and how political they consequentially-slash-inadvertently may appear. Whether it's experienced by his often-first-person narrators or by the male protagonists of his few third-person poems, down to their DNA, the personal is unabashedly homoerotic in Ladouceur's poems.

While puzzling my way through "Masters of the Impossible," I came to understand that to read a Ladouceur poem is by necessity an effort at decoding:

---

14 Jan Zwicky, "A Conversation with Ben Ladouceur," *Contemporary Verse 2*, 40.3 (Winter 2018), 7
15 Ibid, 8.
16 Ibid, 8–9

> Puberty and wartime
> don't count. I don't
> have many years to
> my name. My name
> is Siegfried....
> ...When Wilfred
> died, I was sleeping
> in an armchair.

The savvy reader is meant to realize the narrator, at least initially, is the Great War poet, Siegfried Sassoon, who's speaking of Wilfred Owen, whom he'd met when both men were being treated for shellshock (now called PTSD) at Craiglockhart War Hospital outside Edinburgh. Theirs is one of the most consequential encounters between two British writers of the twentieth century. Owen, with Sassoon's tutelage, would evolve into inarguably the most significant poet of the World War One before tragically dying in action in France a week before hostilities ended. Then, as unexpectedly as Owen's death, the poem takes a surprising turn:

> The Celtic Cross Spread
> has informed me I've
> got one life left.
> My name remains, his
> becomes Roy. Magic
> is our livelihood, our
> gift to the coherent
> world...

Perhaps as a ritual of mourning, Sassoon has now laid out his own cards to foretell his postwar fortunes, the Celtic Cross being one of the most commonly used opening spreads in tarot. In Sassoon's reading of the cards, Owen reincarnates into someone named Roy while Sassoon remains Siegfried, if in name only. Siegfried and Wilfred thus become Siegfried and Roy. Billed as Masters of the Impossible, Siegfried & Roy were German-born magicians active in Europe and North America from the late 1960s to the early 2000s. A tiger named Montecore ended their long-running Las Vegas show incisively when he bit and maimed, but did not kill Roy. "When I began taking lyrical poetry seriously,"

Ladouceur tells Zwicky, "I saw no need for fidelity to a single beloved [or character] within a poem. I was primarily interested in writing entertaining poems, and if accomplishing that goal meant combining friends, exes, acquaintances, etc., so be it, I figured. There still remained an honesty to the poems that way, or a set of complimentary honesties, which I found sufficient."[17]

A poetry of "complimentary honesties" is definitely not the straightforward method of either Rupi Kaur or Billy-Ray Belcourt. Because it's not immediately apparent that the Siegfried and Wilfred mentioned in "Masters of the Impossible" are Sassoon and Owen (their last names aren't used), the reader might fruitfully misconstrue these half-hidden men were romantically involved, even though there's no actual evidence the two Great War poets were ever intimate. Words like "wartime" help the careful reader to unmask their initial identities. The men's possible status as lovers becomes real through their transformation into the tragic Las Vegas duo, who were once described as "the world's most openly closeted celebrities."[18] How Ladouceur guides the reader through rumour, wishful thinking and conjecture (many a gay man would find it wonderfully affirming to believe Sassoon's mentorship of Owen went below the belt) holds the poem together, yet he resists unambiguously confirming what he believes is the true nature of its protagonists' relationship. The poem need not be about anything more than these Ouija-board-like shifts and overlaps in identity engineered purely by the poet's predilection to read in "connections" (if that's what they are) only he is predisposed to see. Whether or not readers make them as well does not strip the poem of its appeal or wit. If they do, however, their successful interpretation may render it queerer and even political. Through Ladouceur's and the reader's joint shuffling of the cards and of the protagonists' names, Sassoon and Owen are given a chance, albeit solely in poetic terms, to live the more open, consummated lives of same-sex couples like Siegfried and Roy, who prospered in the aftermath of the next world war. Card tricks like these preserve their privacy by confirming nothing and this, for Ladouceur, may be "sufficient" as a master of the impossible and the unconfirmable himself. He indulges in wish fulfilment further, or imagines Sassoon indulging in it for him in "Bijoux," the poem following "Masters of the Impossible" in *Otter*: "I dreamt Wilfred lived, he and I / Found a pair of boring sisters

---

17 Zwicky, Ibid, 10.

18 https://www.questia.com/magazine/1G1-111166126/the-truth-about-siegfried-roy-the-duo-have-never. Retrieved November 20, 2018.

// who left us mostly to ourselves, / we wed them." How many pre-liberation gay-male couples similarly hid in plain sight in marriages of convenience? The poem celebrates the necessity of such unions.

The reader being put in the position of eavesdropping on Ladouceur's own privacy haunts *Otter*, however candid a poet he may be. Eavesdropping on candour could precisely be his point. I cannot think, for example, of many recent books of poetry I have read where anal sex is as profusely described: "If I am home, I say so / by closing the bedroom door // behind which we made a game / of keeping the sodomy quiet / all morning long." ("222 The Esplanade"); "His body, like yours, would lie / mute as a plumb / until a vigilant limb came / to a decision. As you might have guessed / I've come to one myself." ("Pseudepigrapha"); and "If you require only parts then my home is a boutique // and I a dildo, a salt lick, a hole in the wall / as high as your waist. It / matters, but if only it had mattered." ("Poem with Long Title"). Ladouceur's is a performative privacy. The tone of voice in all three poems is cavalier, daring the reader to respond in like manner: what's normal behaviour for one person is to be taken as such by another. Ergo, nothing need be political in the mechanics of queer intimacy and should not have been in the past. Oscar Wilde's imprisonment for gross indecency should never have created the conditions through which he becomes "Oscar Wildebeest," as he's jauntily invoked in "Pollen." Wilde should have enjoyed the same privately shared carnal freedoms the two anonymous soldiers in "Nuncle" do: they "made for the nearest bed" after witnessing the traumas of battle.

The pursuit of queer intimacy as a normal behaviour, which neither needs to be hidden nor have claims for toleration made for it, is the cornerstone upon which *Otter* builds its edifice, a cornerstone laid by men like Wilde, Sassoon, and Owen, whose stories Ladouceur takes apart and reassembles in "The Rites of Spring," the book's middle section, and without which his own generation could not now erect the viable lives he describes in sometimes breezily remarked-upon detail. Like the poems of Frank O'Hara, Ladouceur's poems about contemporary queer agency are casually peppered with the first names of friends and lovers known and unknown to one another to suggest if not a close-knit coterie of semblables, then a network of acquaintanceship from which a definable community is born, which "590 Lisgar St." amply illustrates:

...I remember that photograph
everyone liked, with the ice cream vendor

out of frame, in which I look like a thug, Ryan
looks like a model and you look like a
child. Remember heat from the tree whose heat

was from the green season. Remember being shaken
awake, asked about *the bright intruder*. You'd been
dreaming. No apology because sleep is different.

The community the young men of *Otter* have made for themselves is so secure
it's not by necessity exclusive or exclusionary, unfussily admitting heterosexual
cohorts and admirers to its satisfied number. In "At the Movies," the narrator af-
fectionally acknowledges his ne'er-do-well ways of an earlier, perhaps less-self-
aware phase of his life journey:

> ... Annick
> always hoped to make out
> with a nameless stranger
>
> as a box-office bomb blared
> to an otherwise empty
> auditorium, as the score of violins
>
> swept in to mute the audible
> saliva. Now Annick is married.
> She wrote me a letter
>
> cinematic in its exposition:
> *You faggot, I loved you. Of all the men*
> *You could have been, you went only halfway.*

In "I Am in Love With Your Brother," the queer best man in his after-dinner
speech toasts the bride and groom:

> Richie, while your soul is at its smoothest
> and most forgiving. I did love him, the crimson acne
> flecked across his neck, he was like a man
> a guillotine had made an attempt at.

And later:

> Caroline, Richie
> is one hell of a guy. You would do best to keep
> his body firmly in yours, how seas contain boats
> for he is only stories to me now.

The poem speaks to a cheerful ease among peers, irrespective of where their affections may be aimed, the high points of attraction unashamedly aired. By using Sassoon's, Owen's, and Wilde's first names, Ladouceur grandfathers them in. As queer forefathers, they stand in for so many others who had less famously blazed the way for *Otter*'s contemporary protagonists. They have a history to acknowledge; as a queer writer Ladouceur recognizes a canon of queer figures upon whose writings he crafts his own.

Ladouceur's expanding circle of actual and literary intimates is a luxe he shares with his readers. The relationship he fosters with them is not too different from what O'Hara defines as the one between the poet, poem, and the poem's subject in "Personism: A Manifesto":

> But to give you a vague idea, one of its minimal aspects is to address itself to one person (other than the poet himself), thus evoking overtones of love without destroying love's life-giving vulgarity, and sustaining the poet's feelings towards the poem while preventing love from distracting him into feeling about the person. That's part of Personism. It was founded by me after lunch with LeRoi Jones on August 27, 1959, a day in which I was in love with someone (not LeRoi, by the way, a blond). I went back to work and wrote a poem for this person. While I was writing it I was realizing that if I wanted to I could use the telephone instead of writing the poem, and so Personism was born. It's a very exciting movement which will undoubtedly have lots of adherents. It puts the poem squarely between the poet and the person, Lucky Pierre style, and the poem is correspondingly gratified.[19]

---

19 Frank O'Hara, "Personism: A Manifesto," *The Selected Poems of Frank O'Hara*, Donald Allen, ed. New York: Vintage, 1974, xiv.

Just like many of O'Hara's poems, many of those in *Otter* are addressed to a single named or unnamed person, and they speak to intimacies shared dispassionately in order to preserve the "life-giving vulgarities" to which love and love-making make those involved prey. Ladouceur could have texted (rather than telephoned) the addressees of his poems, but chose not to; indeed, smartphones and texting come up often enough in *Otter* and text exchanges give structure to poems like "Grans Vals." Like O'Hara, however, Ladouceur ends up writing a poem because it's what poets do to prevent the beloved (and love they share) "from distracting him into feeling about the person." The poem is a more accurate transcript of the emotions; unlike the poet, it cannot be swayed by his interlocuter's pleading, begging, contempt, or any other contaminating sentiment an actual exchange by text or FaceTime could introduce. By "Lucky Pierre style," O'Hara means the poem, as in a sexual threesome, is the middle party, "both penetrated by the person behind them and penetrating the person in front of them simultaneously"[20]—an allusion not universally understood when O'Hara wrote his manifesto in 1959—and the poem could just as easily be the middleman between the poet and the reader. Though "Lucky Pierre" does not necessarily refer to gay ménages, I cannot help but believe O'Hara chose to camp it up tongue-in-cheekily for the cognoscenti. His frivolous tone, or what Zwicky calls his "unserious seriousness,"[21] finds its echo in Ladouceur's offhand yet precise, sometimes deceptively throwaway tenderness. Certainly, his poems are intermediaries between himself, the poems' addressees and his readers.

The shell game Ladouceur plays finds its apotheosis in the book's title, *Otter*, a creature unmentioned, as previously noted, from first page to last in a menagerie otherwise containing armadillos and gem-encrusted turtles, over which the poet desultorily casts his zookeeper's eye. Like Lucky Pierre or the handkerchief code gay men used in the 1970s to communicate their preferences while cruising for sex, "otter" features in a still used gay-male lexicon of verbal tags to denote attitudes and body types. According to John Hollywood, a popular U.S.-based blogger, otters tend to be thin or athletic, hirsute (if as shaved and sculpted as topiary), and attracted to bears, their more corpulent animal-kingdom brethren.[22] Otters can be of any age, Hollywood argues, but other sources

---

20 Lucky Pierre (https://www.urbandictionary.com/define.php?term=Lucky%20Pierre). Retrieved on November 23, 2018).

21 Zwicky, Ibid, 10.

22 John Hollywood, Gay Men: Are You a Jock, an Otter, a Bear, or a Wolf? November 20, 2107. (https://pairedlife.com/dating/Gay-Men-Are-you-a-Jock-Otter-Bear-or-Wolf.

suggest they tend to be less hairy than he indicates and also younger, though not as juvenile as twinks, a putatively hairless category time forces all men to shed by their mid-twenties. And their attentions may not be exclusively directed at bears. Interpreting Ladouceur's title through this typology makes it meaningful. The majority of men in *Otter* are young and comfortable in their pelt-bedizened or depilated skins. Many may best be described as being on either side of the cusp marking the transition from being a twink to someone slightly older and more schooled in the ways of the gay-male body. The bloom of their youth is still evident, even if its bud is but a memory. Despite my present mixing of animal and vegetable metaphors, the poems in *Otter* can be read together, if not as Ladouceur's coy version of *The Picture of Dorian Gray* (or his queer poetic version of a bildungsroman), then as a group portrait of a cohort of gay men who are entering their prime. Though if *Otter* were a group portrait, should it not be called *Otters*?

What constitutes being in one's "prime" brings me back to the passage by José Estaban Muñoz that Billy-Ray Belcourt chose as his epigraph for *This Wound is a World*: "When I go extemporaneously, I lose myself." The potential loss of self, which Belcourt maps so eloquently for queer First Nations people who struggle to find themselves while the pernicious legacy of a colonialism far from being on its last legs does its best to erase them, is at complete variance with the self-confident world Ladouceur sketches in *Otter*. To mitigate the coma-inducing effects of settler culture, Belcourt speaks plainly while at the same time finding succor and support for his observations in the ideologies of theoreticians he admires and in the Indigenous resurgence prophesized by his ancestors, nurtured by his elders, and championed by his peers. Ladouceur, on the other hand, delineates a queer culture populated by like minds aware the pathologies once diminishing them no longer have the necessary public sanction to oppress. The past's legacy is never to be forgotten, as his poems about Wilde and Sassoon attest. By "like" I don't mean the only minds for which Ladouceur feels any affinity are gay-male or even same-sex; he's drawn to minds appreciative of difference and therefore queer. To preserve difference, to make it private, and to prevent it from being freighted with the rigor mortis of agitprop, Ladouceur speaks in a sometime opaque language as if it were a lingua franca or even a neo-Polari.

Retrieved on November 24, 2018.

In her tribute to the late José Estaban Muñoz in the *Los Angeles Review of Books*, New York-based journalist Emily Colucci outlines his theories about queer agency: "Understanding the temporality of queerness as outside of straight time's present, which Muñoz refers to as the 'here and now,' Muñoz's queer utopia consists of a drive toward a future, or as he writes, a 'then and there.'"[23] The idea of the here and now vs. the then and there gains authority in the worldview of *The Wound is a World*, where Belcourt's presence as a young First Nations queer individual is compromised by the unacknowledged persistence of colonialism (and its invasive homophobia) and counterbalanced by strategies of resurgence (including love-making, as described in "Okcupid"), where the "then" in "then and there" embraces the survival of age-old Indigenous perspectives and posits them as the someday-healed world of "there":

> but this was different
> because time stops
> and is made anew
> when two native boys
> find each other's bodies
> and write poems about it afterwards
> because each kiss was an act of defiance
> a kind of nation-building effort
> our bodies were protesting
> dancing in a circle
> to the beat of
> a different drum
> that was also a
> world in and of itself

Muñoz also addressed what Colucci describes as the queer community's (and mainstream culture's) "colourblindness" to other coexisting identities, in a way affirming Belcourt's "version of disidentification is neither a complete identification nor a hard-lined rejection or counteridentification, but a politically

---

23 Emily Colucci, "Vacating the Here and Now for a There and Then: Remembering José Estaban Muñoz," *Los Angeles Review of Books*, March 31, 2014 (https://lareviewofbooks. org/article/vacating-now-remembering-jose-esteban-munoz/#!. Retrieved on November 8, 2018).

generative middle ground in which an individual both takes on an identity and reveals its fragile construction."[24] Anyone who reads *This Wound is a World* cannot fail to come away from it with an improved grasp of queer First Nations experience and how by necessity it leads to a "fragile construction" of self. Through such constructions, supported by the decolonizing Indigenous resurgence, the wound is seen and shall continue to be and become a world.

In comparison, the future is now in Ladouceur's emphatically confident *Otter*, though this now is "outside of straight time's present" because the equities fought for and won in settler culture during the long, sometimes dark decades after Wilde's incarceration have vouchsafed this outsideness. It can at last rub shoulders with a more cognizant, less heteronormative straight contemporary moment, though, to echo Ladouceur's conversation with Zwicky, mainstream society may not permit queer experience to stay personal. Perhaps it's still not yet commonplace enough to be anything but political and won't be considered everyday until straight insiders look up from their set ideas of tolerance to notice how the world really is. In the meantime, it's necessary, according to Ladouceur in *Otter*'s closing poem, "Goodbye, Cruel World," to keep

> the world away from us
> with barriers of sponge of latex of wool.
> We wore earplugs at the venue.
>
> We wore condoms as the day broke.
> We wore toques whose pompons
> leapt off—*goodbye, cruel world!*—
>
> because that year the cold came
> quick. All of that is water now
> as in, under the bridge.

For Belcourt, in "Love is a Moontime Teaching," the heart-stopping, un-Instapoetry-like poem that closes *This Wound is A World*, the persistent depersonalizing cruelties of the past cannot be left in the dust because the present is still stuck in reverse, intent on erasure:

---

24 Ibid.

the body is a myth
is the only good news the doctor gives you when your cells run amok
amok is the border the skin doesn't remember
how to secure anymore
anymore is the feeling you get when a police officer
pulls you over because he thinks you're driving a stolen vehicle
a stolen vehicle is the nickname you give to love.

The cruelties Belcourt is obliged to roll his window down for are definitely not water under the bridge.

2019

Poetics of Orienteering: Some Remarks on Sexual Disorientations

Whether we are writers or readers, we locate ourselves in poems through a comprehension of word choices, how they act as signifiers in order to carry valences of meaning.

When it comes to sexuality, the mainstream position even today is compulsory heterosexuality. For most, by default, heterosexuality is the accepted first measure of what it is to be fully human.

Marginalized people, in this case those who are marginalized on the basis of gender expression, sexual orientation and/or sex identification, can choose to accommodate mainstream aesthetics or to conflict with it.

The poetics of the beautiful: a tendency from an aesthetic point of view to create poems that are examples of sanctioned beauty. It is a poetics necessitating the composition of poems about queer experience, for example, that are aesthetically pleasing and therefore less threatening to non-queer audiences. The cultivation of the beautiful can be dangerous, for this approach may unwittingly accommodate and even foster an ill-conceived, blind, and even shallow empathy among certain seemingly tolerant, but sometimes self-deluded heterosexuals who believe themselves to be liberal and open-minded. The beautiful potentially shields them from undiluted realities that might otherwise make them uneasy. In response to poems that cause them discomfort, they might express this uneasiness through the posture of critique, complaining that the poems are excessively personal, are more therapeutic in motivation than aesthetic, are overwrought or, worse, overwritten and not beautiful. Many queer writers may write the beautiful to protect themselves. The beautiful becomes a mask unrelated to the life of the wearer. On the other hand, poems written to be beautiful sometimes have a subversive utility. They anaesthetize the non-queer reader and therefore allow for the transmission of previously unknown and unimagined experiences. Nevertheless, the beautiful suggests closure, that by the end of the poem everything is all right or safe.

Related aesthetic environments to the beautiful are the inclusive and the representative. Both often describe experience using mainstream frames of reference so that marginalized experience can be recognized by those whose own experience is not marginal in the same way.

The poetics of discomfort endeavour to disrupt the assumptions of the (straight or straight-acting) readers' potential for complacency, for their high regard for their own tolerance. Poems of discomfort aim to create social unease. The readers' responses to such discomfort may be to arrest it (its anarchic disordering of the mainstream ethics is criminal), to silence it (it is social noise). Poets of discomfort, even if they are writing love poems, want to challenge complacency, forcing readers to examine their own internal discourse, to consider why they feel uncomfortable.

The poetics of disorientation aim to reproduce the disorientation queer poets may feel in a heterosexist society, to create an environment where straight or straight-acting readers lose track of themselves. It also aims to disorient queer readers out of their acceptance of the status quo, should they default to being socially subtextual.

The poetics of orienteering seek to locate readers in the wilderness of the queer poet's reality wherever and whatever that may be, the poet deploying the positions, references, and vocabulary natural to that reality, defining the beautiful and the not-beautiful in their own terms.

1997

PHANTOM DIARY

Queer Rose Country

THE MOUNTAINS, FOOTHILLS, AND open prairie of Alberta wrought how I first came to see the world. The contours of its light clarified the standard against which I'd measure all later landscapes, the darker traces in my birth-place's nature making it inevitable that I would leave. The dislocations, initially brief, began early. I would come to see the differently lit shadows they cast as proposing alternatives.

When I was a very small child in the early 1960s, my mother took me from our home in Calgary to see my grandmother in Victoria. I remember playing in the sand at Willows Beach, three or four blocks from her peak-roofed house. I could see the ocean and Mount Baker from her upstairs bathroom if I stood on the closed toilet seat. In 1968, my parents sent me to Pioneer Pacific, a boy's summer camp on Thetis Island, an hour farther north on Vancouver Island and off the coast from Ladysmith. One afternoon we canoed over to an even smaller island—an island off an island off an island—and slept beneath the stars at the edge of a First Nations burial ground. In the faint penumbra of Vancouver's lights miles to the south, campers and leaders alike were unaware our tempor-ary presence could linger as disrespectful of the spirits at rest nearby and of their descendants who continue to watch over them.[1]

The next summer, I got shipped off to Pioneer Ranch, an affiliated camp on Crimson Lake in central Alberta, west of Red Deer. I wondered at the time if its overpopulation of leeches could justify the lake's bloody-sounding name. The camp happened to coincide with the moonshot, a neologism coined to capture the decade of machismo it took to rocket Apollo 11 to the Earth's sole natural satellite on July 20, 1969. In an effort of mimicry engineered to appeal to pre-adolescent boys, the camp leaders staged a raft race to an island in the middle of

---

1   In the late 1980s, when I was at work on poems probing my childhood in Alberta, I wrote a poem called "Indian Graveyard, Gulf of Georgia, 1968." All these poems are collected in *Designs from the Interior* (Anansi, 1994). I was sent to Camp Pioneer Pacific because my grandmother had decided that she couldn't live alone anymore, so chose to move in with my family in Calgary. My mother had gone to Victoria to help her pack. She would end up in a nursing home suffering from dementia for over fifteen years.

the lake, our listing journey there and back accomplished in a couple of sunny hours rather than in the eight leisurely days it took Apollo's crew. The raft race and banquet afterwards, during which we tried to make out the actual landing on staticky televisions plugged in for the occasion, are the only happy moments I can summon up of those two unendurable weeks away from home. A boy living down the street from our house, who would break my arm the following year, had been assigned to my cabin. Like the moon, the camp had no atmosphere and I held my breath—until one hot afternoon I was found miles from camp along a gravel road, dehydrated and gasping for air while attempting to run away. My mother later observed that the Stetson-wearing Alberta boys were much "rougher stock" than those from "genteel" B.C. families, to whom Pioneer Pacific had tipped its hat. To this day, I don't know upon what she based this distinction that so facilely linked geography with social praxis, but it gave me comfort, however short-lived.

A third—and more lengthy—dislocation to B.C. came almost a decade later, in 1978. I transferred from the University of Alberta in Edmonton to complete my undergraduate degree at the University of Victoria—and to find out if I could write. The next five years I spent on the west coast as a putative adult, student, and not-yet journeyman poet would leave an enduring, lightly placed footprint on my already stepped-on spirit. Though I'd grown up landlocked and overshadowed by the Rockies, the flat disc of the Pacific was, in its potential for emptiness, not too different from the plains. Victoria became the primer that sealed the plaster Alberta damaged to prevent it from bleeding through the more opaque layers of colour to come. In due course opportunity would take me to Ottawa, where I chose to live for almost two decades. When I look back, the dislocations in between where I started and where I settled in Ontario and truly began to grow up were necessary, especially in the character of their in-betweenness, for they allowed me the distance I required to re-invent or re-vision myself as someone other than who and what my place of origin and initial becoming, in its dearth of possibilities, tried to convince me I was.

Identity, in my experience, depends on flux, is as much about placelessness as it is about place. Moving east taught me I am more of a westerner than I ever felt myself to be as a teenager. While I was never about to cancel any emotional Crow Rates[2] by exorcizing the prairies from my psyche, I never once saw myself

---

2   For details about the Crow Rates and their impact on the development of the west, go to
     https://en.wikipedia.org/wiki/Crow_Rate

returning to either of Alberta's two major cities, however abundantly they may have changed.[3] Yet, if I were ever to indulge a long-time dream to move back west, and more precisely to coastal B.C., I was afraid I would feel out of place. My years in Ontario had brought to light a perceptible eastern inscape.[4]

When I left the plains, I had not yet negotiated terms with myself as a sexual being. Alberta's emotional climate had been far too wintery for that kind of awakening, at least for me. I defined myself as liking girls—"straight" was not a term I knew back then—because that was expected, though by fifteen I had already had sex with another boy my own age. However natural that furtive brush with Eros was, it scared me. Four years later, a lifetime to an adolescent, I found myself attracted to a close friend at the University of Alberta. A force more insidious than my conscious self guaranteed that I would misread what my response to him could mean, recasting it as something not carnal but solely (if you will forgive the pun) of the spirit. If roses symbolize erotic love, then in my case, the wild Alberta rose can only stand for a love my anxieties had hoped to nip in the bud, or at best, let shrivel before it could open and spread its intangible scent.

This tendency to deny myself roses was a long time in the making. At Banff Trail Elementary School, my grade-four classmates and I were taught the rudiments of place. We learned to distinguish plateaus from deserts, began to recognize the slow, disparate shapes of the continents, learned to spell the awkward names of out-of-the-way capitals while local winds blasted snow against the multiple-paned windows of our classroom. We were asked to colour in the white spaces ruled off by the mimeographed map's pre-existing boundaries. Clutching a rapidly worn-down crayon, I knew that pink stood for something called "Empire"—or was it "Commonwealth"? —over which the sun would never set.

---

3   Unsurprisingly, when I spent nine months in Saskatoon as writer in residence at the public library, I felt a sense of recognition that overwhelmed me. It was the boulevard elms and poplars, the bitter January cold, the fierce blue skies, the fiercer sun, and the shattering crunch of snow, like Styrofoam. When you leave behind the place that has compromised and tormented you, you lose everything else about it you may have unknowingly loved.

4   My suspicions were confirmed in 2004 when I moved back into one of the neighbourhoods where I'd lived as a student in Victoria. However much I may feel affirmed by my proximity to the ocean—it's a block away from my apartment and I can see it from my balcony—I have never felt wholly at home on Vancouver Island during the fourteen years since my return. I'm too much of a nomad to feel fully at home anywhere, though now, if all the years I have lived in Victoria are combined, I've spent more time here than anywhere else, including Alberta.

The predominating "pinkness" of the world map I was exposed to might equally have suggested pink clouds and an artfully arthritic decline into twilight.

In the school yard, I was taught that boys shouldn't like pink. Any boy who did skipped Double-Dutch with the girls. At home, I played with my sister's dolls with increasing guilt, though undressing an emasculated G.I. Joe was considered butch—and acceptable. I learned my geography lessons well enough to guarantee that only the dry Alberta air would make my nose bleed. A young woman in ermine looked down on us obliviously from a faux-gilt frame above Mrs. Zechariah's desk. In Wolf Cubs, I swore allegiance to the Queen, but never to queens.

Some of us boys were drawn together, however, in ways we were unable either to recognize or acknowledge. Three of my childhood friends, two of whom I've known since before I was ten, turned out in adult life to be as gay as I am. Alberta provided us with few words to know and love ourselves by, and none of us live there anymore. During puberty, I was labelled without labelling myself: "pansy," "sissy." Though I got good marks in school, I was a "cocksucker," never cocksure. What could the labellers see that I did not? It took me years to find possible words for what I feel; my imperial, Anglican "fuck-you" arrogance and fear of humiliation constrained me. In the mindset of my adolescence, the three most isolating insults were "chink," "bohunk," and "fag."

The landscape—physical, social, emotional, aesthetic—that we are raised in imprints us with an arcane vocabulary whose symbolism we spend the rest of our lives deciphering. It is a vocabulary whose richness or poverty determines how we come to describe and discover ourselves. Because of the life I knew in my first landscape, which is a time more than a place, it took me years to feel even marginally at home in my body and to acknowledge the signs that had long been telling me who I was. My vocabulary—be it composed of words, sensations, gestures of the body, or simply the most elemental of ideas—had first to be supplemented by what I came to learn after I left. This made me see Alberta as I'd first known it for what it was: a sexual hinterland where the missionary position was the epitome of household efficiency.

However central Alberta may have remained to my imagination, never once while I growing up did I think of it as "centre." It was forever off-centre: life happened in other places. Anything occurring there, or here (…where am I?), in the imponderable moments of my own life, was null in the shadow of that life. This half-conscious awareness of being peripheral was deepened by my parents' newness to the province. My mother's roots were in Ontario and British Columbia, military and mannered. She married an RAF pilot training at the Patricia Bay air base north of Victoria during the Second World War. She followed him to England, where they lived for ten years and where my two elder sisters were born. Though my father seldom talked of his British homeland, he made its monarchic primacy felt. I was my nuclear family's sole Alberta-born original, and we lived in a remote part of Empire not of the Commonweal. Even when I ate supper at my parents' dining-room table, the heirloom silver flatware we used made me feel home was faraway. I never felt any "blood" connection with those around me, whose beliefs and family life were differently formed.

The task for some queer writers is, in part, to recast straight aesthetics, to expose its lacunae in order to restate them in terms that attempt to exclude less. According to Margaret Atwood in *Survival*, Northrop Frye suggests that

> in Canada…the answer to the question 'Who am I?' is at least partly the same as the answer to another question: 'Where is here?' 'Who am I?' is a question appropriate in countries where the environment, the 'here,' is already well-defined…. 'Where is here?' is a different kind of question. It is what a man asks when he finds himself in unknown territory, and it implies other questions. Where is this place in relation to other places? How do I find my way around in it? If the man is really lost he may also wonder how he got 'here' to begin with, hoping he may be able to find the right path or possibly the way out by retracing his steps. If he is unable to do this he will have to take stock of what 'here' has to offer in the way of support for human life and decide how he should go about remaining alive.[5]

For queer people who were raised in or find themselves in places like the Alberta of my youth, the known environment is overshadowed by straight, mainstream hegemony whose answer to the question "Who am I?" is, by design, quite limited.[6] For many gay men and lesbians, whether they are writers or

5 Margaret Atwood, *Survival: A Thematic Guide to Canadian Literature*. New Edition. Toronto: Anansi, 2012, 10–11.

6 Look to today's Russia, which banned the "spread" of "gay propaganda" among anyone eighteen or younger. Look to Uganda, where being queer is an offence punishable by death. And look to the Ontario of Doug Ford's "Progressive" Conservatives, which has replaced

pipefitters or vodka drinkers, "Where is here?" must be restated as "Where is queer?" or at least as its derivative: "Where is straight-acting?"

And we go looking for it.

Eventually.

Here or elsewhere.

Elsewhere and here.

I grew up in Charleswood, near the university in Calgary's northwest. The Rockies formed an early western limit to my thoughts, and Highway 1A remains my favourite approach. It veers downhill past Cochrane toward Ghost Lake and Jumping Pound, then swerves archetypically into my flesh. Even as a child I would believe I could stand on my bed, gaze out the window, and there they'd be, waiting. Mountains: distant and sentinel, but patient and reassuring. Each spring their dusty indigo insouciance was echoed by the windblown slopes of prairie crocus in the foothills. The mauve chrysalides would poke through slowly browning grasses, shy heads bowing as they opened.

I believe our first landscape imprints what's porous and visceral inside us, shapes the nervous system's involuntary responses. Words rise through the body, which is geologic, stratified—layers of place, of family, silted over by subsequent successive futures. The oldest words, as they well up, conjoin with others more recent. Meanings blur. After I grew up and moved beyond the provincial borders of my imagination, Alberta, or rather my Alberta and everything that occurred there, continued to assert itself, imposed its template on all later geographies. My answer to the questions they pose is physical. I am comfortable in cities where the land overwhelmingly intrudes. In Ottawa, the Gatineau Hills across an Ottawa River broader than any prairie river I'd grown up knowing, offered a discomfiting reassurance. In September the maroon haze incandescing up their flanks, as the sugar maples turned, both disoriented and delighted me. Something inside linked this purpled fluorescence not to autumn but to spring.[7]

Over the years, whenever I returned to Calgary to visit my family long enough to spend an afternoon on my own, I could not help remarking on the proliferating signs of queer community to which I had not been privy—if they'd been there to be noticed—while growing up. To echo Atwood, I was more able

a recently updated approach to sex education that discusses gender identity, gender expression, and same-sex marriage with the blinkered strategy used in 1998.

[7] The Olympic Mountains across the Strait of Juan de Fuca from where I live now in Victoria in certain lights are also often lilac or mauve, but they are in Washington, another state of mind and country completely.

to find my way around. There would be several shelves of familiar gay-male and lesbian titles to peruse at Books'N'Books on 17th Avenue. One time I stumbled on a travelling exhibit of lesbian erotica at an artist-run gallery on 12th Avenue. I never had enough time to myself to explore in more depth—or, should I say in my most fey un-Alberta voice, to go orienteering.

This emergent local here-ness was always something to uncover from a distance. Prior to a visit home in the pre-Internet 1980s and early 1990s, I would look up Calgary and Edmonton in the latest queer gazetteers and travel guides circulated by the Ottawa Public Library and never fail to be struck by the unexpectedly rich listings of queer-run or queer-positive social services, bed-and-breakfasts, restaurants, phone lines, and advocacy groups in addition to the inevitable discos whose collective life expectancy was even then shorter than that of most gophers. Long before Grindr, dancing was the foundation of queer culture, along with a phone line and a rogue cell of the Gay Liberation Front. Of course, the neutrally worded guides listed the safe and unsafe places to go cruising, several of which must have been known to the many and the few from times unremembered.

The queer social geography of my first cities was still not as rich or diverse as what could embrace you in Vancouver, Montreal or Toronto—or even Ottawa, but the changes since I had left Alberta clearly represented a beginning. Had any of the stitch-and-bitch knitting circles for men listed in the guides met while I was still a provincial resident way back when, I doubt, ostrich that I am, that I would have noticed or cared. Had I joined one, would my life have unfolded a different roadmap, with fewer dislocations and detours?

I now ask myself: where lies the queer rose country I long for[8]? A run-off-sluiced oasis that my writing over the years has been dedicated to locating and reclaiming? It must have existed among the cowboys and behind the

---

8   "Wild rose country" has been the provincial tagline on Alberta's licence plates since my adolescence in the early 1970s. In 2014, the Progressive Conservative government of the time attempted to replace it with "alberta.ca" under the pretense of making safer even the most out-of-the-way highway or gravel road. That the very right-wing Wild Rose Party served as their official opposition in the Alberta legislature is a far more likely reason, with an embattled government not wanting to give their popular opponents widespread publicity on millions of plates stopping and starting in traffic jams in the province's biggest cities. Needless to say, the optics of the change were not on the government's side and it soon backed down. Now that the PCs and the WRP have merged as the catchily named United Progressive Conservatives to oppose the province's first NDP government in the May 2019 election, the tagline has been stripped of disconcerting taint.

palisades of the earliest white settlements and before, it existed peaceably as two-spiritedness among the First Peoples—where it has persisted despite the efforts of residential schools and every possible colonizing force. My Alberta is a time capsule of the late-50s to the mid-70s, buried deep under my foundations, one that I sometimes plunder—only to reseal badly, the mouldy, fading papers and photographs differently jumbled.

Absent so far from this personal archive is any reference to Everett Klippert. He was the last person in Canada to be arrested, charged, prosecuted, convicted, and imprisoned for homosexuality. And, like me, a former Calgary resident. Four years younger than my father, he grew up in a neighbourhood close to the city's centre and a short drive from the subdivision where my family permanently established itself in 1961. After leaving school at the end of grade eight to help his recently widowed father support a family so large it could form its own baseball team, Everett worked for almost nineteen years, first in a dairy and then as a city-bus driver, before being arrested on charges of gross indecency—legalese for being accused of having sexual relations with other men. Twice he was sent to prison, in 1960 and 1967. He good-naturedly didn't dispute his first conviction, and upon his release four years later, he willingly relocated to the Northwest Territories to shield his family from any consequent shame, working as a garage mechanic's helper for Consolidated Mining. In 1965, he was arrested again on the same charge and given a choice of pleading guilty or being charged for arson, the crime for which he was questioned initially. The Supreme Court of Canada's 1967 decision to uphold a lower-court-assigned psychologist's recommendation to condemn him to indefinite detention as "a dangerous sexual offender" led to a surprising outcry. Sympathy for Everett, aired and promoted by the press nationwide—even by the Calgary *Albertan*, a paper my parents read—prompted the Liberal government of Pierre Elliott Trudeau to decriminalize consensual sexual relations between two members of the same sex in May 1969, several weeks before the Stonewall Riots in New York, the drag-queen-led rebellion that launched the gay-liberation movement, colouring past homophile activism as polite, quasi-law-abiding antecedents. Trudeau's government took its legislative inspiration from the United Kingdom. Two years earlier, the Commonwealth's apparent flagship amended the laws that for more than a century saw Oscar Wilde and thousands of other men crushed by two years of hard labour. Despite the changes to our own criminal code, Canada did not release Everett from prison until 1971.[9]

---

9   The details of Klippert's story, one which changed the direction of the history of the queer

None of Everett's unfortunate story could have found a way to impress it-self upon me as a child, but it must have floated in the air just as thickly as the cottonwood fluff to which I have remained supremely vulnerable—if not more sensitive to the undercurrents that pulled him down, since my pollen allergies are mercifully seasonal. His ill-treatment, so close to hand, is the green screen across which I now see my adolescence was projected. It doesn't take a stretch to imagine my younger self as a shadow puppet in the thrall of hurtful social forces. How unaware I was of how acutely any misinterpretation brought to my unself-conscious actions—a predilection for playing with dolls, a tendency to sit with my knees together, a chance glance in the wrong direction—would extend into my early adulthood and later post-Alberta life.[10]

Queer rose country, however irrigated, is an imaginative territory being re-covered by those who continue to live there and by those who have been raised in or have moved from other places and situations into a geopolitical landscape tempered by external influences that began to assert themselves after my depar-ture. My creased roadmap of Alberta has become so worn, it falls apart in my hands. My Alberta both is and is no longer. It revises but does not erase what for me was, and remains, a learned vocabulary of shame.

community in Canada, can be found on the Calgary Gay History Project website (https://calgaryqueerhistory.ca/2012/10/17/ calgarys-role-in-decriminalizng-homosexuality-in-the-60s/; retrieved on July 21, 2018). The History Project also posted a month-long commemoration of Klippert's life in November 2017 to mark the fiftieth anniversary of his being declared a dangerous sexual offender (https://calgaryqueerhistory.ca/2017/10/05/klippert-month-week-1/; retrieved on July 21, 2018).

10 I knew nothing of Klippert's life when I delivered the original version of these remarks at the Writing Alberta conference at the University of Alberta in September 1996. His story only came to my attention in the spring of 2016, when the federal government announced it would review the cases of gay men convicted of sexual offences prior to their decriminalization in 1969 (https://www.theglobeandmail.com/news/politics/ottawa-to-consider-pardon-for-gay-men-convicted-under-pre-1969laws/article28927302/). Again, Canada has followed the example of the United Kingdom, which extended the pardon it gave to Alan Turing, the breaker of the Nazi's Enigma Code and father of the computer, to the rest of the wrongly convicted on January 31, 2017; Oscar Wilde was among the 50,000 affected (https://www.telegraph.co.uk/news/2017/01/31/turings-law-thousands-convicted-gay-bisexual-men-receive-posthumous/). Klippert's unasked-for role in the advancement of queer rights has both darkened and lightened my feelings about the province where I was born and grew up. It would have been remiss of me not to create a place for both him and my feelings, an admixture of pride and despair, in the updated version of this essay.

But wait: back in December 1978, seven years after Everett obtained his freedom and when I was in Calgary for Christmas after my first semester studying creative writing in Victoria, I went dancing at Murt's on 9th Avenue with Carl, one of my three aforementioned, "turned-out-to-be-gay," childhood friends. The club exists no more, but its discreetly marked black door once opened onto an ill-lit space filled with smoke and men dancing solely (again forgive the pun) with men. I recall little else about that night except what I was wearing, which I can only describe as the campiest pair of tan leather boots I've ever had the honour to own. Calf-high, with zippers up one side and clunky platform heels, they catapulted me into atmospheres far too thin for me to sense a change in air or in myself. Atmospheres I denied breathing in or noticing. Who was I kidding if I didn't notice I stuck out even here? I was hardly Candy Darling, but some part of me must have wanted to skip queerly forward, self-denying, exhibitionist glam boy that I was. It would be another eight years before I kicked up my much-lower heels. I'd felt so out of my depth despite how I chose to dress—to stand out as well as to blend in?—that I never went back or searched for another Murt's in Calgary.[11] Queer rose country is a void I fill in: with words.

Carl, on the other hand, came out to himself with saner flourish, no doubt slept with more than a few handsome urban cowboys he'd meet at places like Murt's until, within a year or two, he fell love with the man he has, as far as I know, lived with ever since.

I never thought love was possible in Alberta.

This is the stuff that poetry is made of. If you want to know more about the queer rose country of the late-1970s, perhaps you would do better to track down Carl.

1996/2018

11 Had I gone back to Murt's or decided to explore the gay bars in Victoria when I returned to university after the turn of the New Year in January 1979, I would now have the pleasure of considering myself as an alumnus of the long defunct Queens's Head, Victoria's legendary gay bar that established itself on Head Street in Esquimalt, not far from the army base my maternal grandfather commanded during the Second World War.

My Emily Carr

"Every existence has its idiom."

—Walt Whitman

SITTING IN THE DINING room of Emily Carr House, a living-history museum that occupies the artist's birthplace at 207 Government Street in the heritage neighbourhood of James Bay, a few blocks south of Victoria's historic core, I remark on the contemporary art on the walls. Jan Ross, the resident curator, explains that when Emily returned from art school in San Francisco in December 1893, this room was her studio. Ross exhibits Indigenous and other local artists here in tribute to Carr's frustrated desire to open a "People's Gallery" in the 1930s and thumb her nose at the exclusionary Island Arts and Crafts Society.

I accept the cup of tea Ross offers. In exchange, I comment how it hardly ever escapes my daily awareness that I walk along the same streets that Carr did, however changed they would appear to her since she since last strode them. My apartment in a 1970s-era walk-up is only a few blocks away. What would I have passed while coming here today that she would have also recognized?

One way to understand Emily Carr, Ross agrees, is through her James Bay addresses. Except for periods of study abroad or years in Vancouver, she spent most of her life within a short walk of where she was born. Starting from a "here" isolated from the aesthetic movements of her time, Carr evolved a transcendent vision. For Ross, how she managed this is an almost unanswerable question. According to art historian Doris Shadbolt, Carr's "instincts were [for] homing,"[1] whether home was Victoria, for which, in her darkest years, she felt abiding rancour, or whether it was found in the remote coastal places she sketched from 1899 to 1930. The natural world upon which the city impinges inspired a pride of place she transformed at fame's onset into "a fierce and broader Canadianism."[2]

1   Doris Shadbolt, *Emily Carr*. Vancouver: Douglas & McIntyre, 1990, 10.
2   Shadbolt, 11.

It is now thirty-two years since the publication of the first edition of *West of Darkness*, my book of poems in the voice of this iconic artist. It is also thirty-five years since I completed the final manuscript and forty-one years since I wrote my first poem about Carr. Though I knew from the start that I had found in her a subject that would preoccupy me so completely I could write a book-length work, it was Robin Skelton who first affirmed "the importance of being Emily." I was Skelton's student at the University of Victoria for three years and his friend until his death in 1997, almost twenty years after we met. He anticipated the place that Carr would take in my life as a poet and often cajoled me to press on when I needed pushing, once cautioning me to finish by a certain All Hallows. That particular All Saints' Day passed, but, Robin clearly saw how formative my connection to Carr was. How prescient was he, though? Could he have then imagined how abiding this connection would become in the decades ahead?

Emily became my muse and my anchor for six years, and she locates me still. The poems I wrote in her voice all those years ago continue to speak to me with conviction about the west-coast landscape that today surrounds me, and it's Emily's voice that I still hear speaking them, never my own. I have maintained an ongoing relationship with her built upon years of familiarity and association. Whenever I walk along the ocean I never fail to see the seascapes that long ago inspired her. I like to think that some of the puppies being exercised by passing strangers could be very distant descendants of the dogs she raised. I continue to browse, if not always read, the countless biographies and artbooks about her that have been published since my own book first appeared in 1987. Whenever I have the opportunity to travel, I enjoy making time to see any temporary and permanent exhibition of her work at museums across the country. While I have managed to view almost every major canvas and drawing, there's always some new surprise as works held in private hands are lent, donated, or sold to public institutions. It intrigues me to consider her accomplishment against the surrounding landscape of whichever city I am visiting, deracinated from the west-coast one that had moved her.

• • •

Jan Ross's family resides on the top floor of Emily Carr House while the main floor and gardens are open to the public. Watching her daughters grow up in the artist's birthplace, she has gained fresh perspectives on the Carr family's daily life, finding her own family's habits echoed in Emily's written accounts of her childhood. As a parent, Ross can imagine how Richard Carr must have worried about his precocious daughter straying into the forests that encroached on early Victoria. Even nearby Beacon Hill Park was still largely wild when the artist was a child. In *Growing Pains*, Carr describes riding her pony into "the deep lovely places that were the very foundation on which my work as a painter was to be built."[3] She often observed Indigenous people beaching their canoes below the nearby Dallas Road cliffs. Yet her own mother felt intimidated by the trees overshadowing the house, her foreboding hard to comprehend today, a few manicured blocks from the Empress Hotel.

When the Carrs arrived in 1863, Victoria had 2000 white residents living on what is now acknowledged to be unceded territory of the Songhees and Esquimalt First Nations. The larger Songhees village across the harbour was home to 3000. Richard Carr had made his fortune during the California Gold Rush. Initially, he returned to England to make a home for his family. However, after a life of adventure, he found retirement at age forty-three unsatisfying, his restlessness aggravated by the deaths of two infant sons. In Victoria, Emily's father established a business in the town proper on Wharf Street. This Italianate-style house where Ross and I compare notes rose within walking distance on Carr Street (now Government Street). He built it for his English wife, whom he had met in San Francisco while he was prospecting, and for their two California-born daughters, on four acres of land south of the original settlement. Emily was born in an upstairs bedroom on December 13, 1871, the year the amalgamated colonies of Vancouver Island and British Columbia entered Confederation. Emily was her family's second-youngest child, and because she was the last of the three "Canadian" girls, they nicknamed her "Small" (the two elder were known as "Bigger" and "Middle"). In the parlour she learned her prayers under the tutelage of her increasingly stern and ever more religious father. She made an easel for her bedroom from branches he had pruned from the cherry trees. She was always contrary, but it was to her family she would return from the after-school drawing lessons she was allowed in the belief that her aptitude could be shaped into a ladylike pastime.

My interest in Emily was seeded in me early on by my mother. In 1965, when I was Small's age or, more exactly, close to the same age as the little girl her readers fall in love with in Emily's memoir about her childhood, *The Book of Small*, I needed to compile a scrapbook on great Canadians to fulfill a requirement of

3   Emily Carr, *Growing Pains: An Autobiography*. Toronto: Fitzhenry & Whiteside, 2004, 14.

my Blue Star for Wolf Cubs—I was a member of the 31st Beavers in northwest Calgary. Providing magazine clippings about Emily and others, my mother helped me with the wording (I still have the scrapbook):

> Emily Carr was a painter and writer who was born in 1871 in Victoria, B.C. where she lived most of her life. She died there in 1945. Her home was the 'House of all Sorts.' She kept lots of animals, especially cats which she loved. She painted many Indians who were her friends and loved her and called her 'Klee Wyck'—the laughing one.

How my eight-year-old self determined that a dog-loving Emily raised cats, I have no idea! She, meanwhile, began to stake her place in my imagination, interleaved somewhere between Lester Pearson or Pauline Johnson, Colonel James McLeod or Robert de La Salle, Sir Wilfred Grenville or Stephen Leacock, who was my godfather's uncle. More important was the enthusiasm for Carr that my mother shared with me. When I moved to Victoria in my early twenties, Emily's life was one of the few local legends familiar to me. I gravitated to her.

Carr's parents died two years apart when she was in her teens. In 1890, impatient to escape her sisters' perceived tyranny, she convinced their guardian to send her to a San Francisco art school, where she learned the basics. At home in 1893, she supported herself by teaching children art, earning money for study in England. She lived through several dispiriting years there from 1899 to 1904, having chosen a London school no longer at the fore of European art practice. Fleeing a lifelong abhorrence of large cities, she deepened her skills studying in Cornwall and elsewhere, but when her health collapsed midway through her stay, she came home feeling a failure. Her sisters found the cigarette-smoking, foul-mouthed, portly woman who disembarked from the ferry unrecognizable. In England, she chose art over love; her future at home portended "spinsterhood."

Soon after her return to Canada, Emily moved to Vancouver, where she gave popular art classes and participated in what passed for a local art scene. During a cruise to Alaska in 1907, she saw totem poles *in situ* for the first time and met an American who supported himself by selling his paintings and sketches of the Northwest "Indian" villages to buyers in New York. Carr envisioned that documenting the Indigenous peoples and places she loved for posterity could be both livelihood and vocation. Over the next two summers, she sketched villages within reach of Vancouver and as far north as Alert Bay, and, in 1910, travelled to France to equip herself with "the New Art," as she called it. Though she fell ill again and never led *la vie bohème*, her sense of art's possibilities was forever transformed. No longer would she paint what biographer Maria Tippett calls "faithful and pleasing reproductions of the picturesque."[4] Instead she grasped that art should not imitate nature but be its realization. Her palette brightened and her forms loosened, so much so that she felt rejected by audiences when she exhibited her "French" work in Vancouver in 1912 and new work in 1913, having applied her new aesthetic to Indigenous subjects sketched as far away as the Queen Charlotte Islands. That her detractors did not favour her choice of subject was equally disheartening.

Just prior to the outbreak of the First World War, Carr, in her mind misunderstood, left Vancouver and returned to Victoria. Around the corner from her birthplace stands "The House of All Sorts," which I'd mentioned by name only in my entry about Emily in my childhood scrapbook and which she would coin as the title of a memoir she published almost thirty years hence. It is the rooming house that Carr built at 646 Simcoe Street on a lot carved from the original family land. Planned as an income property, with a suite and studio for herself, it never adequately supported her. She spent fourteen years scrambling to make ends meet, solidifying her reputation as an eccentric trailed by dogs around town, who pushed a pram full of animals, including her monkey, Woo, in a dress. Though she painted through these years, she never ventured far. Art gradually lost its primacy; it had dried up, according to her later recollections of this time. When she moved into Hill House, as she then called it, she was full of hope. "On the generous slope of the attic roof I painted two Indian eagles. ... They were only a few feet above my face as I slept." She felt these comforting presences "belonged to the house for all time"[5] and indeed they are still powerfully there, though the rooming house, albeit still standing, looks derelict. According to Jan Ross, Indigenous artist Floyd Joseph predicted that "those eagles' wings will flap and lift the roof right off with them."

In 1927, after hearing reports of a woman who had painted Indigenous villages, National Gallery director Eric Brown visited a skeptical Carr in her rooming-house studio. Stunned, he invited her to participate in the *Exhibition of Canadian West Coast Art, Native and Modern* planned for that year and

---

4   Maria Tippett, *Emily Carr: A Biography*. Toronto: University of Toronto: 1979, 76.
5   Emily Carr, *The House of All Sorts*. Toronto: Clarke, Irwin, 1971, 9–10.

made arrangements for her travel to Ontario for the opening, where she was the best-represented "modern" artist. She met several Group of Seven members, feeling immediate kinship with Lawren Harris and very disposed to his belief that art "was not a product of the intellect or the result of academic training," according to Tippett, "but the intuitive response of the artist to a higher spirit."[6]

. . .

In the decade immediately after *West of Darkness* was published in 1987, Indigenous and non-Indigenous critics began to voice their reservations about Carr's depiction of Indigenous culture. The controversy about how colonialism displaced First Peoples from their own narrative, however, was not in the air that I knowingly—or ignorantly—breathed from 1978 to 1984, the years during which I wrote about Emily. Only later did I become aware that her legacy was increasingly a target for criticism because she had found inspiration for art in the totems and villages of the Pacific Northwest's First Nations, a term she would not have been familiar with. Tsimshian-Haida scholar Marcia Crosby, in her landmark 1991 essay, "The Construction of the Imaginary Indian," asserts, that Carr's "paintings of the last poles intimate that the authentic Indians who made them existed only in the past…These works also imply that native culture is a quantifiable thing, which may be measured in degrees of 'Indianness' against defined forms of authenticity, only located in the past."[7] I have never been directly accused of any error in judgement for choosing to write about Carr's interpretations of and relationship with Indigenous culture, but when I first became conversant with the justified arguments advanced by the proponents of cultural appropriation, I anticipated slights and became sensitive to— and even paranoid about—any insinuation that I had consciously or worse, unconsciously, annexed experience more in the purview of Indigenous artists working in any creative discipline. Castigating myself for being indifferent to, or ignorant of, any prior claim to my intuitively chosen subject material, I feared being accused that I had stolen and misinformed a readership more deservedly theirs.

---

6   Tippett, 150.

7   Marcia Crosby, "The Construction of the Imaginary Indian," *Vancouver Anthology*, Stan Douglas, ed. Vancouver: Talonbooks, 1991, 285.

Any accusations of cultural appropriation that could be levelled against *West of Darkness* do have a few stinging, shadowy antecedents. While I was writing my first Carr poems in the late 1970s, a friend questioned why I wanted to write what she called "white Indian poetry," which in her opinion seemed to be inappropriately fashionable at the time and was being written by many poets, Seán Virgo and Susan Musgrave among them. "White Indian poets" were accused, often by other white or settler poets like my friend, of commandeering Indigenous traditions as their own shamanistic space rather than accepting the challenge of exploring the spiritual concerns of their own time through the frame of our own culture. In my own defense, I argued that "white Indian aesthetics" were not in sympathy with what I was trying to accomplish with these poems, so I resisted the label. Instead, I was attempting to understand a white female artist who was in awe of the accomplishments of the original inhabitants of her own country. She was aware and critical of the destructive influence of settler society on Indigenous culture and saw her desire to paint Indigenous villages and totem poles *in situ* as one way—but not the only way—to create a record of their moving presence, a record I was sure she would argue that she was not creating on her own, but alongside Indigenous and other non-Indigenous artists. To ignore the Indigenous themes in Emily's work would have been to misrepresent her.

The years during which Carr painted were certainly devastating ones. Disease, displacement, and poverty had reduced the Northwest Coast's population of Indigenous peoples by eighty percent in the first century after contact. By 1915, fewer than six hundred Haida occupied two still habitable villages and by 1929, the number of Indigenous peoples living in B.C. had fallen to 22,605.[8] In contrast, the total provincial population rose from 392,480 in 1911 to 694,234 in 1931.[9] The two censuses loosely bracket the two principal sketching trips that Carr made to the north coast in 1912 and 1928. Because she revisited some of the villages on her second trip, she saw how they had changed for herself, and she feared for the people that remained. As the American-born, Simon Fraser University historian, Douglas Cole,[10] argues in "The Invented Indian, the

---

8 Douglas Cole, "The Invented Indian, The Imagined Emily," *B.C. Studies* 125/126, Spring/ Summer 2000, 150.

9 http://www.bcstats.gov.bc.ca/StatisticsBySubject/Census/2011Census/ PopulationHousing/BCCanada.aspx; retrieved November 27, 2018.

10 Douglas Cole (1938–1997) wrote a number of books on B.C. history, including *From Desolation to Splendour: Changing Perspectives of the British Columbia Landscape* (with

Imagined Emily," "Carr's sense of the 'vanishing Indian' was not imagined. It seemed [to her] an inexorable truth verified by all known experience. She saw the deserted villages—they were no myth—and she was witness to the tilted and rotting poles. She regretted their demise, whether to the forces of nature or to museum collectors."[11] Her paintings and sketches can be seen as a different way to "collect" and, as Cole observed, they manifest as a version of the "salvage paradigm," but unlike the anthropologists who relocated the material heritage of Indigenous peoples to inaccessible vaults in distant places in order to "keep them safe,"[12] Carr, by sketching or painting them only, left all she saw in place. In later years, she recounted her travels in the written sketches that, when gathered together, became *Klee Wyck*. These literary sketches included vivid, affectionate, and always grateful portraits of the generous Indigenous men and women who shared their stories, acted as her guides to the even remoter sites where she wanted to paint, or simply were hosts who offered her a bed for the night. Her efforts to paint what she saw of Indigenous life were not solely for herself, as Cole contends, attempting to substantiate this observation with a quote from Carr's sketch about her visit to Kitwancool: "I want to make pictures of them, so that your young people as well as the white people will see how fine your totem poles used to be."[13] Her employment of the verb "used to," tellingly betrays she harboured fear that the solid ground upon which the resurgence of Indigenous cultures we are witnessing today from coast to coast to coast was built was in fact quicksand. However, "used to" does not imply that she believed Indigenous peoples would disappear or be assimilated. Her paintings, among many stimuli, she may have hoped, might help remind future generations about who they are. Cole nevertheless felt that art historians who insisted that Carr appropriated Indigenous imagery without recognizing the continuing vitality of the people who created it focused too narrowly on the paintings, which are vulnerable to justifiable as well as erroneous

---

Maria Tippet, Toronto: Clarke Irwin, 1977); *Captured Heritage: The Scramble for Northwest Coast Artifacts* (Vancouver: Douglas & McIntyre, 1985); *An Iron Hand Upon the People: The Law Against the Potlatch on the Northwest Coast* (with Ira Chaikin, Vancouver: Douglas & McIntyre, 1990); and *Franz Boas: The Early Years, 1858–1906* (Vancouver: Dougls & McIntyre, 1999).

11 Ibid.

12 Ibid, 151.

13 Emily Carr, *Klee Wyck*. Toronto: Clarke Irwin, 47, as quoted by Cole in "The Invented Indian, The Imagined Emily," 160.

interpretations, and did not take into account the fuller story her published writings and unpublished journals provide.

That's Cole's perspective. For others, Carr's minimalistically limned, sometimes romanticized reminiscences about the Indigenous peoples she knew shall never ring true and therefore read as damningly insubstantial. In her foreword to *Unsettling Encounters: First Nations Imagery in the Art of Emily Carr*, which University of Guelph professor emerita Gerta Moray published in 2006, Marcia Crosby writes about her grandparents, Clara and William Russ, who were Carr's guides on Haida Gwaii. In *Klee Wyck*, Carr referred to them by fictitious names, Jimmie and Louisa.[14] Comparing Carr's anecdotes with her own deeper knowledge of her grandparents, Crosby feels that their "shared history and memories[, which they had passed on,] are not the same as Carr's personal memories, which had entered into the public memory long before she began writing *Klee Wyck*. All written accounts, lectures, journals, memoirs, autobiography, news reports, art history, exhibits, catalogues, and her texts of creative non-fiction figure as representation, lying somewhere between history and imaginative discourse. That is different from the memories of someone who is part of a community of shared rememberers."[15] I can't believe that Carr would disagree with this assessment of her book; Carr, herself, was a severe critic of her own creations. She would have been more than happy, I think, to defer to and learn from anything that Crosby might choose to share, should they ever have had the opportunity to meet. It is sobering nonetheless to consider how much it must rankle when the travelogues of a stranger like Carr, whose reputation appears to have largely been made by interpreting a culture that was not her own, come to be the only window that the world decides to look through to get a hazy glimpse of how your own kin saw where they lived and you, as their descendants, see it now. I am using "rankle," fearing it completely underplays the strength of emotion felt in response.

Cole's assessment of *Klee Wyck*, I must admit, does closely describe what I recall of my sense of the book when, as a twenty-one-year-old, I first read it while researching the poems I wrote for *West of Darkness* in the late 1970s and early 1980s:

---

14 In *West of Darkness*, Crosby's grandparents' correct names are used. As a young man, I had wanted to give them their proper place in the record of Carr's life I aimed to create.

15 Marcia Crosby, "Foreword," *Unsettling Encounters: First Nations Imaginary in the Art of Emily Carr* by Gerta Moray. Vancouver: UBC Press, 2006, vii.

What emerges is an apparently unselfconscious portrait that records, with the artful eye of a sensitive observer, the Aboriginal people she meets. They live in Carr's present, not in an ahistorical past. The Haida she describes are not "imagined," seldom traditional, and certainly not stereotyped into a false authenticity. An occasional note of wistful regret over the disappearing past intrudes, but the people she describes live in partitioned houses, engage in the commercial fishery, even prepare herring roe for the Japanese market. They live in a world of missionaries, cannery bosses, schools, policemen, and Indian agents.[16]

Klee Wyck and Carr's other autobiographical writings, as I perused them, so inhabited me, that they fundamentally shaped how I saw and described her paintings. Always, in every poem responding to a particular canvas, my goal was to create a transcript of what she *might have* been thinking during the heat of creation. I now acknowledge that it did not occur to me to be sensitive to and filter out any inaccuracies about the Indigenous cultures of the Northwest Coast that I unconsciously laid down in words in my struggle to be true to Carr. Based on my research, I instead grappled solely with the challenges of evoking how she saw the people, villages, and totem poles she visited and painted. Today it feels regrettable that, beyond establishing what she understood of Indigenous culture, I did not search out reliable sources through which I could have modified her and my own impressions and, thus equipped, put Carr's cultural understanding into more appropriate context—though I'd only have been repeating in my own way what she tried to do herself. As Cole points out, "the fact that Carr incorporates Aboriginal peoples into her own conception of who she is is not contestable, nor, for that matter, is the fact that Canadians incorporate Carr's images and writings into their conception of what Canada is."[17] While writing about Carr's life and art, I was certainly that kind of Canadian. I became progressively less so in the decade after I came out as a gay man in 1985 and came to understand how the nation state, which I had been taught to love and which in my name had resolved to assimilate First Nations and appropriate their stories and traditions as its own, had also tried to orchestrate—

16 Cole, 153.
17 Ibid, 162.

for different reasons, employing different strategies, and arriving at different outcomes—the erasure of its queer citizenry.

In an essay T. S. Eliot wrote in 1919 to argue why *Hamlet* is an artistic failure, he coined "objective correlative," a term that's clearly held sway since as a shibboleth of modernism:

> The only way of expressing emotion in the form of art is by finding an "objective correlative"; in other words, a set of objects, a situation, a chain of events which shall be the formula of that *particular* emotion; such that when the external facts, which must terminate in sensory experience, are given, the emotion is immediately evoked.[18]

When writing the poems in response to Carr paintings, I saw their elements to be employed as signposts pointing readers toward an understanding of her experience, imbuing each one with my sense of her response to her chosen subjects. When reading *Klee Wyck*, I recall noting two narrative lines, which were at variance with each other. One rose and traced her growth as an artist; the other fell, tracing her sadness about the challenges facing Indigenous culture. Her increasing assurance as an artist was palpable, as was her concern for the men, women, and children she met during her travels. I saw the Indigenous subjects she painted as touchstones I rubbed to evoke her despair. The poems I wrote, I realize now, had very little to do with the Indigenous subjects themselves, even though I worked hard to understand the import of what was carved into the poles she reproduced in her paintings. Consequently, I'd like to amend Eliot's term ever so slightly, recasting it as "subjective correlative." By this I mean that creators, often without thinking, arrange the objects attracting their interest into patterns imbued, if not overwhelmed, with their own experiences. The grief I wrote into the paintings I described in *West of Darkness*, while no doubt based on evidence culled from Carr's memoirs, letters, and journals, perhaps had less to do with her grief or with how the Indigenous people she'd encountered felt about their own predicament. Empathy, while connective, takes us only so far.

---

18 The text of Eliot's essay, "Hamlet" can be found on The Poetry Foundation website (https://www.poetryfoundation.org/articles/69399/hamlet. Retrieved August 8, 2018). Eliot collected it into *The Sacred Wood: Essays on Poetry and Criticism* (London: Methuen, 1920). The italics are Eliot's.

Carr's paintings gave me a visual vocabulary to experience any grief I may have felt in my own life and to hide it in plain sight. It may have been an unnameable grief that I needed to externalize, even to dissociate myself from. Those of us who have written in the voice of another person come to acknowledge that doing so permits us to express feelings that may find no other outlet. Readers may solely respond to the sometimes-believable mask we have assumed, but it's our own issues, insights, and preoccupations, however much we hope it appears otherwise, that have claimed centre stage.

A new generation of Indigenous writers, artists and critics are now bringing their own perspectives to Carr and to her Indigenous-inspired work. In January 2017, while visiting with friends in the Lower Mainland over New Year's, I spent an afternoon at the Vancouver Art Gallery, where I lingered with the Carrs displayed in the rooms that are devoted to her work on the fourth floor. Hanging in tandem was an exhibition called *We Come to Witness: Sonny Assu in Dialogue with Emily Carr*.[19] Assu, a Ligwilda'xw/Kwakwaka'wakw artist whose ancestral home is on Vancouver Island, near Campbell River, was raised in North Delta, in the sprawling suburbs of B.C.'s Lower Mainland. The exhibition, which ran until April, featured his "intrusions" into Carr's paintings of Indigenous subjects drawn from his *Interventions on the Imaginary* series. In each print he digitally superimposed ovoid, s-shapes, and u-shapes rooted in Kwakwaka'wakw style on her paintings as graffiti-inspired tags. Later, on his website, I read his artist statement, which explains that through

> "[the shapes'] insertion…into the images, both the landscape paintings and the Northwest Coast design elements are changed. The landscapes become marked by the spectre of Native presence and the NWC design elements, traditionally two-dimensional in appearance, acquire the illusion of depth through association with Western principles of perspective. I see these bold interruptions of the landscapes as acts of resistance towards the colonial subjugation of the First People."[20]

---

19 *We Come to Witness: Sonny Assu in Dialogue with Emily Carr* (https://www.vanartgallery. bc.ca/the_exhibitions/ exhibit_assu.html. Retrieved on August 6, 2018).

20 Sonny Assu, *Interventions on the Imaginary* (https://www.sonnyassu.com/pages/ interventions-on-the-imaginary. Retrieved on August 6, 2018). Assu has posted a gallery of the images from the series on website at https://www. sonny assu.com/gallery/ interventions-on-the-imaginary.

He asks his viewers and himself,

> "Could Emily Carr's work be viewed as deeply political? She fought against the aesthetic and gendered bounds of the Group of Seven? She painted "Indian" life and territory into her work, oddly working both within and outside of the salvage paradigm."[21]

Assu dedicated one painting in the series, *Choke on an Ovoid*, which "intervenes" into Carr's *Strangled by Growth*, to Coast Salish/Okanagan artist Lawrence Paul Yuxweluptun because his art "combats the colonial whitewashing of Canadian history. But it also acts as a nod to Carr, who had a genuine interest in recording the daily lives and places of a diverse group of people she greatly admired."[22] Unlike the Group of Seven, she did not represent the land as empty or emptied of its original inhabitants. Nor does Assu wholly exonerate Carr of erasure. How could he resist doing so when one of her paintings, *Graveyard Entrance, Campbell River* from 1912, depicts his grandmother's village. "The personal connection to this work," he explains, "made the intervention [as *What a Great Spot for a Walmart*] particularly satisfying."[23] Displacing her evocation of his ancestral home with the apotheosis of contemporary commerce exacts a calibre of poetic justice so impishly perverse that, had she been alive to shop in Costco or Walmart, Carr would have been as amused, I suspect, by his disruptions of her picture plane in this and other paintings as she would have been appalled. The homogenizing influence of big-box stores would have been abhorrent to her, just as her paintings are to many Indigenous people. Assu's humour makes his work read as less harsh toward Carr than the judgements of her detractors a generation or so older than he is, Crosby, say, or a multiracial cohort of critics within the art-historical community. To echo Cole, Assu has not "essentialized her as the White colonizer."[24] By tagging her art, however, he encourages, if not cajoles, his viewers to see Carr anew through Indigenous eyes and through the history of colonialism, of which her work is a visible as well as a visual legacy. In making space for Carr's "admiration" for Indigenous

---

21 Ibid.
22 Ibid.
23 Ibid.
24 Cole, 159.

people and culture, Assu is nonetheless not dissenting from Crosby's negative characterization of the late-nineteenth-/early-twentieth-century artist's intentions. Instead, in his artist statement, he makes clear the direct link between "Interventions on the Imaginary," the series title of his Carr-inspired prints, and "The Construction of the Imaginary Indian," the title of Crosby's essay.[25] His dissent involves building upon the Tsimshian-Haida scholar's pioneering work by occupying visually the critical space that she had conceptually mapped out about Carr in the early1990s. Assu is performing necessary culture work I could have not imagined myself doing forty years ago when I first picked up my pen to write about an artist to whom we both pay very different forms of homage.

I take to heart Crosby's understandable reservations about Carr and feel *heartened* by Assu. I admire the humour and play he brings to his interventions into and reclamations of the psychic space that Carr had "claimed" for herself. Were I to write *West of Darkness* now, I'd like to believe that I would honour what a generation of Indigenous critics like Crosby continue to say about Carr's "use" of Indigenous history, culture, and experience by taking care to seek advice from my Indigenous peers in the writing and visual-arts community about the very different poems I would write today.

• • •

Despite her star turn at the National Gallery of Canada in 1927, which re-attuned her to her vocation, Carr preserved a feisty, if grudging, sense of her own isolation. Always looking for opportunities for "fresh seeing" that would allow her to better realize her chosen subjects, she nonetheless opened herself to diverse influences, including Seattle artist Mark Tobey, who struggled to teach her about Cubism. In contact with and recognized by her peers, Carr participated in national and international shows, enjoying several solo exhibitions during her lifetime. In the 1930s, she set aside Indigenous themes, finding spiritual fulfilment in forest subjects as well as in seascapes recognizable to anyone walking along the Dallas Road cliffs. In 1936, Emily traded Hill House for property elsewhere in the city and rented 314 Beckley Street, several blocks west in a working-class area of James Bay. The house is now gone, and, even with gentrification, the area feels less upscale than where, mere blocks away, the Carr family had settled almost six decades earlier. In 1937, she had the first

25　Assu, ibid.

of several heart attacks, which curtailed her trips far afield to sketch, though, at her sickest, she nevertheless painted propped up in bed. Her energies focused on her long-time interest in writing, through which she recast happy and dark times. Her autobiographical sketches came to the attention of Ira Dilworth, a CBC producer, who helped her shape them, broadcasting many, and undertaking to find her a publisher.

While writing *West of Darkness*, I was very aware that I was a man writing in a woman's voice. I took as my model the narrator of Sinclair Ross's *As for Me and My House*, whose voice, although one constructed by a male writer— and who coincidentally was also gay—is, from the first sentence, believably a woman's. At the time I would have been more than satisfied if I were able to equal Sinclair Ross's accomplishment. I was also aware how profoundly Emily, as a woman artist, surmounted the challenge put in her way by patriarchy, so I attempted to work that theme into the poems. Once, at a literary event soon after the book was published, a female academic asked me if it were suitable for me, as a man, to appropriate the voice of a female artist. Hers seemed to me to be an easy question inspired less by curiosity than intellectual fashion. I pointed out that Emily left more than ample record of her own voice through her writings and that my challenge had been to equal that voice, and perhaps, through a facsimile of that voice, to "re-voice" certain things that she consciously and unconsciously distorted in her reminiscences. I felt that I had written in Emily's voice, knowing my book existed alongside and subordinate to, rather than in place of, the inspiring books she wrote. I saw what I'd written as an attempt at empathy, not a theft.

During the years that I was looking for a publisher, I met Carol Pearson, who, when she was a girl, had taken art lessons from Carr and who had been one of the executors of Carr's estate. She was then living in Kingsville, Ontario, on the next farm over from a friend of mine at library school at the University of Western Ontario (now Western University). One weekend in the spring of 1985, Tim brought me home with him from London so I could meet her. After Carol read the manuscript, she pleased and relieved me greatly by saying that my poems caught the cadences of Carr's voice exactly. As a token of the real Carr, she gave me a tiepin that her father, Richard Carr, had once worn. A little bit of silver filigree festooned with a single chip of lapis lazuli, it sits among other small trinkets I keep in my bedroom in a wooden box atop my grandfather's tallboy. A few months after the book was published in August 1987, I received a letter from Mrs. J. Murray Speirs; it was clear from the shaky signature and the turns of phrase that she was elderly. Her husband and she had donated *Edge of the Forest*, the painting reproduced on my book's cover, to the McMichael Canadian Art Collection in 1969. A work of oil on paper, Carr executed this painting of a tree, likely a Douglas fir, against a vibrating blue sky in 1935. In my opinion, it's from her best period, when she painted the coastal forests solely from her own perspective, unmediated by any tradition but her own. The Speirs must have bought it from Carr soon after it was complete, and who knows, it may have been a condition of the McMichael's permission agreement with Penumbra Press, the book's initial publisher, that the painting's donor should receive a copy of *West of Darkness*. While reading my book, Mrs. Speirs told me in her letter, she felt as if the woman who had inspired it had walked back into her living room almost fifty years after she'd last seen her.

• • •

Over the past four decades I have had a lot of time to think about my motives for writing what in Canada would once have been called a documentary poem. The rapport I struck with Emily—or rather Emily struck with me—matured me as a writer, or I so believed, with self-congratulations thinking my apprenticeship was over. (It had barely started.) By example, as a writer and painter, Emily showed me that art matters only if what is rendered is true to the spirit of the subject. Without that spirit, no precision in detail, no flourish in technique, is worthy of attention and should be viewed with suspicion. The Emily I present is not unlike the actual woman, yet the two ladies do have their differences. "You should not have said that," each Emily might censure the other.

"Avoid outrageousness and monstrosity. Be vital, intense, sincere. Distort if necessary to carry your point but not for the sake of being outlandish. Seek ever to lift the painting above the paint."[26] I stumbled upon this passage in the late 1970s, sitting in a café one rainy afternoon somewhere along Johnson Street. Her journal enchanted me; and I found myself referring back to passages from it again and again. These words formed the basis of my approach to the writing of what I came to see as a portrait and later as a self-portrait of the persona I'd chosen for myself. (The subtitle of the book's first edition was "a portrait of Emily Carr;" in the subsequent edition, it became "Emily Carr, a Self-Portrait.") The woman who sat for me demanded a style that fit her. What emerged is

---

26 Emily Carr, *Hundreds and Thousands*. Toronto: Clarke, Irwin, 1966, 48.

representational rather than purely factual, impressionistic rather than exact. She despised art that betrayed nothing of the artist.

Another writer once asked me why I would want to write poetry in the voice of an artist rather than draft a critical essay about that artist's work, implying I had made a strange aesthetic decision to proceed as I had. At the time I had no real answer to give her except that it had not occurred to me to do otherwise. Upon reflection, however, I soon realized the obvious: that art criticism and poetry have entirely different aims. The former stands outside and evaluates and the latter sits inside and experiences. *West of Darkness* was never intended to be a work of art history. Perhaps the question was posed out of an unexpressed belief that my creative motivation to write about Carr was parasitic. I could contend that all art is parasitic, for much inspiration is based upon vicarious if sympathetic observation. I could also contend that good art only emerges out of how well we use our medium (language, paint) to mediate and explore what we have come to learn at one remove. My decision to use a persona to make art was simply a more obvious and simpler one among the many aesthetic choices that writers make to address their material.

To understand what actually did motivate me to write *West of Darkness*, it is perhaps useful to connect it with Margaret Atwood's *The Journals of Susannah Moodie*, a book-length poem that inspired me enormously. Where Atwood's protagonist is "bushed" by the uncompromising Ontario wilderness of the early to mid-1800s, mine views the natural world of the Pacific Northwest as a sentient, benevolent force that is the incarnate expression of Carr's God. Though I may have read something unintended into Atwood's characterization, I wrote *West of Darkness* as a refutation of Moodie's and perhaps Atwood's sense of place to illustrate a different kind of survival (to repeat, yet again, that bankrupt Canadian literary cliché). Instead of Atwood's "Your place is empty,"[27] I wrote "The land is not empty."

How little I understood at the time I wrote this line the ways in which it would resonate today. It concludes a poem about *The Clearing*, the last painting Carr is known to have completed. Carr, as I imagined her, is tired and humbly preparing for death. I had intended my readers to infer that she felt, despite the disappointments that living causes us to accrue, that hers had been a full life worth living:

---

27 Margaret Atwood, "A Bus Along St. Clair: December" in *The Journals of Susannah Moodie*. Toronto: Oxford, 1970, 61.

Yet I cannot say
this solace of trees

rippling in circles
around me

has left me unscarred.
I am tired.

Circles widen.

The land is not empty.

Now the concluding line is easily read as Carr contradicting the enduring attitudes her contemporaries mostly held, British immigrants or the children of
British immigrants like her, who, unlike her, saw the land they'd come to oc-
cupy as stripped of any discernible markers of civilization, and who saw nothing amiss in stripping the waning remainder of its original inhabitants from
it in order to exploit its bounty and to "rechristen" its points of interest with
a nostalgic overlay of European names. While it's not an interpretation that I
could have anticipated, at the age of twenty-seven when I finished writing *West
of Darkness*, it's one I know to be perfectly in keeping with how Emily Carr felt.

• • •

In 1940, Carr's Beckley Street landlord decided to sell. Perhaps no longer wanting to live alone even with a maid, she moved in, uninvited, with Alice, her sole
surviving sister of nine siblings. Built on another family lot at 218 St. Andrews
Street, the tiny home is visible from the back windows of Emily Carr House.
Alice had run it as a nursery remembered still by a few of her now near-
centenarian charges—including one of my mother's friends, who recounts
how Miss Alice would often take small children for the night, tucking them
each into a "little bed" that she'd made up while their parents indulged in
something we now call personal time by going dancing at parties hosted by
the Empress Hotel.

Carr published *Klee Wyck* in 1941; it won a Governor General's Award the
following year. Despite hospital stays, Carr published two more well-received

books and drafted *Growing Pains*, an intentionally posthumous autobiography. In 1942, she went on a final sketching trip in Mount Douglas Park, then north of the city. In December 1944, ill health forced her to relocate one block from where she was born, to St. Mary's Priory, a seniors' home that took over the James Bay Inn during the Second World War. When peace came, it reverted back to being what today is Victoria's third oldest hotel and once the home to the JBI Reading Series, the populist roots of which Carr would have appreciated. On March 2, 1945, almost three months after her seventy-third birthday, Emily passed away there, close to home and the now-tamed park and ocean cliffs that first kindled her imagination.

• • •

After I completed *West of Darkness*, at some point that is vague to me now, I began to question the legend surrounding Carr—"a little old lady," as she described herself, "living on the edge of nowhere," "a paste solitaire in a steel-claw setting"—and wanted to correct what I then perceived to be distortions, realizing she had contributed to her own creation myth through the memoirs she published in the last half-decade of her life.

Whose version of her life should I accept? I found myself wondering.

Hers?

A response that skirts many issues.

Or her biographers?

Another strategy that betrays too many of her secrets.

In the end I absorbed something of all points of view, or all the points of view of which I was aware, but what I came up with is only another version. Its composition occurred in a past more than half my present age away, when I was a young man whom I doubt I can recall with any accuracy and who knew almost nothing when he measured his small cache of knowledge against the wisdom Carr had earned over the course of a sometimes sheltered, always adventurous life. I still believe what I wrote between the ages of twenty-one and twenty-seven is faithful to the woman herself, the one who is at the heart of her. I know I composed out of respect.

By chance, in the late 1990s or early 2000s, I met a descendant of Ira Dilworth, Emily Carr's CBC editor and literary executor. We bumped into each other at Market Station, a gay bar on the first floor of a nineteenth-century stone building near the intersection of George Street and Sussex Drive in Ottawa's

Byward Market. On Thursday nights, men could pack into this pocket-square-sized bar with such alacrity the temperature inside would rise thirty to forty degrees above what the flash-frozen streets we followed to get there goaded us to escape. On that indifferent spring evening, the pub looked demoralizingly empty when I peered in before deciding to sit at the bar next to one of the only customers, a middle-age man uniformed unpromisingly in office drag. How we started exchanging pleasantries about Emily Carr is lost to history, but I soon learned that in addition to appointing Dilworth her executor, she'd willed him the rights to all her published and unpublished works. The father of the man whose knee brushed up to mine had inherited the rights to *Klee Wyck*. Dilworth had left one of her books to each of his nephews and nieces. By this time, though, all of her writing was in the public domain. By the way the man spoke it was clear that this tangible family connection to Carr's legacy awed him still, even though he'd known about it since he was a boy. I thought privately that the three of us—Carr, Klee Wyck, and the little boy I was—had come a very long way.

How would Emily Carr have perceived me had she known me?

How would have Klee Wyck?

I began to speculate about this impossibility soon after *West of Darkness* came out and I had come out myself. Would she consider me to be an appropriate biographer? Or autobiographer? Would she consider me a good person? How would she judge me for being gay, a homosexual, or whatever moniker she would have used to describe a man like me? Would she question my right to tell her story?

Such considerations never occurred to me while I was writing about her. The voice I heard her speaking through me while writing these poems was warm, benevolent and searching, and not judgmental in any way. Nor did I define myself as gay at the time I was at work on *my* Emily Carr. Consequently, it is only in the years since I began living "openly," as one used to say about men like me, that I have come to see Emily as my drag persona. How she would hate that! Given that most drag artistes lip-synch retro disco hits or show tunes, my choice of drag identity is particularly iconoclastic. Maybe my prim Miss Emily could go clubbing with Miss Chief Eagle Testickle, an avatar of Cree artist Kent Monkman, who un*reserve*dly and in impossibly lofty high heels rampages buxomly through his paintings, films, and installations to set ablaze the erasures of settlement in bold borrowings from and crafty reworkings of the techniques and palettes of artists renowned in the Western canon. I am very sure that Miss

Chief would have to order me an Uber before my maquillage started to run in face of the heat from the dance-floor lights.[28]

In any case, perhaps my forty-year connection to Carr through *West of Darkness* is the cause of my anxieties about her good or bad opinion of me. Or are these anxieties the self-conscious frailties of a Dorian Gray uncertain what his portrait betrays about his own soul? Who is *West of Darkness* the portrait of anyway? Its subject or its author?

Perhaps both. We all hope that those we love will favour us with returned affection, that they will see something of themselves in how we see them.

1987–2019

---

28 Friend Miss Chief Eagle Testickle, 8 Aug. 2018, https://www.facebook.com/ MissChiefEagleTestickle/.

"Conditions Attached to the Driving of Motor Vehicles by the Holder of a Provisional Licence"

WE FOUND HIS BRITISH driver's licence in one of the musty, dilapidated boxes passed on to us by his widow. She took advantage of his passing to clear their house of all his clutter, which had irritated her for more than two decades. Until she died in 2007, two years after he had, boxes of his possessions and family papers would be unexpectedly, if regularly, passed on to me by her or by one of her sons from her first marriage. My sisters and I would rough-sort their contents into clean, archival boxes that now sit five-high and three-across in the hall of my apartment in the James Bay neighbourhood of Victoria. In 1983, after a thirty-year career as an accountant and systems analyst for Shell Canada in Alberta, he retired to the city of my college years. By good fortune I moved back in 2004, a year before his death.

Box after box in my hall is layered with photographs and the surprisingly worthless stamp collection that either his father or grandfather had started in the nineteenth century. Others hold the papers of my great uncle who had captained a White Star ship in the golden age of ocean liners; bundle after bundle of our ancestors' letters; and the genealogy charts he would maintain in a clear, precise script. He had attempted to trace the generations preceding us as far back as records would let him, when, lacking any further leads, he turned his attention to the even more obscure, but pinpointable East European antecedents of his second wife's family. A few of his clothes now hang in my closet—the tuxedo and coats of a man whom I had always supposed to be physically larger than I am, yet which fit me perfectly across the shoulders. The sheep's-fleece-lined, leather, RAF flying jacket and leggings that our mother had always referred to as his teddy-bear suit is now stored at my sister's in Calgary, though before we packed it away, she photographed me wearing it. If anything, it felt too small. When he wore it, flying reconnaissance above the North Sea, he must have been a winsome twenty-two-year-old; I am now a settled fifty.

Though the distancing rational mind accepts as *a priori* that death is inevitable, it's nevertheless disturbing to face the fact that a life, especially one as essential to my sisters and me as his was, truly ends up being finite. Its unfathomable essence can be stored away in a few banker's boxes like relics in an ossuary. Though I can extend the life of those shirts of his that I have chosen to keep for their retro appeal, he can never again add anything to the boxes in my hall. They house all that is left of the oddly precise shambles of his steel-trap mind, whose reverence for family seemed to ignore his living children in favour of the shady or upstanding personages from whom we descend, his real legacy to us. It is difficult not to consider his papers and ephemera as equivalent to the detritus uncovered in a midden. Their hieroglyphic signifiers, like those carved into the Rosetta stone, demand the expertise of our languishing memories, as well as speculation and hearsay, in order to crack open the riddle of who he might have been and of who each of us has become in relation to our loss of him and to one another.

His British driver's licence surfaced among an arbitrary collection of pens, wallets, envelopes, tie pins, watches, and alarm clocks, perhaps the haphazard contents of a desk or dresser drawer hastily tipped out. It is unlike any licence I have ever seen. The red clothbound and hardcover booklet measures two-and-half inches wide and three-and seven-eighth inches tall. Its front cover bears a corniced insignia of some sort in black ink, with "DRIVING LICENCE" printed declaratively beneath. There is no photograph of the licence's holder inside, but instead a flipbook of annual renewals is glued in place like ascending layers of the geologic record, the most recent of which having expired on November 27, 1953, nine months after he (a Londoner by birth), my mother (a Canadian), and my two British-born sisters left England for Canada. Eight years after V-E Day, my mother brought them "home" to opportunities only a country undevastated by war could offer. The trip back was a return for him as well. He'd met and married my mother on Remembrance Day in 1942, after completing his pilot's training at the Patricia Bay air base north of Victoria. Through her family connections he obtained employment in the spring of 1953 with the Shell Oil Company in Edmonton.

This most recent renewal in his British driver's licence bears my parents' last greater London address: a block of flats that still stands across the Thames from Hampton Court and where they brought my second sister home from the hospital after she was born in 1951. It's a typical British apartment building of the mid-twentieth century, yet nine years ago, our mother couldn't remember exactly where it was—46 Hampton Court Parade, in East Molesey, Surrey, according to his licence—when, on a mother-daughter trip back to England, she showed my sister around a neighbourhood she would have been too small to recollect after our family moved to Canada. For our mother, absence erased the block of any locatable distinction that had, forty-six years before, made it stand apart as familiar from the others around it. Growing up, I gained the perhaps false impression the decade she'd spent in England was the happiest of her marriage to our father.

The earlier renewals glued into the licence could provide us a with a skeleton key to all his addresses in England from the time he learned to drive to his emigration to Canada, but because they are affixed one on top of the other, we would destroy the little booklet trying to prise them apart. Fortunately, only little licks of glue were sometimes applied when a few of the sheets were added, so with care they can all still be partially lifted away to reveal a very few salient if fragmentary details. It seems there were no renewals made during the Second World War, years when he either didn't drive or hadn't required a civilian licence.

The particulars of his first (or primordial) driver's licence, dated 10 August 1939 to 8 November 1939—a provisional licence that, having grown up in Alberta, I would call a learner's permit—establish that he was then living at the YMCA on Great Russell Street, near the British Museum. This was something I already knew, a detail in a mysterious life that the little red booklet for once confirms. In the last weeks before he died, when illness had so shaken his natural reticence that he indulged us with what for him were rare, extravagant, long-winded reminiscences. He narrated his daily walk from the Y to the Air Ministry, where he was a civilian employee before signing up. He would stop, he recalled, on Fleet Street to watch boys not much older than himself unload mammoth rolls of newsprint from horse-drawn carts into the printing plants of the London dailies. This brought back a memory of my own, when he had once shown me a letter he had written to his mother during the Battle of Britain. He liked to shove tantalizing bits of paper under the unwary noses of his adult children when he wanted us to know something he thought pertinent about his past. In the letter, he recounted looking out his window at the Y to catch sight of a Heinkel 111 at the very moment it was shot down over central London. Even though I had not seen the letter in years, I could still see him as that nineteen-year old vividly brought into being by what he had written down in the summer of 1940, full of a naïve curiosity despite the carnage he had begun to witness, a young man for the first time out in the world, supervised neither by parent nor housemaster at school.

All through my life I have wondered about what he must have been like as a person when he had reached whatever age I had just attained—a boy of eleven with a stutter in a West Sussex public school, a youth working for the Air Ministry, a bridegroom of twenty-one watching the Rockies go past as he travelled by rail with our mother from Vancouver to Halifax to catch a troopship back to England—but I have never had much to go on. Once I'd surpassed the age he was when I had started to form clearer memories of him—he was almost forty-one when I turned five—I could flesh him out more plausibly. Or maybe I could only imagine what a man of forty-five in the 1960s might have felt simply because I had at last achieved the same ambivalent age in the early 2000s. If I manage to live longer than he did, I will truly enter uncharted outer *inner* space.

The little red licence must have fit in his hand as easily as it does in mine; it is so small that I can imagine him losing it inside the capacious pockets in those baggy Alec-Guinessesque flannel trousers he always wore in snaps taken of him in the years before the Festival of Britain. Rubbing against his tobacco pouch, the cloth cover might have taken on his brand's sweet scent—that is, if he smoked a pipe back then, as he did while I was growing up. Though the little booklet's scant compendium of attributes is open to our interpretations and is victim to a kind of phantom nostalgia—mine in particular, since I was not alive during the years of its use—my sisters and I have no idea what the licence meant to him and why he had kept it. He would come to keep so much, to which so little recognizable importance adheres.

Did it make him think of where the years it embraced—1939 to 1953—had taken him, from London to Victoria, from the skies he flew over occupied Europe to a quiet life across the Thames from the palace of that other old-school adulterer and first defender of the faith, Henry VIII? All we know is that he thought it worthy of retention, so we choose to keep it too. It is an object he may have valued for its occasional utility during its active life, years during which he never owned a car, and he may have then handled it with no real thought of the future—like so much else that he has left us, it seems, almost by accident.

2007

Adding Nothing to the Flow:
Greening The Pregnant Man

WHEN I WAS A small boy not much beyond kindergarten age, I very much wanted a little brother. I don't remember putting any thought into how I might get one. I had no clue about procreation, and I have no memory of begging for a sibling of the male variety from my parents. Nor had I ever heard of partheno-genesis: the Virgin birth was not much of a mystical Anglican Sunday School concern for me as an inattentive Christian wannabe at St. Cyprian's in north-west Calgary in the early 1960s. I was more entranced by the possibilities not yet spelled out in the cloudless Alberta sky above me and over Nose Hill just to the north of where I grew up. A pudgy child until I had my tonsils out at age seven, I was happy to pose and resolve my own cosmological riddles without input from others. I saw no role for my mother and father in my hypothetical brother's care and upbringing, let alone in his making.

He would come out of thin air, like many of my better daydreams. I alone would be responsible for changing him, dressing him, and feeding him, and when the time came, sending him to Banff Trail Elementary School, the 31st Beavers Wolf Cub pack, junior choir practice, and wherever else that appealed to me. He would also be spared the humiliations of Cowboys and Indians, hockey, and football. He would be my little doll to love, one no doubt cast in my own image without a thought of his own—doesn't that sound like parent-ing?—a baby who could live and breathe at my prerogative through the long lonesome airings of my imagination. In this captivating fancy, the evaporation of which I can't trace past any convulsive emotional heat wave to the present residue, I don't ever remember my little brother crying or having a need I couldn't answer.

My only other bout of paternal feeling came almost two decades later, in 1979, when a girl I was sleeping with missed her period. I was a confused twenty-two year-old, a nascent poet exploring the metaphorical potency of my own poetic argot, and still not fully cognizant of my more natural interest in men. A couple of weeks before, an acquaintance at the Saskatchewan School of the Arts in the Qu'Appelle Valley, an hour's drive east of Regina, had tried to point the way towards enlightenment when he read my cards and foretold only a long line of males trailing ahead of me into my future. I refused to follow the breadcrumbs he tellingly scattered. For the girl, our short and intense summer-school romance was an adulterous one, and she swore she would not keep any complication we might have inadvertently spawned that could ruin the charmed life she hoped to continue leading with a husband who was absent until the fall. As a counterpoint to her temporary hysteria that she was truly "with child," I considered raising our potential son or daughter on my own, leaving out, just as I did when I was six, every bit of salient detail, such as the more plausible likelihood of an abortion, or how we would break the inconvenient news to her husband upon his return, or how any bundle of joy might be passed over to me while leaving their relationship intact as a hymen. Of course, there was to be a lot of bloodletting of a sort, for her period did eventually come, with the scare over and the secret of our fling unspilled, but for a time I was an inept expectant father glad to make plans.

Other than my phantom boy-child brother and my bastard love-child never-to-be, I have no other recollections of wanting children. Six years after my sloughed brush with pregnancy, I came out, ending what I have since characterized as my gulag-friendly stint of sitting in solitary confinement (i.e., in the closet) with the tortuously bright light on full blast. It was 1985, and though I was then living in Ottawa, that most provincial of national capitals, I was in great company. Rock Hudson had just gone public that he had AIDS, a diagnosis that was then an automatic death sentence. It was also his first frank admission to his fans that he was a homosexual after a decades-long, humpy, and square-jawed career of pillow talk with the likes of Doris Day, Elizabeth Taylor, and Susan Saint James. On the evening news, I remember watching his jet land in Los Angeles when he returned from Paris after the iffy experimental treatments he had tried at the Institut Louis Pasteur proved ineffective. In retrospect, it was a good time for me to come out, for, unlike a lot of my friends who had done so a few years earlier, I do not have many AIDS dead to mourn and remember. Caution and circumspection seem, for the gay men who came out around the same time, to have been the greatest prophylactic against death.

However, I probably did feel tainted—at least in theory, for I have never tested positive, though like most gay men I have had a few scares. Still, anxiety did put my genetic material under wraps, not that I had any plans to put it to its religiously sanctioned, original purpose. I even went along with guidelines that stopped gay men from donating blood, a prohibition still in force, though

HIV knows no gender. With apologies to the inventors of the contraceptive pill, which is a Johnny-come-lately on the "only-connect" scene in comparison to the timeless luxury of being queer, twentieth-century homosexuals had prided themselves on their innovation of separating the risk of procreation from the lark of recreational sex, especially those men sexually active from the post-Stonewall years to the onset of AIDS. Yet, like teenagers born too late for the sixties, many gay men coming out in the eighties would look back with envy to the barrier-free hedonism of their immediate elders and therefore tested the limits to which safer-sex strategies could be pushed. Some of us may have been as heedless as we dared, but we were undoubtedly less carefree. The rest looked to settle down with the right man and to mimic, if not in our bedroom antics, then in the sheltering domesticity of our increasingly oblivious, sweet-tempered straight neighbours. The demand for equality rights that Trudeau responded to in 1969, when he decriminalized consensual sex between two, but not three or more, members of the same gender, generated momentum through the next four decades, culminating, as much as Stephen Harper may rue it, in the victory to enshrine same-sex marriage in law.

Into domesticity and marriage may come the unfamiliar, overly percussive sound of small feet, though the closest that some of us have ever approached to having children is through the tender role-play of daddies and boys at the heart of many stable gay relationships. If memory serves, when I came out, the prospect of a gay couple adopting an actual flesh-and-blood child seemed a distant dream. Many gay men and lesbians had progeny from previous straight relationships that they continued to rear, but if I ever then gave a thought to paternity it must have seemed beyond my grasp (and tip of my erect penis), for the only way for me to have had a child would have been to conceive one outside of any relationship I might have been in—and with a woman, a possibility upon which I had at last closed the door after years of bewilderment. To knock on it again solely for the sake of posterity would be to solicit an invitation to open and enter Pandora's Box.

Posterity has never mattered to me. I am an only son of an only son and, when I was younger, it appealed to me that I was the last of a hereditary line. My father was the product of a broken marriage, as was his father, and my parents separated after I left home. With the arrogance of young adulthood, I thought it more fruitful not to perpetuate chromosomes that have been trumped by failure for at least three generations. My two older sisters and I knew from experience that, though children often hold the lapsing conjugal relationships of their parents together far past their sell-by date, the shelves are always cleared in the end. If the children are adults, obligation may even force them to get out the Mr. Clean (always a gay icon) and mop up the mess left by the pater and mater.

Being gay removed early on the pressure to reproduce that society, if not my parents, might have exerted upon me had I been straight. It provided me with a mental coitus interruptus in more ways than one, though it would take me years to admit that I have sadly repeated in several of my more promising relationships with men many of the learned patterns of behaviour I had hoped to avoid. Of course, thinking that my family would peter out because I chose not to fulfill my biological destiny as the only male of my generation is nothing more than a risible patriarchal construct. My elder sister took her husband's name. In having two daughters (one of whom is a genetics counselor who took her husband's name and has two sons of her own), she ensured that the genetic legacy of our ancestors would carry forward, but under a succession of other names in much the same way that Eaton's and its many historic locations survive despite bankruptcy protection and takeover, albeit with no brand recognition under the imprimatur of Sears. As a gay man conversant with the fluidity at the nexus of identity, I should have known better than to get blinkered by labels other than Armani or Jones of New York.

Of course, should I want to have a child who shares my chromosomal make-up, it is now refreshingly possible, and I could keep any vestigial procreative imperative I may feel within the purview of an extended same-sex-like relationship. Many gay men donate their sperm to lesbian couples, most often at one remove through artificial insemination, and even to couples they know. The trio of expectant parents may choose to go as far as to conceive one child with one of the women, then later on conceive a second child with the other in order to guarantee that the siblings are biologically related and share the same father. Both single gay men and gay men in relationships have been known to contribute their spunk, and some lesbian mothers will allow the donor and the donor's partner to be involved in their children's lives, though it is true that other couples do not want such complications, preferring to rely on a suitably screened, but anonymous donor. And complicated is what three-way parenting can turn out to be, even humourously so. A lesbian couple I know had wanted to choose a gender-neutral first name for their daughter as well as to give her the last names of all three of her parents until they realized the result—"Lindsay Leary McDuffie Rimmer" is a good approximation—would sound more like a law firm or a cabal of accountants. The little girl, now nine or ten, is known by one and all by a name like Leticia.

Despite the new possibilities for parenting, I still do not want to have children, but this does not mean that I don't have any interest in them. I took great delight in watching my nieces grow up. One of my favourite memories of all time is of a visit to Edmonton in 1979, when I was still an itinerant student, and woke up to their expectant faces looking down on me when they were two and five. Their mother, my sister, had told them they could watch me sleep but not wake me up. And already I have amusing memories of my two great nephews that will entertain me till the grave. I am grateful that society, through strenuously fought-for legal precedents, has been forced to allow gay men and lesbians more ways to experience the very satisfying realities of parenthood, realities that for me will always be vicarious—and, to paraphrase the poet Lorna Crozier: a garden going on without me. Frequently, I observe small children lolling in the countless enormous strollers that clog up bus aisles and sidewalks (a friend calls them SUVS) or are left parked to one side at the Starbucks in James Bay, the Victoria neighbourhood where I live, while their parents order elaborate coffee drinks with names far beyond my ken. The realization that I will be long dead by the time these squirming, crying, or wonderstruck byproducts of love have attained my present age never fails to be sobering. Thirty-one years ago I did write a poem called "The Pregnant Man" that opens with this echoey evocation of conception and the womb:

I've let you in,
filled empty marble halls,
arching silences that have lasted generations.
My doctors will be shocked.
Hitler will be shocked.
They never knew I would give birth
to a new age.

Despite the wry drumroll, my child-bearing years are well behind me.

However, I can't completely let go of an anarchic belief that I once more zealously adhered to and shared with my peers: that queerness issued a challenge to mainstream society, one that goes far beyond merely trumpeting the splendours of procreation-free sex. On one Earth Day many years ago, it came to me as a life-affirming insight on Parliament Hill, while overlooking the Ottawa River, that we could shore up our pedigree by expounding far and wide that gay sex is green sex. Unlike the galvanizing frivolity of sex for sex's sake for which we are best known, ecologically neutral sex is uplifting and in no way gratuitous. To quote "Watershed," another of my poems, "we add nothing to the flow." This makes us good citizens. Yet, as more and more gay men and lesbians have biological children or without legal impediment raise children conceived with earlier straight partners, I have to acknowledge that this aperçu is no longer in the strictest terms valid and might even sound passé or smug.

Still, I am captivated by the sentiment behind it, for if being gay or lesbian is about anything, it is about having the self-consciousness to accept ourselves as we are. "Gay sex is green sex" may be nothing more than T-shirt sloganeering, but if it might point to a way to transform self-knowledge into global awareness, then why not go for it? No one, gay or straight, can deny that the planet's exploding population will soon outstrip its ability to support us all and that our uncontrollable appetites, including for sex, are compounding the effects of climate change, habitat destruction, and wasted resources. While a wanted child conceived in love cannot be anything but a welcome child, and must be a child we all want to protect and cherish whether we are its parents or not, there are still countless children worldwide conceived in the heat of passion who are not—or did I buy into too many lies during my prairie childhood about kids starving in China? Not placing another life on the planet should be seen as a virtue equal to the urge to perpetuate the species.

To avoid smugness necessitates a willingness to acknowledge that not having children of our own does not give us license to avoid caring for and taking an interest in the children of others around us. As a childless gay man who, while grocery shopping, sometimes catches himself watching young parents sheep-dogging their knee-high charges past distractions on the lowliest of shelves, I am well aware of the absence of these disorienting biological imperatives in the immediacy and dailiness of my life. This does not mean I have lost touch with what it means to be a child or with the child in myself, however wayward and recalcitrant he (or she) may seem to be to those who choose to know me even a little. Inside this ever-more myopic fifty-one-year-old body, I am sometimes still that all-seeing six-year old daydreaming his life away. Although I no longer want a younger brother or a thirty-year old boyfriend who is also my son—now doesn't that sound like some perverse dynastic relationship worthy of a minor Egyptian pharaoh?—I can still muster the last of my energy to help shoulder change in what's left of this world. Or at least to make a plea for it. To be aware of children is to be aware of the Earth, and whether our sex is green or not, we must take care of both.

2008

The Pain Closet: Outtakes from a Phantom Diary

I stepped into an avalanche,
It covered up my soul;
When I am not this hunchback that you see,
I sleep beneath the golden hill.
You who wish to conquer pain,
You must learn, learn to serve me well.

—Leonard Cohen

Sunday, October 30, 2016

Last night, after a long day of puzzling rectal pain so deeply set and illuminating that it gave actual teeth to the word "viscera," I struck on a likely way to dislodge it. Stretched out on my living-room floor just before 12 a.m., I drew one knee up and, grasping it with my hand, pulled it across my trunk, holding it in place for sixty seconds, in order to unlock my hip joints—if indeed they were locked. I repeated this simple stretch three or four times with both knees. Slowly, the bottled-up ache began to rise from my entrails, like a mute, stubborn djinn, as mystifyingly as it had cached itself there, hours before.

Why don't I think of solutions like this one earlier than I do, especially when a guerrilla army of physiotherapists have put me through years of anti-terrorist training to prepare me for victory in pain's contested territories: diet recommendations, exercises, stretches, and controlled breathing? Inaction is one of chronic pain's enigmas. A perverse form of magical thinking, it reminds me of one of my sister Pam's cats, a seal-point Siamese. Over thirty years ago, when he was a kitten and so tiny he could stand up in my palm, he swallowed a threaded needle he must have found to play with, in plain sight, without anyone noticing. Any movement must have been so painful that he became still and unkitten-like, more like an octogenarian—in cat years—resigned to sleeping his life away in self-induced stupor. Such inertness—the annulling of the self by pretending not to be present—is what pain, physical or mental, often leads to. Pam took him to the vet, who detected the needle—in an X-ray, a black line ruled through his oesophagus—and removed it. After the incision healed, a zipper of dark brown fur grew in against his otherwise tawny cream throat, lingering there, unopened but undiminished, for the rest of his long life. As I write this, I realize my poor sister, who died in 2015, never knew it was me who had dropped that needle. Pain leaves its mark and keeps its secrets.

As I repeated the stretches, my mood rose as the ache altered. It was not gone, and is there even now as I write this, but, happily, much dissipated. I often worry that what I have dismissed as a routine pain might at last be symptomatic of something more insidious. I am so used to peculiar manifestations of bothersome discomfort—a hair-thin skewer jammed into the tip of my tongue or at the end of my penis, where my chronic pain began nearly thirteen years ago; radiant heat coursing up and down my arms and legs, as if they were being roughened by industrial-grade sandpaper; a tightness in my SI joints so vice-like I'm racked inarticulate—that I fear my endurance will one day mask something fatal. My chronic pain will kill me because I am prepared to live with physical annoyance—any annoyance—for both the short and long term. Because I am affected by everything, I pay heed to nothing.

This open-mindedness about suffering requires a discipline that poetry has taught me. I must sit through whatever "it" is—doubt, lack of confidence, delusions of eloquence—to get the work done. Pain and poetry are conjoined twins, standing shoulder to shoulder like the twins in smocked dresses that Diane Arbus photographed in 1967, which Stanley Kubrick referenced famously in his 1980 film, *The Shining*. Like his little girls floating down the halls of the hotel where he set his movie, pain and poetry float up out of nowhere and discomfit one another as much as they do me. Pain can make sitting at my desk to write tortuous—standing is not much better—yet, draft after draft, I put aside my body and its once and future perfectibility in order to make something out of the nothing that life sometimes is.

Monday, October 31, 2016

Today I renewed my costly prescriptions that run out every three months. Here am I, a poet who must take a drug called Lyrica, which if it is the laudanum of the twenty-first century, hardly makes me a twenty-first-century Coleridge. The side effects empty the aquifers from which poetry springs, not replenish them, for I experience dizziness, drowsiness, and wandering concentration. I have taken Lyrica for eight years and often feel my writing has less and less focus. Sometimes this Catch-22 doesn't seem worth it: frustratingly, Lyrica blunts but does not dull my peripheral neuropathic pain.

Instead, I face down a slowed but still fierce ball of pain whose volleys—burning, tingling, numbing—target me, as if my body were a wall in a racket-ball court and my pain an athlete in dire need of conditioning. I am pummelled so routinely and so randomly that I can't remember what it's like not to insouciantly return pain's missile-accurate serve. Right now, a breastplate of incandescence radiates from my sternum—a warmth almost pleasant, as if I were being wrapped in hot towels in a dry sauna after the racquet-ball match is over. I can largely ignore my pain symptoms unless they become so acute that they succeed in blocking out all other thought.

I am a worthy opponent, however, for my pain and the drugs I take to reduce it. The concentration I muster, a product of over three decades of unbroken writing, is equal to a constancy of pain that might defeat someone less single-minded. Is this a good character trait? I'm not sure. When I first began to write, I boiled a stovetop kettle dry so often while revising poems that the bottom fell out. This was after the kettle had been whistling, unheard by me, for a long fifteen minutes. How's that for lyrical?

Saturday, November 5, 2016

On Wednesday, I had an appointment at a healthcare centre an hour's bus ride away. Though it was socked in by drizzly fog, on a clear day it must have an unparalleled view of the water—the San Juan Islands rising like jagged chips of malachite out of the cobalt Salish Sea. My family doctor had sent me there to have my left foot evaluated. I was born with flat feet. The right one was clubbed, and now, at 59, the dramatic congenital pronation of my left and once better foot has caught up with me. Specialists have told me that the way my feet cause me to stand and walk could be contributing to my chronic pain. Any potential I might have had to be a speed walker shall remain unrealized, I suppose. It's perhaps a good thing that, as a poet, I'm a marathoner well-conditioned enough to go the distance.

The doctor I saw knew Pam professionally, and, like her, she qualified in the early 80s. My sister, the person I was closest to, had a stroke on January 16,

2015. Three days later, I sat at her bedside in the ICU at the Foothills Hospital in Calgary after life support was removed and, holding her hand, felt her pulse quickly fade. She was—is—six years older than I am and had watched over me from adolescence onward, playing a key role in having my chronic pain diagnosed, treated, and made more manageable. In the fall of 2008, after I'd confided in her about my symptoms, she flew me to Calgary from Saskatoon, where I was living at the time, and arranged for several of her colleagues to examine me. They determined that I had a deviated coccyx, loose sacral-iliac joints, and a misaligned symphysis pubis. These misalignments conspired to cause the ligaments, holding me together like well-cinched metal cables, to droop across and irritate nearby nerves. Eventually, my crossed wires blew circuits and burst into flame.

Through a kind of narrative forensics of questions and answers, they figured out that a spill I'd taken twenty-one years before may have set my chronic pain in motion—the clumsy butterfly that led to my later hurricane. In March 1987, when I had just started working at the National Museum of Science and Technology in Ottawa, I sat down on a geriatric office chair. It flew out from under me, and I dropped hard, ass-first, onto the concrete lunchroom floor. I have no memory of the agony that oppressed me like an Old Testament god, but my supervisor, who'd witnessed my fall, sent me home, after making me complete an incident report for what in Ontario they now call the Workplace Safety and Insurance Board. I came back to work the next day, apparently fully recovered. I was not yet thirty and physically resilient.

Three months later, I had a hernia repair. Two weeks after that, the incision popped open. The surgeon who'd performed the operation happened to be in the hospital when, terrified, I returned by taxi. The emergency ward called him down, taking him away from whatever he had been doing—pinning tails on widows, declawing juvenile delinquents…who knows, but he was not pleased to see me. Rather than expressing any surprise or sympathy, he instead rolled his eyes and asked me if I might have been exposed to AIDS—which dumbstruck me. I had never told him I was gay. Too disarmed by the nasty implications of what he'd said and too scared of what I saw when I looked into my open wound, I had no answer. In silence, he sewed me back up with black suture and sent me home. Within a day, the incision became infected and I obtained from my family doctor the antibiotics that I feel he should have prescribed. AIDS made the 1980s a very dark decade. Once I'd recovered, the pain that the surgery had intended to address persisted, as if someone was slowly pounding a nail stored in the freezer into my groin. Pam's colleagues deduced that the nerves caught in the scar tissue of my complicated wound could be referring pain throughout my pelvis and beyond, like malicious telegrams sent across the icy Atlantic from Signal Hill in St. John's.

A chronic-pain diagnosis, despite the potential life-long implications, came as relief. Previously, a urologist had interpreted my symptoms as prostatitis, leaving me with the impression that the pain I felt through my urinary tract was largely untreatable. According to him, it would increase and decrease in strength, waxing and waning like the moon for the rest of my life, but without its predictable cycle. He never once discussed pain control with me. I have subsequently learned that many urologists know little about the impact that musculoskeletal injuries can have on the systems for which they are supposedly the most expert. This is especially true for men with injuries like mine—pain referred through the urinary tract, not originating from it. More credence is given to pelvic pain experienced by women because that region of their bodies is pulled out of shape by childbirth—or so the gender politics were spelled out to me by Pam and her colleagues. As a frontier guide into medical incognita, she had been an outlier. Her comprehension of the body was experience-based, deepened over years of observation and trial and error. Mainstream medicine appears baffled by or oblivious to pelvic-floor maladies, regardless of who is floored by them. Experienced as a stickpin jammed into the glans penis, my pain was initially thought to have been gifted to me by an STD. Almost a decade since my diagnosis, doctors' attitudes have begun to change. The physiotherapy clinic where I go for treatment now offers programs to address male urinary incontinence. That said, despite the number of healthcare professionals initiated into the occult mysteries of the human pelvic girdle, the child is more commonly mother to the pain, not the father.

Pam opened the clinic door through which I found the doctors and physiotherapists who have transformed my chronic pain into something tolerable. Strangely, my daily pain comforts me because it reminds me of her, physical sensation more bearable than the mental anguish of loss. I talk about her with many of the practitioners I see because most of them knew or know of her. This offers solace, though the doctor I saw today about my foot seemed to resist any conversation about my sister, as if she did not want to address an aspect of my pain outside the narrow purpose of our doctor/patient relationship. Though no doctor possesses boundless reserves of empathy, this saddened me.

Sunday, November 6, 2016

Every time I sit at my computer to write, I court pain. Sometimes, to my surprise, I experience no symptoms while starting on a new poem, but this is not usually the case. Eight years ago, I managed to sit through the day-long composition of "Shade," a poem I wrote just before my chronic pain was diagnosed and which is now collected in *Polari*, by mentally looking askance from what I was feeling. Casting my attention past the body's—and the mind's—vanishing point is akin to putting your Jeep into four-wheel drive in order to inch up a steep, snow-packed slope. By involving myself in the poem's complicated metrics—eight stanzas of eight lines, each of which is eight syllables long and knitted together by a challenging ABBAACAC rhyme scheme—I crested the hill, despite the black ice, driving myself beyond what the poem had cruelly put my body through—wildfire through my genitalia, heat flashing up my back until it formed a shackle around my neck, the tips of each flame hellishly licking at my cheeks, a final flicker blackening the tip of my tongue. Perhaps my attraction to formal poetry, which upon reflection coincides with the intensification of my chronic-pain symptoms in the mid-2000s, has provided me with a way to contain and control what my body expects of me, the pliancy of poetic form sculpted into a body cast, at best, or rigged up as a metal brace, at worst.

In 2010, Pam took me to see one of the *Body Worlds*[1] exhibits that continue to circulate around the globe. That summer, it stopped for three months at the Calgary Science Centre. Billed as "the original exhibition of real human bodies," it displayed corpses that the people who'd once occupied them had bequeathed to the Institute for Plastination in Heidelberg, Germany. They had "declared during their lifetimes that their bodies should be made available after their deaths for the qualification of physicians and the instruction of laypersons.... Their selfless donations allow [the institute] to gain unique insights into human bodies."[2] Each one is preserved, dissected, and posed to reveal a particular condition or aspect of biomechanics for public consumption—as a tennis player, for example, or a dancer, the body freeze-framed at a particular point of motion. Pam wanted to walk me through my own malady, in a sense, by pointing out the various soft-tissue structures and musculoskeletal arrangements implicated in

1   Accessed December 11, 2016. http://www.bodyworlds.com/en.html.
2   Accessed December 11, 2016. http://www.bodyworlds.com/en/body_donation.html.

my pain, hoping it would be enlightening for me to see what was happening to me from the inside out rather than just suffering its insidious effects.

Though the majority of the dioramas were mawkish and the use of the donated bodies a trivializing of their humanity, I found one display astonishing. The deceased's nervous system had been painstakingly excised in its entirety from the flesh and hung from above like an unclothed wire mannequin. The spot-lit nerves looked as warm as candle wax. As they converged and diverged from one another, meshing together or thinning out frail and fugitive as rootlets, the nervous system they wove into a single whole looked like an array of cities viewed from space, glowing through the dark with the light of human connectivity. The lower torso was at its most brilliant in the pelvis—a near equal to the brain's luminous and distant megalopolis.

Profoundly moved, I later drew upon my awe to compose one section of my poem, "A Built Environment," also found in *Polari* and written in heroic couplets:

What tool will strip free cut, shorted-out nerves
Conduits of feeling few alive observe

Pared from bone, but as they're picked apart
From flesh, the exposed ache unrolls a chart

Of failed continents, painful, tender wastes
Glimpsed from space, built-up expanses laced

With nightmare glimmers of snarled village slights
Converging at the groin in blinding light

A blaze of agonized urban sprawl mapped
By satellite, agonies in time lapse?

This afternoon, after a few hours' work on a new poem, I went for a swim. Lap after lap, I could not extinguish the fire that sitting at my computer had sent roaring up my legs from ankle to groin with such agility that, like a fleeing, terrorized bear lit on fire, it could leap across my pain-free back to my arms as if across a useless firebreak.

I have had to modify the way I swim. The breaststroke's whip kick bothers my pelvic floor. Flip turns are too risky: the flip itself is manageable, but pushing off the wall irritates my SI joints. Long ago, I stopped swimming 1500 metres without pause. Now I alternate between front crawl and backstroke; every five lengths I walk two, repeating this routine nine times. The touch turns at either wall are half-rhymes—in contrast to the rimes riches of the flips—in the sixty-line poem I swim three to four times per week.

Swimming and poetry require discipline—and it's a balancing act for both. How much should I ignore my pain; how far should I give in to it?

Friday, November 11, 2016

In Victoria, it's been raining since the beginning of October. Yesterday I had so much pain I was too tired and disappointed in the weather to write down the diary entry I had composed in my head while working at my job as editor of *The Malahat Review*. I had woken up early feeling fine, so took advantage of the extra hour before leaving for work by prepping to make gazpacho, chopping up tomatoes, onions, cucumber, and red pepper. I'd purée them when I got home that evening.

While standing at the kitchen counter before showering, my pelvic floor began to ache. I felt as I were being raised high in the sky on a pole, its blunt end goring me between the legs, my body a wooden horse on a celestial merry-go-round, revolving too quickly, no other horse in sight, the lack of a canopy leaving me open to the elements, the air thin. No stretch, exercise, or drug could hope to slow me down or bring me back down to earth.

I dissociated from my pain, as is my habit, got dressed, and caught the bus to work. Proceeding north to the university, I entered the words of the book on my lap—Paul Monette's selected poems—savouring each syllable, losing myself in his dramatic monologues: Hansel addressing Gretel; Edna Saint Vincent Millay resisting the amorous appeals of Edmund Wilson; and Noel Coward camping it up for the benefit of Marlene Dietrich—all the while listening to Joni Mitchell on my iPod, all her studio albums on shuffle. This made for a total of 343 songs to shield me from the university students talking to friends on their cell phones. Mental stimulation, not drugs, always sets me free. My pelvic-floor pain was a bass drum counterpointing Joni's plangent soprano, its percussive hip-hop reverberations like floodwater slicked with gasoline, my nerves set alight. I arrived at the *Malahat*'s office and strove to be both pleasant to my staff (something that I am not always equal to) and productive (I always am). I concentrated on the magazine's business, my mind willfully not in communication with my body—software rising above hardware, and the day passed. Stopping at a coffee shop downtown, I wrote a poem. Once home: dinner. CBC Radio One, my spirit guide. Pain. Two a.m. Bed.

I woke up after five hours' sleep. My body felt blank, as if it were an Etch-A-Sketch someone had shaken to erase the previous unbecoming picture. Who knows how my pain will next turn the knobs? What likeness will it draw of me today?

Wednesday, November 16, 2016

I began seeing a new physiotherapist in mid-October who specializes in the pelvic floor. Over two appointments, she's taught me a series of breathing exercises to make mine more mobile, which I must perform every day, and has begun to release internal tension with a finger by inserting it inside my rectum to locate the tight, deep-set muscles. As with any new therapist, I've had to recount my medical history and inevitably also talk about my sister, which, together, always heighten the emotional intensity of the appointments. Appointments with this new therapist are particularly draining because I am naked below the waist under a thin sheet on an examination table while she puts on her latex gloves.

She's focussed me more than my sister or any other physiotherapist on the role that my hernia scar has played in my chronic pain, urging me to start looking at it, to speak to it even, while softening the underlying scar tissue by massaging it with my fingers. I have to admit that for decades I have avoided it in the bathroom mirror after showering, my eyes skittering away like cockroaches should they chance to scuttle across it. Now I force my gaze to linger while I press my thumb into its deep indentation, a diagonal rut slashed from the jut of my right hip to the pubis. It used to be rhubarb-coloured before other therapists treated it with novocaine, acupuncture needles, or hypodermics that pierced through the skin to release the bound-up fascia. Now, when kneading it every morning before dressing, I can't believe how tender to the touch it is, amazed how after thirty years it is still a reliquary for so much hurt. At her insistence, I apply as much pressure as I can muster, and over time it's become less and less sensitive.

The pain my scar has long harboured brings home to me how significant it is to my pain—its cryptic representation on my body. I am also re-experiencing the anger I felt at the time toward the homophobic surgeon who hacked me up, as well as the fear and shame I felt at being stigmatized as a potentially diseased "faggot" while he stood above, looking down in judgement upon my split-open body. How different would my life have been had he been more compassionate as well as competent? How many other patients has he harmed? I met him for the first time in his office a month before the surgery. His waiting room was so small that there wasn't enough space to provide chairs for the patients queued up to see him like airplanes waiting to land at an over-subscribed airport. More of us were standing than were sitting. It had struck me as a bad omen.

Saturday, November 19, 2016

Though I have had varicose veins in the calves of both legs since my teens, they have never bothered me. Eighteen months ago, a physiatrist—again, a colleague of my sister's—suggested that they may be yet another factor in my chronic pain: maybe adhesions their ballooning causes have balled up the fascia like discarded cellophane? It took twelve months to see the vein specialist, who four months ago recommended further investigation before he could decide on a course of treatment. If it ain't broke, don't fix it.

The ultrasound technician required forty minutes to map my veins, with an accompanying audio-guide—my body is a museum that specialists like to curate. At key points, say at my left or right groin or at either knee, the sensor eavesdropped on my blood as it sped back to my heart. It sounded as if she—or we—were testing new components in a wind tunnel, say a wing for a solar-powered airplane, to confirm how aerodynamically sound it is. Of course, it is my unsoundness that's being sounded out.

The technician had just moved to B.C. from Ontario with her family. We passed the time by comparing notes about Victoria and Barrie:

> *Technician:* Everyone here gripes about the Colwood Crawl, even though it takes less than half an hour to drive downtown. Try commuting north on the 400 in rush hour—more like rush hours.

> *Me:* Yeah, they think driving from Esquimalt to Oak Bay is really going the distance.

> *Technician:* I could do it with my eyes shut if it weren't for all the seniors behind the wheel here.

Me: You might have your eyes closed but they're all blind. Myself, I was made for winter driving.

Technician: We came here to get away from snow.

Me: Yeah, but you've moved to an earthquake zone. Wherever you live there's always something that screws things up.

For a moment, we both got lost in thought—or maybe she was concentrating on the task at hand: my bloody veins. The so-called "Big One," for which the government has brainwashed us into stockpiling cans of tuna and stale bottled water, is fated to rend the planet's surface at a far grander scale than any cataclysm my body has thus far put me through, even if the strength of what rips at my fault lines is often off my own private Richter scale.

Me: What's a little shaking, anyway, compared to freezing rain?

To last on the "wet" coast everyone cups a flame of optimism between their hands in order to face up to the weather and to deny what we are assured is only a matter of time. In my faulty state, I couldn't begin to tell the technician how wholly I identify.

Wednesday, November 23, 2016

Being in pain is a lonely experience. Fortunately, it is invisible to nearly everyone I interact with in my day-to-day life. I will myself to separate from my pain in order to honour the social contract I'm entering to with others by being and feeling *genuinely* cheerful. This allows me to enjoy the best of what each day offers and to take advantage of any opportunities that might come my way.

I know another writer who's on a similar path. He too is suffering from pain that is the consequence of a fall, but unlike me he hasn't had someone like my sister to lead him through the labyrinth of medicine and pain management. Today, things are not going well for him. In my reply to his email, I went on at length about how our stoicism is unremarked upon by others; if they don't notice, then we've pulled off our daily magic trick one more time and should consider robbing banks. I suggest that we find ourselves suffering inside something I have coined the "pain closet." The closet exists because our pain is not something we want to draw to anyone's attention, in part because we fear we'll be misunderstood, dismissed as hypochondriacs, or perceived as damaged goods that must be carefully and therefore contemptuously handled. As he said in his next email: "The number of times I can hardly think straight, yet I don't say a word.... The fear that if we give in even a little bit, we'll be pushed aside and never approached again."

After I came out as a gay man in my late twenties, I would contemplate the long years I had obstinately stayed in the closet while knowing who I was and what I wanted. I used to describe those pupate years as sitting in the closet with the light on.

Friday, December 2, 2016

I had four medical-related appointments this week, all of them in the early morning. There is no additional credit for the extra struggle involved to arrive on time, especially before the sun has risen. The Rubik's cube of my weekly schedule, as it sped up, was a bewildering, exhausting blur. No one saw my hands moving as the time slots, noisy as an automatic weapon, clicked into place.

On Tuesday, I saw the vein specialist, who revealed that my deep veins are in as poor condition as he had guessed and that I must start wearing compression stockings. On Thursday, I picked up my new orthotics, which, before they were trimmed down to fit my shoes, looked as unseaworthy as boats ferrying refugees from north Africa to Europe. The note from the doctor to accompany my insurance claim described my left foot as "severely deformed." I didn't have the fortitude to ask if the extremity of her language—no pun intended—was purposely hyperbolic to help substantiate the justice of my request for reimbursement.

On Wednesday, between these two appointments, I saw the pelvic-floor physiotherapist. She gave me yet another exercise after sticking her finger for an extended period of time up my butt. That evening I saw the counsellor I've met with every other week ever since my sister died. He assured me that as physical pain is dealt with, the suppressed psychological pain associated with it can often emerge as well—that the two are linked—and that we should talk this out too. There seems to be no humiliation, or revelation, to which my body is not prepared to expose me. The paradox of chronic pain is best understood by contrasting the relief experienced knowing that, despite everything, it will not kill me, with the undying hope felt, when it's extreme, that it will.

For the past month, I have been turning over the fact that I have no idea how to distinguish the normal aches and pains caused by ageing from those that are chronic-pain-related and consequently are more natural, a product of time, and not the consequence of misadventure. Most of the treatments I receive are painful, if transiently so, and I always tell my therapists that there is nothing that they can do to me that my body can't do worse—and, therefore, they should drop all caution and "have at it" with unapologetic alacrity. Chronic pain has taught me not to shy away from agony if it can't be avoided, if it gets in the way, as if I were steeling myself to put my hand on a live stove element—which I have done once by accident, so this metaphor is not theoretical to me, but something seared into my memory and understood by the flesh. It's like writing a poem that suddenly reveals an unwanted personal truth. I learned early not to palliate my lines by dumbing them down in order to draw a rosier picture of myself.

I long ago accepted that chronic pain will be an unwelcome companion for the rest of my life, not something that can be permanently unplugged like my mother's electric iron or the laugh track in some annoying sitcom in which I have reluctantly agreed to play an uncredited role. Sometimes, when Netflix is turned off for the night I rue that chronic pain will be my sole companion, for it does not invite intimacy or make it easy. One recent boyfriend, so intent on his own pleasure, failed to understand that the parkour-like rigours he wanted me to perform with him could render me incapable of walking away from his libidinal obstacle course, let alone have me jumping for joy. Even the gentlest of floor routines poses a challenge for me.

In the fall of 1983, I'd enrolled in a master's program at Columbia University in New York and had the unexpected good fortune to study lyricism for a term with the Russian émigré poet, Joseph Brodsky. In a class of forty, very few of us had the nerve to speak, let alone the temerity to answer one of the questions this chain-smoking future Nobel Prize laureate might pose us. Attending his every word, I learned by his example how to read a poem line by line, how to imagine my way into the insights, technical or thematic, that possessed the poet while he or she was in the throes of inspiration. We listened to him move through the precise workings of his favourite poems by Hardy, Frost, and Auden as if he were articulating a shadow scaffold in order to show how each poem's struts had so seamlessly—or perhaps painstakingly—come to fit together, the actual poem left free-standing for us to admire. For an hour I became Thom, Bob, or Wystan, of whom he was so enamoured that we never finished reading the rest of the course's syllabus, which included my favourite poet, C. P. Cavafy.

One afternoon, cigarette in hand and with several butts in the ashtray beside him, he explained the difference between Victorian and modernist poetry by contrasting paintings of a young woman—say one by Dante Gabriel Rossetti and another by Wyndham Lewis. The nineteenth-century poet would describe the woman standing for her portrait in terms of the expensive silk of her summer dress, the slant of her straw hat on her head, the sparkle of her jewels, the lustre of her hair, and the motes in her eyes. The twentieth-century poet, ever more economical and forward-thinking than his or her male antecedent, would choose one detail, say the ribbon in her hat, and let its satin curves and curlicues, however distorted, stand for her.

This is where I depart from Brodsky, I'm afraid. To cope with my pain, I need to dwell on every last detail, sketch out the woman in full—the way she holds her head, the small clutch tucked beneath her right arm, the delicate downturn of her wrist, the daydream behind her opaque blue eyes—as well as the background she stands before, whether it is real or not, or merely some scrim hanging against a softly lit wall in the artist's studio. I can never let the pain that I may feel for the rest of my life become me or let this part of me represent the whole. I am not that enamoured of synecdoche.

I would even leave the ribbon out, its sinuous flicker of discomfort best ignored in favour of greater prospects. This attitude, I hope, is not too unlike the view with which "A Built Environment" concludes:

Men attenuate every ziggurat
Nosing through lit cityscapes, habitats

They keep adding floors to, alert, adept
At welding struts to buttress untried scripts

Fritted into the buildings' skins, all glass
A lyric hypothesis with impress

Equal, if planned, to imagination
Beauty a scaffold laddering passion

Toward an unplumbed sky to balance in—
All vistas departing from its blueprint.

Life is something I must strive to live despite pain. Pam once told me that many of her patients could never bring themselves to adopt such an expansive outlook. They allow daily life to become small and drugged up, detached from the passions that once fuelled them. I'd rather be in pain and happy than in pain and not. Chronic pain has become my vocation with the same odds for success or failure that poetry has. With both I take the long view.

2017

SNOW ANGELS

SNOW ANGELS

Fluid Epiphanies: Margaret Avison's "The Swimmer's Moment"

I AM AT THE pool, swimming lengths, as I have several times a week for over a decade. It conditions the mind as well as the body. The regular rhythms of back and forth, departure and return—butterfly, backstroke, breaststroke, free-style—perform a wordless, concentrated discipline that aims for perfection. By which I mean: whatever perfection I can imagine. I have never been in better shape, with a sense of form I wish I had taken an interest in when I was twenty, the age I began to write seriously.

When I first took up swimming, it was the endorphin-induced meditative state it calls forth that ultimately hooked me. The sport has allowed me to trans-plant my innate reserve—the cell of solitude I came to know well in the writing of my poems—to the social confines of the public swimming pool. Sometimes I chat with other regular swimmers. Or we simply acknowledge one another with a nod, if only to let the faster go ahead.

For years I have pulled my body through water while revising poems in my head or working through some other anxiety, wondering if the swim-mers around me are similarly caught in their own singular cycles of reflective thought.

We are all getting somewhere.

Or not.

• • •

Margaret Avison's "The Swimmer's Moment" has haunted me for thirty years:

> For everyone
> The swimmer's moment at the whirlpool comes,
> But many at that moment will not say
> "This is the whirlpool, then."
> By their refusal they are saved
> From the black pit, and also from contesting

The deadly rapids, and emerging in
The mysterious, and more ample, further waters.
And so their bland-blank faces turn and turn
Pale and forever on the rim of suction
They will not recognize.
Of those who dare the knowledge
Many are whirled into the ominous centre
That, gaping vertical, seals up
For them an eternal boon of privacy,
So that we turn away from their defeat
With a despair, not from their deaths, but for
Ourselves, who cannot penetrate their secret
Nor even guess at the anonymous breadth
Where one or two have won:
(The silver reaches of the estuary).

I often find its tune, stripped of words, circulating behind my freely wandering thoughts as I dress, walk to work, or swim. For a while I don't know what it is until a phrase breaks through—"'This is the whirlpool, then'"—and I know where I am: once again immersed in Avison's dangerous water, "at the rim of suction," imagining the "ample, further waters" ahead. My rapport with the poem is immediately re-established, and I often recall how I initially responded to it while taking a first-year Canadian literature course. Avison articulated for me a sense of destiny I have never completely lost—not just to be a poet of substance but, more significantly, to be a fully realized human being. To become the latter—and even the former—meant braving the sacred tests that life presented. To do so—and survive—would place me in an exclusive, enlightened company—or so I thought then. Success was by no means guaranteed.

I have since made occasional allusions to the poem in my own work, for example in "Hidden Structure,"[1] a complicated, book-length poem about identity and desire, which I wrote in my early twenties:

---

1   Ekstasis Editions published "Hidden Structure" as book-length poem, with paintings by
     Miles Lowry, in 1984. It was recollected in *Great Men* (Quarry, 1990) and in *The Boy with
     the Eyes of the Virgin* (Nightwood, 2012).

But men,
they are the surge and break of
luxuriant storm. I am

drawn into the vortex
whether I will it or not.
What is this power?
We sink into each other,

emerge into the calm
glittering stretch of our arm

"Hidden Structure" is a plain-spoken, public appeal for understanding by a young man coming to terms with his sexuality. The courage alluded to in Avison's poem to "dare the knowledge" powers every word I forced out on a typewriter over the six months it took me to complete the first harrowing draft. For me, the allusion is apt, for I was attempting to "penetrate" and expose my vertiginous, bracketed, "secret" self.

• • •

I have now clocked twenty-five lengths, concentrating on the correct freestyle entry position of the right hand as it slides under the surface while the left hand accelerates beneath me toward my feet, palm-flat and perpendicular to the swimming-pool floor.

• • •

I experience "The Swimmer's Moment" rather differently now, in the most literal sense, since I became a swimmer.

For one thing, I am now very conscious of the poem's geometry. First, there is the gaping verticality of the whirlpool itself, which, to my mind, is an inverted isosceles triangle that may or may not draw under those willing to risk its "ominous centre." Second, "the silver reaches of the estuary" suggests a horizontally oriented isosceles triangle. Its two equal sides swiftly open away from the downward-pointing apex of the first triangle, in a rush of exhalation bearing away the few transported souls toward their well-earned enlightenment. It is the movement suggested by these two triangles that animates the poem and anchors its central theme of risk and spiritual discovery.

In contrast, I am struck by the horizontal near-ellipse (ellipsis?) my years of swimming laps have come endlessly to describe.

• • •

I have been working on my breaststroke. I glide as far as possible to reduce the number of strokes per length, touching the soles of my feet together after each whip kick, pointing my toes, teaching myself to angle both feet powerfully like oar-blades.

• • •

For me, swimming creates a world of silence, apart from the words churning through my head, one perhaps not too different from the "boon of privacy" that Avison mentions.

"Boon" means "advantage" or "blessing." Secondary meanings are "gift" or "favour." It has been traced back to Middle English, originally meaning "prayer," which, in my reading of the poem seems eerily appropriate. As an adjective, "boon" means "close," "intimate," "favourite," with an antecedent Middle-English meaning of "jolly," harkening back to Old French (*bon*) and Latin (*bonus*), meaning "good." The OED offers "boon companion" to exemplify usage. Has anyone ever said that?

For me, "boon" is the poem's most puzzling word, especially as "defeat" succeeds it so closely. Are swimmers who recognize and decide to brave the vortex, only to fail, nevertheless blessed with a kind of partial knowledge?

And how is it that something as negative-sounding as defeat turns out to be something so innately good—though the nature of this good is incommunicable to us by those defeated souls who possess it?

This ambiguity gives the poem its anxious, cautionary bite, especially for readers like me who have come to identify with those who are turning blandly, blankly, at the whirlpool's edge. I derive great comfort that the narrator—"so that we turn away from their defeat"—believes herself to be one of them as well.

While I continue swimming back and forth, I imagine Avison turning at the "rim of suction" and wonder if the other swimmers in the water with me are truly my "boon" companions, all of us made somehow "companionable" within the limits of the pool through our shared *solitary* pursuit?

. . .

It has taken me seven years to master the butterfly. To learn how to force my body down into the water hard enough to rise above it.

. . .

Without dispelling the illusion of simplicity that the poem has, I find Avison's careful line breaks, varying line lengths, and sure use of syntax carve the poem into discrete and telling unities of meaning that at turns fulfil anticipation or surprise me. The language is unadorned, seldom Latinate—'estuary' and 'anonymous' being two telling, judiciously chosen exceptions—and with a minimal use of adjectives. The conviction in the narrator's voice is emphasized by an even-handed use of half rhymes at line endings (everyone / comes; say / saved; contesting / emerging in) that drops off somewhat as the poem accelerates toward its argentine, arms-opened-wide epiphany—as if the force of its coming overran Avison's careful planning.

Yet the poem, despite the strong, concrete image of the whirlpool, is abstract, even mathematical, not merely geometric as I have come to realize, but also algebraic. The pacing seems so carefully thought through that the individual syllables read as parts of an equation that, because it factors properly, expresses some essential truth. I am always convinced it does by the time I have weighed the values of the last line.

Yet notice how Avison never specifies what that truth is. For me its nature is essentially spiritual, but she does not connect it to any philosophy, ism, or religious sect. It is entirely personal.

Though, for me, it is about process.

. . .

The discipline I learned in becoming a poet has helped me to improve my technique as a swimmer.

The secret to swimming well is to learn how to move through water while creating as little resistance as possible—or, more accurately, to use whatever resistance the body creates to most effect—coupled with a tuned sense of how to vary pace in order to sprint, for example, or to swim long distances.

Ease in swimming is an illusion created by endless revision. The routine of swimming laps can sometimes feel like pacing a cage, but its perfection is also like learning to slip through a crowd effortlessly and unnoticed.

Some (key)strokes are executed in despair.

Others with elation.

. . .

"The Swimmer's Moment" appeared in *The Winter Sun* in 1960, Avison's first book, in which she collected poems she had written over two previous decades, a gradual accumulation of work that suggests a slow and careful writer. I have also read that the poem was composed before her conversion to Christianity, an experience recounted in her second book, *The Dumbfounding*, which appeared in 1966 and, in contrast to her first, seems to have been written quickly.

When I was younger, I saw life leading toward some single transformative, all-caps-EPIPHANY that would assert the direction of my future, an epiphany of the quality I would have inferred from Avison's poem, and which, though her father was a Methodist minister, she experienced definitively later in her life.

Now I am more circumspect and content myself with smaller, less corrective transfigurations—life-affirming and soul-destroying ones alike—that happen with regularity, though they are sometimes so tangential that I do not recognize and remark upon them until long after they occur.

Nothing is absolute; everything is contingent.

So much for destiny.

So much for fate.

. . .

I end my swim on my back. Though it's easier to breathe since I'm now supine in the water and can note the position of the sun through the skylights, I have found backstroke demanding to master. Comparable to walking backwards, I risk speeding headfirst into the wall if I miscount my strokes. To not look back asks me to have faith in myself, if not wilful blind trust.

• • •

The great pleasure in appreciating art is to make it new constantly over the course of our lives.

Life's concerns have conditioned me to read "The Swimmer's Moment" in subtly different ways over the length of my career as a writer, as have my laps in the pool. What new readings will I bring to it and how will the future further shape my understanding and response?

What will the parentheses embracing the last line of the poem over time contain?

2006

Angels and Pilgrims

WHEN LALA FIRST TALKED of a Saskatoon friend who was about to visit Victoria, I didn't catch her friend's name because I was still not adept at following her elliptically spoken, Polish-inflected English. In the fall of 1978, I'd not known her long, having just arrived on the west coast that September. My ear hadn't acclimatized to the charmed tonalities in her turns of phrase.

Annschuhmigullski! she enunciated.

Aynzuhmygahlskee? I mumbled back.

The syllabic spell was alchemic: this friend must be a warrior-queen chieftain, a Scheherazade who had beguiled her sultan. Lala's cultured elocution had scrolled this personage inside curlicues of a vaporous, sibilant perfume. Once I came to know both women, who'd met in Saskatchewan after emigrating from a devastated postwar Europe with their husbands in the 1950s, I saw how the love of story had bonded them. The fabular part of me relished curling up by the fire of their imaginations, eyes drifting open and closed while I listened.

At last the friend arrived.

Lala's Tudor-style house on the Esquimalt waterfront welcomed her terrace by terrace, salon by flung-open salon. Lala and her husband may have arrived in Canada as displaced persons, but today they presided over manicured gardens of Pappas grass and hydrangea that looked across the Strait of Juan de Fuca at the Olympics Mountains as they breached through the marine layer like snow-barnacled humpback whales. The University of Victoria, where Lala and I had met in Robin Skelton's third-year poetry workshop, had invited the friend

---

I wrote this memoir about Anne Szumigalski more than twenty years ago and almost twenty years after the events it narrates were first set in motion. When I originally set pen to paper (or, more accurately, fingers to computer keyboard), I had only intended to recount the milestones in our friendship. I did not realize, as I do now, that what I was really describing was the art of mentoring she practised, her imprint so light it was almost unnoticeable. When I met her through our mutual friend, Lala Heine Koehn, a poet who also played a role in my literary apprenticeship, little could I have known that over time Anne would school me in the craft of mentorship by teaching me how to believe in myself. Since I completed "Angels and Pilgrims" in 1997, it has taken me another two decades to grasp how Anne limned for me a vocation that includes helping other writers recognize and further their own voices.

to read. Posters announcing her reading around campus helped me sound out her bedizened name: *A-n-n-e* [First word] *S-z-u-m-i-g-a-l-s-k-i* [Second word]. Spelling's alchemies have always offered comfort.

I had come to Victoria that autumn on a pilgrimage. Not knowing how long I would stay, I rented short-term lodgings in one of three rooming houses run by Mrs. Steers, owner and landlady. She overwhelmed them with gardens whose Japanese lanterns and hollyhocks I soon discovered she dried and sold from a rickety backyard garage. When I strode up the walk through this narcotic profusion and knocked on her door to view the room she advertised as available, I knew nothing of her powers. She greeted me in a soiled dark-navy parka. Her colourless eyes held mine, face cropped by greying cinnamon hair, a grin angled across thinly rouged lips.

I was enchanted.

And convinced she was an artist.

I learned from other tenants that with her husband's pension from the Navy she had purchased the houses after he'd married her, a putatively winsome but calculating girl from rural Manitoba. By the time I moved in, he'd slept for years on a cot in the back hall of the largest of the three while Mrs. Steers, whose smile I came to believe could steer anyone anywhere, collected rents, running houses and lodgers alike into the ground to achieve the apotheosis of gloomy, uninsulated splendour. Without even testing the stove or noticing that there was no sink, I took the room and plunged into my future, having enrolled at the university to see if I had any talent to write or lead what I thought to be a poet's life.

Twenty years later, I mention Mrs. Steers because, as I write this, I could be describing the heroine of an Anne Szumigalski poem: the tale of a gardener who neglects her tenants while potatoes soften in the cellar, unfathomable eyes adrift at the ends of tentacles blonde as moonlight. "The house collapsing, her husband composted under icy loam," the poet laments, "She crushes dried eucalyptus leaves from her garden into the filthy clouds of her bath."

But I digress.

Lala hosted a party in Anne's honour on the same evening that the poetry group she'd started met. When Lala had invited me to join it, her invitation was issued point blank, like a threat. With Anne ensconced in a wingback chair as if it were the Peacock Throne of the Mughals, each member read one poem like children in a grade-school recital. Apart from the East European pastries and Russian tea that Lala served with raspberry syrup in shot-sized crystal tumblers cradled in brass holders, I don't remember much else, but Anne remarked on

how much she liked what I had read. As a novice writer stranded on an unfamiliar island that high tide might lift like a rudderless dingy and cast farther adrift,
I found her words anchored me.

Because Anne would read in Victoria several times over the five years I lived
there as a student, our friendship grew, and our paths also sometimes crossed
elsewhere in Canada. I was in the audience when she read at Harbourfront in
1980 during an international poetry festival. My confidence in my own writing
grew during those years, a result of the discipline that comes from being expected to have a new poem ready to workshop every week. In my last year at
the University of Victoria, I wrote a review of Margaret Atwood's *True Stories*,
Phyllis Webb's *Wilson's Bowl*, and Anne's *A Game of Angels* for *From an Island*,
the student-run journal that the writing program published during my time. I
called the review "Victims, Saints, and Angels." Of Anne's work I said:

> She sees all of human experiences mirrored and purified in a
> child's heart and, most importantly, in the child in herself and
> in the hearts of us all if we take the time to listen to their ecstatic
> songs.

She later told Lala that it had surprised her how well I seemed to understand
the substance of her work. Anne and I never once discussed the review, but
over the years a regard developed between us that involved an interest in each
other's work.

By 1989, I was living in Ottawa and an associate editor of *Arc*. A review by
Douglas Burnet Smith of Anne's books to date, which founding editor Chris
Levenson had commissioned, led me to propose that we devote an issue to
Anne's many accomplishments:

> In all of Szumigalski's work as a whole, it's not just that the situ-
> ations are bizarre, that we are shocked by the matter-of-factness
> with which these nightmarish occurrences are presented. We are
> haunted by them; haunted because they attack and overturn our
> expectations—about poetry and about life. They never ask us to
> understand them; they ask us to accept.[1]

---

1   Douglas Burnett Smith, "She Do the Police in Even More Voices: The Poems of Anne
    Szumigalski," *Arc* 23, (1989), 69.

In my enthusiasm as a novice editor, I volunteered to approach Anne for some poems. She contributed three texts, as she called them, including "Purple," of which this is a short excerpt:

> The chaffy seeds fall as we watch. Who could believe the urgency of that scattering? More than a poet desires fame or a traveller his bed, each one of these seeds desires its own resurrection. But why should God, who after all did not heed the desperate prayer of his only Son, spare even a moment's thought for a loosestrife seed?[2]

I also arranged for William Robertson, a fellow Saskatoon poet, to interview Anne. In reply to a question about "what kind of communication is poetry," she was very clear:

> I consider the whole of the universe as a poem, and that it's being read, or listened to, by innumerable minds or innumerable entities. That's how I see the world. So, I can't say what kind of communication it is. To me it's fundamental. That's the way the universe is made, and in my perhaps slightly perfunctory reading on physics of different theories of the universe, I haven't found anybody to contradict me in saying that the universe, and whatever more there is, is a poem. That any idea that any reader or listener could have is in it and it's possible for everybody to read it.[3]

E. F. Dyck, a poet, University of Saskatchewan professor, and former editor of *Grain*, contributed a theoretical article about the "situation of place"—or "topos"—in Anne's poetry:

> she distinguishes between "place—the external landscape" and "space—the internal landscape." We need not read Szumigalski's

---

2   Anne Szumigalski, "Purple," *Arc* 23, (Fall 1989), 22–23. Anne republished "Purple," along with the other two prose poems in the issue, "The Cranes" and "Jesus," in her next book, *Rapture of the Depths* (Regina: Coteau, 1991). Only "Purple" and "The Cranes" were included in *On Glassy Wings: Poems New & Selected* (Regina: Coteau, 1997).

3   William Robertson, "A Conversation with Anne Szumigalski," *Arc* 23, 1989, 29.

successive figures for the "poet"—rider, bird, space-dweller—as
a thumbnail history of prairie poetry to see that her expressed
poetic includes the topos <place, z>. The pair, place/space, may
be considered either as a version of <prairie, "prairie"> or as a
synecdochic generalization of <prairie, z>.[4]

A drawing of Anne by Heather Spears on the cover and an author photograph
facing the interview rounded out the issue. I organized a reading for Anne with
the Tree Reading Series at the Society of Friends' Meeting Hall in the Glebe,
a neighbourhood south of downtown Ottawa. *Arc*'s press release about the
launch described the issue as a "revealing portrait of the artist."[5]

Much more memorable than compiling the issue and setting up the reading, though it was the first time I had done either, were the hours Anne and I
spent together. I had recently acquired a leprously rusted Datsun from a friend
who had moved back west, and it gave us freedom of the city, even though we
mostly talked late into the night in my apartment. Anne pored over the sketches I'd executed in a life drawing class and listened to a few of my recent poems.

One afternoon she read *Capital Poets*, an anthology of Ottawa writers, in
which my own work was well represented. That night, after I got home from
work, we discussed poetics and motivation. I acknowledged that for me writing
was one way to recover or repatriate experience; Anne suggested that through
writing I recovered *from* experience, an observation that resonates to this day. I
was in the early stages of getting over the second of two years-long depressions
that had troubled me through my twenties. I had now begun to write poems
about growing up gay in Alberta. Anne's discussion of my work that autumn
night, hours after the *Arc* launch, gave me an unknowing foretaste of the impact
her friendship would have. She helped me recognize forces at play in my own
work without probing too far into my particular untamed species of anguish.
Which was as invasive as loosestrife. She validated the space it occupied by
simply letting its "zed-ness" exist, despite being overshadowed by the foothills
of my childhood. To borrow from a poem by Phyllis Webb, which became a
lifelong koan the moment I read it, Anne "thr[ew] a bridge of value to belief, /

---

4   E. F. Dyck, "The Topical Art of Anne Szumigalski," *Arc* 23, 1989, 45.

5   I found a copy of the press release that I must have stuck inside the issue soon after the
     launch. It is printed on a plum-colour laid stock that matches the red used on the issue's
     two-coloured, 1-sided cover. Its DIY feel has nothing sophisticated about it, but instead
     evinces the grassroots ethos of volunteer-run literary organizations.

where, towards or away from, moves intense traffic."[6]

Sometimes that traffic literally does involve cars that slow to a meandering pace, with others piling in for the joyride. In May 1990, before the League of Canadian Poets met in Regina, my boyfriend, Blaine Marchand, and I spent two nights with Anne, sleeping on air mattresses in the living room of her Saskatoon home. Our flight from Ottawa had landed in Regina the week before. As closely as we could in a rental car and as if we were pilgrims, we shadowed the route my great-grandfather had followed, on foot and by boat, having volunteered for the Northwest Expeditionary Force that Sir John A. MacDonald government had raised to suppress Riel in 1885. With an excerpt from his diary as our guide, we drove north from Swift Current, where the army had detrained to march to a paddlewheel anchored in the South Saskatchewan. We crossed the river and drove along gravel roads to Fort Pitt. The site of a battle, all that remains there is a lonely log building, perhaps a remnant of the Hudson's Bay fort, east of the Alberta border on the banks of North Saskatchewan. In the bloody twilight, we sped east to Prince Albert and a day in Batoche before driving to Anne's. Over the thick vegetable soup she'd prepared, the three of us talked in depth about my family's complicated connection to the history Blaine and I had just driven through, as well as of the intricacies of Duck Lake French that Anne knew so well. After dinner, we read poems we'd been working on to one another.

Anne read first. "The Light" recounts the wonder she experienced as a five-year-old wearing her first pair of glasses, which she put on for the first time just before her father switched on a string of battery-powered Christmas-tree lights:

And suddenly: the triumph. It didn't last long but it was wonder-ful. Perhaps the most beautiful sight I have ever seen. A kind of foresight of Paradise, that light of death, that glorious beginning and ending. Where there had been nothing but a just discernible fuzz of dark green there was now a huge fuzz of rainbow light. All colours, no perhaps not, as I remember it was red green and blue. But how pearly that light was. It was dawn in the garden; it was the inside of a thousand seashells. For a moment I forgot my cold legs, my musing state. All I could think of was that light. Then it suddenly went out and I never saw it again.[7]

6 Phyllis Webb, "Pain," *Selected Poems, 1954–1965*. Vancouver: Talonbooks, 1971, 26.

7 Anne Szumigalski, *The Word, The Voice, The Text: The Life of a Writer*. Saskatoon: Fifth

A few months later, I would write to ask Anne for permission to publish "The Light" in *Arc*, having just become the co-editor.

Blaine read next. His first poem evoked a childhood friend's recent death:

Beside me, a schoolgirl in uniform reconjugates
the passé composé of the irregular verb *vivre*.
I rummage through my briefcase, retrieve
the *Selected Poems of Delmore Schwartz*.

The last time we spoke we argued about him.
Such a complex man. The promise of acclaim.
The fears that held him, consumed him:
sexuality, anti-Semitism, rejection.
I found him insufferable; you, more than the sum of his parts.
I thought of your mind, like phosphorescence,
trapped in a body that had not
worked since you were born.[8]

He took on the voice of Caitlin, the wife of Dylan Thomas, in his second poem:

How I hate what he has made me. He who writes:
"O Caitlin, my love, my Cat, my lovely love,"
then spends his drunken self pummelling some bitch.
Legs, feet in the stirrups, it's almost
as if, lying here, I am giving myself to him.
But the doctor is not here for that reason.
His hands run red as he hacks at the foetus.
It comes out bit by bit. Only three months to term.[9]

As a teenager, Blaine had esteemed the Thomases as exemplars of romantic love, and just read her memoir, *Caitlin: A Warring Absence*. He was horrified she'd only had an abortion this late in her pregnancy so she could fly to New York, where Dylan was partway through a U.S. reading tour. She'd wanted to

---

House, 1900, 69.

8   Blaine Marchand, "Life is a Train," *The Craving of Knives*. Ottawa: BuschekBooks, 2009, 53.

9   "In the White Giant's Thigh," Ibid, 61.

sabotage his dipsomaniac womanizing. By the time she'd landed, he was in St. Vincent's Hospital for acute alcohol poisoning and died the next day. Lapsed Catholic boy that he was, Blaine wrote his poem to express lingering awe over-come by sudden disillusion.[10]

I read last. "Pre-Architecture" describes being tested for my Modeller's badge at Cubs. I'd modified Styrofoam my father had discarded after unpacking our new stereo into a "model home." Triangles of cloth from my mother's sew-ing box curtained windows I cut into its sides:

> ...the blueprint
> unfurling in my head as I cut
> windows with a nail file
> pieced together doors
> with toothpick hinges
> from balsawood for a biplane,
> filled each room with empty
> spools for chairs
> matchbook beds and bits
> of old fabric.
> I boast that it is part
> of a neighbourhood I want
> to build up in the hills
> beyond the city
> with a view of the mountains.
> The House of Raymour
> I call it, ranch-style
> with tumbleweed chandeliers
> and a three-car garage.[11]

After a few eyerolls, the leader testing me hastily awarded the badge. My "design sense" made me stand out a little too neatly from my fellow little boys. Anne and Blaine, listening closely and, unlike the leader, asked me if I recalled any

---

10 Blaine collected the two poems he read that night into a manuscript I would edit for him fifteen or sixteen years later. After BuschekBooks published *The Craving of Knives*, it was nominated for the Archibald Lampman Award in 2010.

11 John Barton, "Pre-Architecture," *Designs from the Interior*. Concord, Ontario: Anansi, 1994, 20–23.

other details about my model home whose pride of place deserved mention. Five years later, at my request, Anansi hired Anne to help me prepare *Designs for the Interior*, my sixth collection of poems, for publication, a book that gave a home to this and other poems about my growing queer consciousness. Her comments limned a species of intuitive mentorship that's provided me with a model of how to work with other poets.

Blaine's and my ghosting of my great-grandfather's involvement in the Northwest Resistance surfaced a few years later in "Aqua Poetica," a poem about the North Saskatchewan River and its tributary, the Bow, which flows through Calgary, the city where I grew up:

Moving toward and not forward

beyond Batoche
a man with blood like mine,
my mother's blood hearing

reports of

gunfire carried by sandy and wind-crazed
river cliffs to where he stood
sentinel, in 1885, and seeing nothing,
words I hear

in the blood, the photocopied diary
my lover read
aloud
(over my shoulder) in 1990:
"and time lost rounding the bends in the stream."[12]

Before learning how to read, I was bemused the alphabet could represent the words I spoke daily. The eureka came in Grade 1 with the word "and," which joins us to the world and to one another.

John and Anne, Anne and Blaine, Blaine and John.
River and gunfire, loosestrife and desire.

---

12 John Barton, "Aqua Poetica," *Sweet Ellipsis*. (Toronto: ECW, 1998), 139–40.

I salted my lines with "and" wherever I could:

the word "and,"
intimate conjunction repeated at every

bend in the flow

my first
recollection of this love of words.

Each "and" immersed me in the poem's flow, shooting the rapids that the line and stanza breaks created.[13] This wordplay approaches the wily cosmology Anne's work models.

Seven years have passed since Blaine and I were in Saskatchewan, and, though we are no longer partners, we try to recapture the expansive feeling of those two days we shared with Anne at the annual meetings the League holds across the country. The ease of the time we spend with her stands apart from the rest of the conference. I like teasing her that she always flies home to Saskatoon too early on the last day for me to be fully awake to see her off.

The last time we saw Anne was at the 1995 Governor-General's Literary Awards gala in the entirely beige auditorium of the National Library of Canada, an edifice so blockishly oppressive it looks more suited to the steppes of the former Soviet Union than to the fairy-tale, neogothic pretensions of our Victorian-era capital. To an audience of over three hundred, she read "Goodbye," which opens *Voice*:

How dear to her is the journey of the mind,
flying from dwelling to dwelling,

her feet scraping the tops of the
forest trees as she floats on by,

---

13 "And" did not yet cause me to fully connect the Indigenous peoples' loss of self-determination and the right to their lands with my great-grandfather and his role as small player in the imposition of colonialism. See my essay "Stepping Back in Awe: Honouring Indigenous Perspectives."

exchanging one language for another,
never quite sure of her bearings,
counting the chimneys on unfamiliar roofs.

One day she hopes to understand progression
how it has no end and no beginning,
how nothing precedes or succeeds,
how time is a disc that wobbles
as it spins.

The melody is an old one
played again and again.
All night she is aware that it scuttles
over the pillows like a louse on holiday.

Waking she hears it emerge from her nose,
a hum like paperwasps.

"But that's just the tune," she says,
"tomorrow on my way I'll write the words."[14]

In the future, Anne explained, she would always read from the leather-bound, artisan-tooled copy of her award-winning book of poems. It had been presented to her the day before in Toronto, where the names of all the GG winners were made public. The beautiful, to Anne, is meant to be dog-eared by everyday use.

Every time I kiss Anne goodbye, she asks me when I will come see her in Saskatoon. She has even offered me haven—to recover from the anguish still written in lemon ink across my face. I always say I will visit someday soon.

Anne, you have been constant—like one of those stars in the incalculable sky that has guided travellers for millennia.

Somehow you always know how I am and where I am going.

• • •

1997

14 Anne Szumigalski, "Goodbye," *Voice.* (Regina: Coteau, 1995), 3.

Postscript, 2018

When *Prairie Fire* published "Angels and Pilgrims" in its Anne Szumigalski issue in Spring 1997, who could have imagined she would die two years later on April 22, 1999. After learning she'd left us from Blaine, I called Lala. I still feel the sun streaming through my office window while we talked.

Lala died on December 12, 2017. Knowing her had shaped me differently but as profoundly as Anne had, especially as I was a postwar brat raised by a Canadian mother and a British father who'd seen the war out in England. Lala was the first person I'd met who'd lived through the war in continental Europe. Her accounts of fleeing disguised as a hunchback ahead of the Russians as they closed in on Berlin affects me still. As a relief worker in Europe in 1945, Anne must have understood what Lala had suffered better than most. Blaine emailed me from Ottawa to tell me she had died in Saskatoon, where she'd moved to be close to her five children.

Lala amused me once by extolling one of Blaine's gifts, a B.C. Ferries cup and saucer emblazoned with a crown and the name of the ship upon which it was used: Queen of Esquimalt. All Queen-class boats were named after the municipalities they linked, including the one where I'd known Lala during the years we were close. Through a cup and saucer Blaine found while thrifting in the Ottawa Valley, two queens of greater Victoria were reunited. Anne would have regally shown deference.

Time at a Standstill: Ruth Roach Pierson, Ekphrasis, and the Museum of Memories

In "Woman with Wild Flowers," which falls near the end of *Aide-Mémoire*, Ruth Roach Pierson's second collection of poetry, the narrator—she must be female; shall we call her Ruth?—ponders a figure in the painting of the same name by French post-impressionist Odilon Redon. Ruth tries to meet the woman's almond eyes, comparing them and her oval face respectively to "Natalie's" and "Simona's," two women never again mentioned in the poem or in the book. Looking for similarities appears to be an attempt to make this stranger, albeit a painted one, less strange, even though the women she's likened to are less sketched in than gesture drawings quickly executed in a life-studies class. They are shadows of a shadow. Yet the woman, according to Ruth, has "her own look," her own individuated regard. The viewed and the viewer hold each other's eyes. Acts of looking populate Ruth's poems. She also has her own look, casting her eye (and I) over works of art, the past and present, and the natural world. All sustain her attention. As in a mirror, she catches glimpses of herself that lead to discoveries not always pleasing and sometimes lasting. If we follow the poems' sightlines and meet her eyes, we may even attain a sense of how our own minds and memories work.

Ruth presses on in the poem. Wild flowers she assumes were picked in a meadow are mentioned. The woman's lips are "thin but not pursed." Then the poem turns precipitously, as if Ruth feels the ground become solid beneath her feet. She realizes "the woman stares / at nothing as though unseeing / or witnessing an inner // *clair-obscur*." She does not see Ruth. The stanza break after "inner" enacts this turning, with "*clair-obscur*" radiating through the poem as if the flowers the woman holds with "an unseen hand" had unexpectedly opened. This turning *turns* on Ruth, the painting bringing her face to face with her own tendency toward chiaroscuro, which other poems in *Aide-Mémoire* pencil in.

The impact on Ruth is profound:

.... I stand
and stand before it. Time

at a standstill. She sees.

Sees. Behind her
deepening and spreading, a splotch
of intense yellow.

A consequential word in these final six lines, surprisingly, is "it," for, though "it" must refer to the painting, grammatically it "stands in" for the "*clair-obscur*" or for time itself. "It" and "time" share the same line. Even the effort to describe the effect of "it" preserves its ambiguities. Ruth could be standing before her own inner life just as easily as the woman's. However construed, this transaction between the viewer and the viewed is required for awareness to occur, to have any import.

For anything to happen, however, time must be made to stand still. Odilon Redon, who painted this work over one-hundred-and-ten years ago, has succeeded in doing so, for he's made at least one of his viewers— Ruth—stop. The painting has become a conduit, the woman in it carried into the present while remaining in the past as Ruth pauses, briefly obtaining a sense of her place in time's unstoppable, forward motion. The power of this epiphany is signaled through her scrutiny of Redon's use of yellow, the poem's last word, which she beautifully evokes with the impressionist-sounding "splotch," as it floods the painting's background. The present participles "spreading" and "deepening" make the paint still appear wet, as if Redon were also present and sharing in Ruth's alertness to light and darkness while applying finishing touches to his painting. Art is such a touchstone for Ruth in her apprehension of self and life that she intuitively places herself in a direct relationship with any artwork she views.

While the setting is nowhere described in the poem, Redon's *Woman with Wild Flowers* must hang in a museum. Where else could it be seen, unless in the home of a wealthy collector? Ruth's experience of it reads as a private moment lived in public. The word "stand" allows her to evoke the kind of space a museum creates. By implication, if she were not standing before Redon's painting, she would be moving on. This is how public viewing works: visitors stand (or not) or move on (or not) as they respond (or not) to works on display. If Ruth is anything, she is a gazer. "Woman with Wild Flowers" betrays no sense there is anyone with her while she takes the measure of Redon. She is not stopped before his painting during a busy retrospective, where the crowds would elbow her out of the way. Or maybe Ruth is not on her own. It's perhaps a quiet weekday afternoon and she has come with a friend, who's only a few steps away. They may have chosen to move through the exhibition independently while respecting the order the curators had imposed upon the assembled canvases. Or they may crisscross the gallery, looking at only those paintings that interest them in much the same way a reader sometimes dips here and there into a book like *Aide-Mémoire*, rather than beginning with the first poem and reading through to the last. A stone dropped into a pool, a reader or museum visitor may start in the middle and move slowly outward in ever-more reflective waves. No matter how an exhibit or book is experienced, the path taken through either leads to an impression, or, if not, to clearly articulated insights. Though how a reader or a gallery visitor chooses to recount what they've seen or read need not parallel the way in which they experienced it in real time; the account itself speaks volumes. Ruth writes often about visual art, employing ekphrasis as a tool of self-exploration. She also applies her powers of observation to non-ekphrastic situations, the resulting poems more often than not artifacts of memory.

However a reader comes to view what Ruth writes, a museum is a natural space for her to locate her gaze, whether the collection on display consists of paintings or the caps worn by women who fought for Canada. In 1986, Ruth collected women's wartime stories in *"They're Still Women After All": The Second World War and Canadian Womanhood*, which stands alongside other books, journal articles, and conference papers on women's history that she has written, edited, or delivered during a thirty-one-year career as a historian and feminist scholar. Born in Seattle in 1938, Ruth spent her formative years on the west shore of Puget Sound in Phinney Bay, which is close to Bremerton, the home of a naval base. When I walk along the Ogden Point breakwater in Victoria, I can look south and see Ruth as a girl, sitting in a swing with her nose in a book. She spent one year as a student in Germany before returning to Seattle to finish high school and begin her post-secondary education at the University of Washington, where she studied history. At Yale, her doctoral thesis focused on Jewish identity during the Weimar Republic. Occasionally, only a German word will convey the sense that Ruth wants, like *die Spuren* for "the traces" in "Insignia" from *Aide-Mémoire*. Ruth left the U.S. to join the faculty of Memorial University in St John's, Newfoundland, in 1970; ten years later, she moved to the Ontario Institute for Studies in Education, now a part of the University of Toronto. She retired in 2001 and trained her eyes, so to speak, on a passion long put to one side: poetry.

The intention of the genre, however, makes it a pursuit very different from history's evidence-based depictions of the past. In 2002, BuschekBooks published Ruth's first book of poems, *Where No Window Was*. She chose a passage from Aristotle as an epigraph: "The difference [between the historian and the poet] is that the one tells of what has happened, the other of the kinds of the things that might happen. For this reason, poetry is something more philosophical and more worthy of serious attention than history...." Aristotle's commendation of poetry for providing access to things "that might happen" gives her obsession with memory a changed licence. Perhaps Ruth the poet, unlike Ruth the historian, has the tools to enter into the world of what-if with more confidence. How poetry shapes memory brings into play not certainties but possibilities. The past is less about facts as lived than about how they come to be seen, especially how they were unknowingly lived at the time they took place. Or, as Ruth outlines in "Repeat Performances":

Evening my parents sat out here,
watched the sun leave the river.
A kingfisher chatters, sweeping
in low, following the stream's
curve to his perch in an alder
cantilevered over the water.
There he waits, watches,
dives for his dinner.

Two end-of-day riparian rituals:
his, born of instinct or intelligent habit,
utilitarian; mine,
merely chosen repetition,
not unlike the act of collecting—
one more piece of art deco Vaseline glass
or another 1920s fishing reel—

as though, by this proliferation of the same,
things will be kept as they were.

Is the historian the kingfisher, diving for his dinner? Is the narrator the poet? Of course she is, but, in her pursuit of the poem, she can't rid herself of the habit of collecting in order to keep everything as it was. No historian would want to bring time to a standstill, but a poet might.

"Conceit" casts light on how Ruth perceives her relationship to the process of writing poetry:

> I don't know that there always has to be
> an "I"—camera's aperture, mast
> to cling to, pole to run a flag up,
> auto for the bio. No
> cynosure or paparazzo darkens
> a Casper David Friedrich scene,
> only the drama of oak, soaring mountain,
> sky. Piet Mondrian purged his art
> of all but geometry and equilibrium.
> And may Saul Bellow rest assured,
> the parade of pictures, that play
> of light and shadow philosophers call
> appearance, will soldier on after
> our eyelids are weighted with coins.
> What is our fear: that without an "I"
> there'd be no "us," no "you"?
> Or that beauty's site of being—
> the "I" of the beholder—vanishes
> into the eye of a passing cloud?

Friedrich's dramatic oaks and Mondrian's equilibrium, cleansed of self-consciousness, anticipate Redon's wild flowers. Ruth makes the lovely equation of "I" and "eye" and of "site" and "sight," the latter pairing awareness with place. Ruth is an autobiographical poet with a historian's perspective, wise to how over-focusing on the self inflates one's *self*-importance. Ruth's poetic self is aware of others' selfhood, the "us" of society and the "you" of friendship and intimacy. Her "I" is really many "I"s, the specimen self, which does not speak for others, but presents the details of her own experience so those others may recognize them and feel kinship and difference. Hers is a self that is modest before the inevitability of vanishing into the "eye of a passing cloud." "Eye" also suggests the turning "eye" of the storm, placing the turn characteristic of Ruth's work in the last line.

In 2007, BuschekBooks published *Aide-Mémoire* and in 2008, the year Ruth "turned" seventy, it attracted a Governor General's Literary Award nomination. The transitory nature of life and self becomes particularly acute when Ruth admits in "Though Not Asked" that she returned to poetry late:

> Was it folly to begin writing poems
> when already growing old? Poetry is written,
> I've been told, out of new experience. Well, ageing
> is new, goddamit. The newness of skin
> falling in folds like a stranger's clothes. The throes
> of windedness climbing subway stairs. And then
> looked at no longer with desire...

Although bemused by ageing, Ruth is more a poet of memory who recalls incidents from the past with fresh insight in order to re-experience them as new.

Ruth demonstrates her way of analyzing the ageing self's relationship to time's passage in "Burlap Coat with a Red Velvet Lining." Taking its name from a work of art by Luci Dilkus, it provides a more readable sense of how Ruth visits art spaces than does "Woman with Wild Flowers." Unlike paintings hanging on a wall, contemporary art often responds to and is redefined by the environments in which it's displayed:

> shifting uneasily from foot to foot
> you see the sag of your skin
> in the burlap coat the artist has draped
> over a hanger dangling from the ceiling
>
> the jute, coarsely woven
> basted with makeshift stitches
> is crude cover for the velvet lining
> a fire banked yet ardent
>
> hummingbird-feeder red
> glimmers at the end of each sleeve
> and at the gaping buttonless
> unhemmed front

frayed thread
pooling at your feet

The chord of mortality, so resonant throughout *Aide-Mémoire*, in this poem is plucked plangently. It's as if Ruth's encountering the "newness of [her] skin," as described in "Though Not Asked," "falling in folds on a stranger's body," the strangeness of this perception communicated viscerally through the objectifying second person. She studies the sculpture and responds to the garment's absent body as if it were hers, the coat's sackcloth harbouring her own lingering heretical flame. It's significant that the outer shell is rent and buttonless. The void left by the body hints at anguish that amounts to nothing more than thread looping upon itself on the floor.

The coat, as if it were turning in the drafts coming in through the gallery's door, prompts Ruth to recall a moment from her past, in which another garment takes centre stage:

and you had almost forgotten …
the young woman modelling before the mirror
her mother kneeling on the floor
measuring to mark a full skirt's

hem, the job of daughter to turn
stand still, and holding the pins, turn again
but you loosen your grasp and they spill
rattling into a disordered heap

and your mother's shrill *Why can't you learn
to organize your life!* And you look down
at your moving feet but can't stop
their shifting

The kind of turn that the poem performs is characteristic of how intuitively Ruth enters memory's realm or what might be more precisely called the past present or the present past, a kind of stasis, of time brought forward to briefly stand still, the same way that the woman in "Woman with Wild Flowers" is brought into the present through the act of looking. It's striking that in Ruth's memory, the skirt bells full, unlike the burlap coat, which no one could imagine twirling herself in to gauge its amplitude. Only its red lining offers a sense of any such remnant possibility. Had her younger self, recalled as a fond but strange familiar, "organized" her life appropriately, would she now feel less emotionally rent? She wonders if a firmer grasp on herself and on those slippery pins might have led her to hem the fabric of life's mismatched pieces more neatly.

"Farm Wife, Western Quebec, 1940," the finest ekphrastic poem in *Aide-Mémoire* and one of its most straightforward, also describes an item of clothing and its wearer's mismatching accoutrements. Based on a photograph by Malak, the brother of the more famous photographer, Yousuf Karsh, the poem describes an art medium that, by its very nature, makes time stand still, even though what it records appears to be in motion, as if it were really a documentary film:

> Malak, plying the back roads
> in search of country folk,
> has leapt from his jalopy and asked
> her to pose. But she refuses
> to smile. Spine strained back,
> eyes locked above the camera,
> a sapling against the sky.
>
> From under a man's worn cap,
> its tweed bill twisted to the side,
> her hair, all marcelling spent, hangs
> in slack waves around a face grim
> with impatience at this uncustomary
> standing still. She wears, not trousers,
>
> but a dress, its sleeves deflated,
> paisley pattern sun-effaced,
> a rent at the waist and an isosceles tear
> below the bodice's last button. Meagre
> sheath for a body sharp as a ploughshare
> and gaunt. See the jut of hipbones
> and the ache of veins tunneled
> beneath her arms' bare skin.
>
> She grips the handles of the plough.

While the body is only implied in "Burlap Coat with Red Velvet Lining," the woman in this poem is wholly present. The last button below her dress's bodice counterpoints the burlap coat's buttonless state. The woman is powerful; she'd roll her eyes if chided for not living a more organized life. However battered she might be by poverty, her flesh expresses exactly who she is, "a body sharp as a ploughshare." A realist with her grip firm on the plough, she is unmoved by the photographer's wish for her to appear happy. Ruth's identification with her is palpable, the photograph like memory linking them across time. Does she wish that she unashamedly possessed a like strength?

Shame in response to perceived weakness is an essential thread in Ruth's work, which is not solely inspired by ekphrastic experiences. If the art of memory were to be considered an illustrative gesture equal to the visual arts, it would comfortably fall within the classical definition of ekphrasis, which, according to the *Merriam-Webster Dictionary*, most purely means "description."[1] In "Archival Research as Refuge, Penance, and Revenge," an article that she contributed to the Winter 2007 issue of *Queen's Quarterly*, Ruth describes how the collapse of her marriage became a source of contrition, however socially constructed and imposed those feelings may have been:

> When I asked what we should tell our friends, he answered "Truth is always the best policy." And so the story that was told was of my unfaithfulness, my affair with another man. His infidelities were never mentioned. He became the injured party. And many a person in our shared circle of acquaintances and friends, female as well as male, took pity on him as the victim. I began to feel enormous guilt, nourished by the negative judgments of me I projected onto others or that actually reached my ears.

Ruth has the discretion not to over-freight her poems with excessive detail; the article's frankness comes as a revelation. By comparison, her poems allude to her "moral lapses" tangentially, which serves to heighten the shame felt in response.

---

1   Accessed September 23, 2018. https://www.merriam-webster.com/dictionary/ekphrasis. Interestingly, Merriam-Webster indicates that "ekphrasis" is a "relatively new entry" in its dictionary and notes that the one of the earliest mentions of it is found in the *Iliad*, "when Homer provides a long and discursive account of the elaborate scenes embossed on the shield of Achilles."

Shame is suggested in the first stanza of "The Marrow": "How gauche I was last night!" Deflecting immediately into a description of the rain and of a Man Ray photograph, Ruth acknowledges that

> We see the world
> through a mesh of likenesses, one hooking another,
> until it's impossible to sever the linked hoops back
> to recover the nub, the marrow of a thing.

The world's accreted distractions obscure shame, but it keeps returning, as do other memories, which makes the humiliation she feels particularly sharp: "Opening a book

> closed tight for years, I find your inscription, with its precise grace,
> a reminder not all was lies and strife. Morning dissolves
>
> into afternoon, the rain doesn't let up and I can't shake
> my discontent with that self of the night before. How could
> I so offend? No comfort in the thought I was in disguise,
> a mawkish double, self-absorbed. If only
> I could cast off that habit of mind, the self,
>
> as in a blast of wind, the bare-limbed tree shudders free of rain.

The angst over the largely undescribed incident is so intense that Ruth imagines its perpetrator—herself—as another person whose thinking and behaviour misrepresent her essential self.

"The Unclenching" most acutely expresses the need to atone. Ruth returns to an unnamed city where she used to live, recognizable to many readers as St. John's:

> I traipse the crooked streets
> heuristically, more sleuth
> I tell myself, than tourist,
> climb the steep rise from the harbour,
> the hills barnacled with Paul Klee houses
> like children's wooden blocks brightly

coloured and askew, but braced
against gale-driven rains and snows
and the ropes of fog that spool in
from the sea over Cape Spear
and through the Narrows.

With her "hooded / self, body clenched," after "lurch[ing] into the blizzard's fury," she visits the widow of her first husband, who serves her "peppermint tea. And photos, / dusty, discoloured." After leaving and returning to the storm, she

regret[s] not having asked if he'd still liked
heist movies, the Meerschaum pipe
we bought together in London,
John Berryman poems.

Set in the past—or the present past—in its entirety, "The Unclenching," as a revisiting of memory, is the purest foray of its kind in *Aide-Mémoire*. Ruth's necessary structural turn occurs prior to the first line. The poem unflinching-ly documents her journey to one of memory's most paradox-riven locales, an outpost called regret, and it ends by travelling to one even farther out, called quietude:

By nightfall the wind has quieted,
and stars shine through pinholes
in the cleansed curve of the sky
a few cloud wisps loitering
past the white of the moon.

It's as if the pins in "Burlap Coat" have made pinholes in "The Unclenching" so the stars may shine through. The night sky's scoured curve could be an arc of the earlier poem's full skirt, an arc the stars shall hold in place until every sor-row is sewn together. Ruth, in finding peace about a failed marriage, becomes a flâneur, strolling the once-crooked avenues of her past, made broad, straight, and Haussmann-like by coming to terms. Time's inevitable turn toward death, brought to mind by visiting her first husband's widow, has been stalled for now. How appropriate the cloud wisps are "loitering."

For Ruth, stasis can be happened upon in the tiniest of quasi-aesthetic experiences: in her garden, for example, or when looking outside from an upstairs room, as she does in "Leafing Out":

Outside my window. Aspen
in an ecstasy of photosynthesis:
leaves in the early stages of unfurling
breathe in sunlight,
exhale it back to me,
transmuted into a fresh green, a callow green,
a green so new it still contains
the yellow of the sun.

Stases that arise while contemplating the past may have their own beauty, but those inspired by nature supply *Aide-Mémoire* with its most delectable moments of bliss. Even though no memory process is involved, the movement in "Leafing Out" parallels how recollection works: an encounter with outside stimulus that inspires awareness—some variety of emotional leafing out, melancholic, nostalgic or grief-marked—and delicate, consequential change within. That "Leafing Out" falls after "Woman with Wild Flowers," which brought "time [to] a standstill," is telling. In the iconography of *Aide-Mémoire*, the former poem leads to the latter's wild flowers, as if to reconnect Ruth to her own inner wildness as a young woman who, once upon a time, couldn't organize her life, but now older if not calmer, can reorganize it through retrospect.

For Ruth, remembering is active, equal to living physically in the present, as she acknowledges in "Doing," the book's closing poem:

What to live for, if not
to do? Everyone does.
As in the old song,
even the birds.

But I don't mean
falling in love. No, I'm talking about
labour. *Homo faber*. Meaningful busyness. Even *the vita*

contemplativa is a doing
of sorts, like mulling over,
wool-gathering. However still
the body. And meditation,

cousin to emptying, gleaning,
draining—pail of water,
harvested field, wound.
And remembering, thinking

back. Not merely lively,
but constructive. Look
how we amend and
recast our pasts.

Aide-Mémoire now circles back to "The Marrow," its opening poem. The book's entire backward direction from beginning to end, or from end to beginning, answers a question posed by one of the book's epigraphs—"Why is backward the most beautiful direction?"—a line attributed to Anne Compton.

Retrospect is beautiful because it involves "emptying, gleaning, / and draining," the writing of poems an investigatory tool, an instrument of spiritual meditation, a luminous transcript. The turn in "Doing" takes Ruth back to her childhood bedroom. She invokes herself to "Tear / down and reconstruct

the parental home. Stealthily
I move the young girl's bedroom
to the end of the second-storey hall,

open the windows to sunlight
burning through the mist of Phinney Bay.
Form a half-circle of diminutive chairs,
plop onto each a Raggedy Ann

or Andy, teddy bear, Dumbo,
or ringlet-crowned china doll.
Their eyes, ball-and-socketed glass
or cross-stitched stars of thick black thread,

attend, more acutely than anyone
ever will again, to the child
at the blackboard easel, chalk in hand,
writing words and more words.

In the child, we have the precursor to the poet. Though the former tries early to find her way obsessively through language, she has yet to sense her own small place in the world. The poet she becomes later in life first had to learn how living gives meaning to the words she now uses to locate herself and how the tricks of mind, art, and poetry now permit her to make the past present stand still for a moment so she can speculate with clarity. Based on the facts alone, the historian long ago eschewed the cloying nostalgia that can arise through memory, saving the poet the trouble.

In "The Marrow," Ruth explains that for her "Everything tends toward *aide-mémoire*," which "used to refer to notes, or memoranda, that are taken in order to jog one's memory later…. [It] has also been used as an alternative to the term 'mnemonic aid.' An example of this is the rhyme 'Richard of York gave battle in vain'—the initial letters of which are the same as those of the colours of the rainbow—red, orange, yellow, green, blue, indigo, violet."[2] Though not a mnemonic in this sense, the James Marshall limerick that Ruth uses as an epigraph to *Where No Window Was* captures her method:

A sinister spider named Ruth
set up a photography booth.
 In clever disguise
 she'd lure juicy flies
who too late would discover the truth.

What wryer way to describe how Ruth uses the language as bait in order to snag memories into the present before they fly out of the story. Given her ekphrastic bent, it's apt that the eponymous spider is a photographer. Poetry leads Ruth to unexpected turns in the present, which *in turn* allow her to access and retain the past. *Aide-Mémoire* is a contemporary museum of lived and relived experiences, some of them direct responses to works of art; others, responses to human memory, that most artful of pursuits. As a frequent visitor to

---

2 https://www.phrases.org.uk/meanings/25200.html. Retrieved September 23, 2018.

her own museum, Ruth knows it to be the site (and sight) of her most accurate, speculative, and emotive doing.

2010

The Message Inside *Time Capsule*:
Pat Lowther's Legacy

WHEN I TOLD A friend that I was about to write a review of *Time Capsule* (Polestar, 1997), Pat Lowther's posthumous new and selected poems, he looked at me quizzically and suggested I'd set myself an unrealistic challenge, for how can anyone critique an icon? My friend gave me pause because I'd never considered Lowther to be one. When I conducted a quick search for critical work about Lowther at the University of Ottawa library, I was disappointed if unsurprised to find nothing of substance. After another friend, who is slightly younger than I am and whose reading interests are broad, admitted she was not versed in Lowther's work, I realized that many readers of Canadian poetry only know of Lowther through the handful of poems that Gary Geddes collected in *15 Canadian Poets* × 2. Since the early 1980s and until the publication of *Time Capsule*, her poetry has only been available on the shelves of libraries or found erratically scattered through secondhand bookstores.

If Pat Lowther is an icon, it is because of the myth that draws strength from her disappearance in September 1975, on the eve of the League of Canadian Poets' annual general meeting in Victoria, which she was to chair as co-president; the discovery of her body three weeks later; and the conviction of her husband for her murder in June 1977. Such a narrative is potent enough to be remembered, too often to the exclusion of all else, including of the person she was while alive: a woman and a poet who should have enjoyed the notice and prominence that the gradual recognition of ability justly provides. The League's decision in 1980 to name in her honour the prize that it awards to the best book of poetry by a Canadian woman ironically adds further substance to the myth. Such a well-intentioned gesture encourages us not to forget the woman or how she died—it is the Pat Lowther *Memorial* Award after all—but does it spur anyone to look at the poems? A violent, untimely death felled Lowther when "she was on the edge," we are told in the jacket copy of 1977's *A Stone Diary*, "of whatever fame and success Canadian poetry has to offer." "Whatever" is the operative word. A poet who leaves us just before her ability is recognized and who didn't leave a body of work substantial enough to become the sustainable grist of both long-term popular and academic interest cannot survive in our collective memory without the leverage of a compelling myth.

I first came across *A Stone Diary* at the University of Alberta bookstore soon after it was published. I had only just begun to take my own writing seriously, so would browse the poetry sections of random Edmonton bookstores. I had not heard of Pat Lowther, much less knew of her murder, but the book held my attention. I remember reading the poems with little initial understanding, which hardly mattered to me because the mysterious beauty of the poems enchanted me sufficiently. I was twenty years old, or half my present age. Next spring, I will be older than Pat Lowther was when she died barely two months after her fortieth birthday. To read *Time Capsule* two decades after my first brush with her work is not only to rediscover and refine my experience of it, but also to hold a mirror up to myself. I watch myself recalling my beginnings as a poet and wondering how my own poetry may have changed in response to what I read. It is as a writer marked by my past that I open this book.

Leafing slowly through the book's chronological arrangement, I imagine the countless hours that Lowther spent working at her desk or kitchen table passing in real time. The poems grow lusher, become simpler yet more complex, and ever more sharply representative of the aesthetics, life experiences, and issues that impelled her to write. She becomes increasingly actual to me and speaks in an idiom that, while typical of her moment and place, is more fully her own. I strive not to read the poems with any retrospective intent, as some do, looking for subliminal portents that might reveal Lowther's subconscious awareness of her death's premature and horrific arrival. Rather I endeavour to place her in the historic present, following her through her specific time and space. *Time Capsule* brings her alive. The woman who speaks these poems is not an icon.

. . .

So, who is Pat Lowther, the woman and poet, and what are her concerns? What can the reader glean from *Time Capsule* about her aesthetics? How well did she write?

The present volume contains a selection of poems from the three books published in her lifetime—*This Difficult Flowring* (Very Stone House, 1969), *The Age of the Bird* (unbound portfolio, Blackfish Press, 1972), and *Milk Stone*

(Borealis, 1974)—as well as poems from two posthumous collections—*A Stone Diary* (Oxford, 1977) and *Final Instructions* (*West Coast Review*/Orca Sound Publications, 1980). It closes with a generous selection of previously unknown work from an unfinished manuscript the Lowther family found in an attic three years ago. This section of "new" poems is called "Time Capsule," the working title of the book she was writing at the time of her death. This manuscript's discovery, as well as the desire of many to counter the legend of Lowther's death with the substance of her achievement, makes the publication of this new and selected poems important and welcome.

Lowther is known for her interest in Latin American political struggle in the 1970s, which she voiced in poems of homage to Pablo Neruda and in the masterful "Chacbuco: The Pit," a meditation on the detention by Chilean authorities of political prisoners in a remote mine after the 1973 American-backed coup against Salvador Allende's socialist government. That poem ends with lines I have known by heart ever since I first read them:

And the horrors of the mind
are the horrors of
what we allow to be done
and the grace of the soul
is what we determine shall be
made truly among us. Amen.

Lowther also is known for feminist concerns raised in poems about the relations between men and women, love, the body, childbirth, and motherhood. The human and the natural (especially the geologic), the two worlds of Lowther's poetry, unifies these preoccupations. In "Choice" (from "Time Capsule"), she describes herself as "old, stone-old," but anxious "to build a world within / a world, human." How she mediates the relationship between the human and the natural, often using images drawn from one to evoke the other, gives her poetry its substance.

In "Intersection" (from *A Stone Diary*), the two worlds meet:

At Fraser & Marine, slapped
by the wind from
passing traffic

light standards, trolleys
everything has edges
too real to touch

taxis unload at the hotel
the Gulf station fills them up

the lego apartment block
is sharp as salt

And the sunset is tea rose
colour strained, clarified
between navy-blue clouds,
the moon in its first
immaculate crescent

it's an axis
    double intersection
        transparencies

The natural and human coexist unselfconsciously, the grandeur of sunset, which Lowther compares to a tea rose, that most civilized of flowers, soaking through from behind the grit of the streetscape. However, if a reader is attentive, the way in which the human and the natural intersect becomes clear. Something alchemical occurs, which is both exhilarating and frightening:

the Gulf station
could swallow you like a prairie

you could walk into
that phone booth
and step out between the planets

The immensity of such possibilities excites Lowther. If we can gain access to the natural via the human, she seems to be saying, look at what life offers.

But the two also diverge. In "Two Babies in Two Years" (from *This Difficult Flowring*), Lowther delights in childbirth and childrearing:

Now am I one with those wide-wombed
mediterranean women
who pour forth litters of children,
mouthfuls of kisses and shrieks

their hands always wet and full
in motion

Each is the weaver of her province:
spinning a tight fuzzy world out
of her own body
and distracted mind

The sensuous, almost claustrophobic ambience of female domestic life is evoked in the "smeary congress of kitchens" where mother and children (born and unborn) live "poised on the lip of the spinning / bedroom, kitchen, / vacuum, living/ room" where the firstborn "clings to the cord / of my skirt, afraid yet / of her first step." While obviously procreation is older than the civilized men and women who now bring life into being, Lowther describes it exclusively in terms of the human-made.

In "Coast Range" (from *A Stone Diary*), a poem recalling Earle Birney's "Bushed," Lowther explores the primacy of the natural world, which humanity exploits but cannot wholly subjugate:

The plainness of first things
trees
gravel
rocks
naive root atom
of philosophy's first molecule

The mountains reject nothing
but can crack
open your mind
just by being intractably there

"The land is what's left / after the failure / of every kind of metaphor," she asserts, "[y]ou can gut [it] / blast [it] / to slag / the shapes [it's] made in the sky / cannot be reduced." Lowther admires nature's irreducibility, which transcends our self-interested attempts to destroy it or even contain it with language. She is fascinated by the paradigms that the structures of nature elucidate, existential immutabilities that will outlast us.

Lowther has an especial affinity for our shared human past, exploring it with a lively anthropological, almost geomorphic fervour that I liken to a philosophy of "human geology." This is where the two worlds that preoccupy her—the human and the natural—fully merge. It is best expressed in poems like "Imagine Their Generations" (from "Time Capsule"):

> Imagine their generations a vertical frieze
> the shapes repetitive as an ocean
> the dumb curve of shoulders
> bent to their work, their earth.
> each figure has one hand cupped
> an ambiguous gesture, giving or holding
> corn, metal, pollen, or something intricate
> and bruisable as a lung; or a coal,
> its fragile petals of ash protecting the hand
> from the orange-pink heat
> at the heart of it.

"Feel their shapes in your mind," she extorts, "Imagine now time itself grown dense / as coal, impacted / in that one posture." In "The Dig" (from *A Stone Diary*), Lowther describes the excavation of a site among the lanes of traffic and other conduits of the city where "the ancient world has exposed / a root, large and impervious." Like the diggers who uncover the bones of an almost timeless people, she has "not such love / for the living / who are not finished / or predicted." This "love" of hers allows the bones to tell her—and the reader—stories of men and especially of women whose

> work bent them
> and sex, that soft explosion
> miraculous as rain....

Even their hands
curved around implements,
pounding stones, were worshipping
the cock that made them
round and hollow.

The women address one another and their female descendants, including
Lowther and her readers, asking

Will our bones tell
sisters, what we died of?
how love broke us
in that helplessly desired
breaking, and men
and children ransacked our flesh,
cracked our innermost bones
to eat the marrow.

They question their own legacy. Through this world revealed by the dig Lowther
subtly excavates her own present-day preoccupations with childbearing and co-
existence with men, which are both pleasurable and annihilating. "The Dig" is
perhaps her most complete exposition of the complex feelings she alludes to
in other poems that read as more directly drawn from her own experience of
motherhood, carnality, and love.

In "Woman On/Against Snow" (from *Milk Stone*), Lowther's protagonist
is an Inuit woman:

Figure without landscape,
white with the many names of snow,
she makes her house
of skin and snow.
Alone
For the others are dead,
she is a small Arctic sun
curving space around her.
This world swirls,
changes with every wind.

She must shape the world
by being alive.

Lowther goes on to say that this "first / last human is / poet / shaman / debater / with the universe"; as a mother and midwife who "speaks with the world," she is a model for creativity. The poet, cast in the female mode, is both in touch with the timelessness of life and aware of the power of language to engage polemically with the cosmos. As a woman concerned about the adversity that other women faced regardless of culture, Lowther identifies with how her protagonist makes the best of life's difficult weather. Many readers of this poem today would consider it an oversimplification for Lowther to see this woman—and perhaps herself—as lost or abandoned. Even though she writes with apparent empathy because she assumes that she and her protagonist share similar concerns, Lowther nonetheless does not appear to have considered that the woman could bring an as-nuanced, but different, and culturally specific interpretation to her own experience. "Woman On/Against Snow" must be understood as a poem of its time.

Lowther's human geology finds visceral expression in the title poem of *A Stone Diary*:

Last week I became
aware of details
cubes of fool's gold
green and blue copper
crystal formations
fossils shell casts
iron roses   candied gems....

Today for the first time
I noticed how coarse
my skin has grown
but the stones shine
with their own light

Like silts that mounting pressure transforms into sedimentary rock, life experience leaves its geologic record in the body. Yet the stones, which are mentioned earlier in the poem and whose abrasive surfaces bloody the narrator's hands as she arranges them in "ritual patterns," thus making pictograph-like "blood prints," "grow smoother / and smoother." They stand as metaphors for the poetic process itself, through which the poet, like others before her—whether they are her immediate ancestors or from past millennia, the bloodline uniting her (and us) to them being the humble blood that should harmoniously bond all humans to one another—attempts to record and refine the details of a life.

The mysterious turning to stone that the narrator's rough skin suggests is best explained in passages of "Last Letter to Pablo" (from *A Stone Diary*), an elegy to Neruda, her aesthetic mentor, who died mysteriously in the aftermath of the 1973 Chilean coup:

Always earth was
your substance
grain, ores and bones
elements folded in power
humans patient as time
and weather;
now you too lie with skeletons
heaped about you;
our small crooked hands
touch you for comfort

From the deep hollows
water comes out like stars;
you are changing, Pablo,
becoming an element
a closed throat of quartz
a calyx
imperishable in earth

To become an element, to become elemental, is to enter into a state of al-most-preternatural being; for Lowther, Neruda exemplifies this best, in death as in life. To become aware of the planetary cycles of which we are naturally a part—rather than apart from—we must also recognize how those forces move within us. In "Notes from Furry Creek" (from *A Stone Diary*), Lowther records that

When the stones swallowed me
I could not surface
but squatted
in foaming water
all one curve
motionless,
glowing like agate.

I understood the secret
of a monkey-puzzle tree
by knowing its opposite:
the smooth and the smooth
and the smooth takes,
seduces your eyes
to smaller and smaller
ellipses;
reaching the centre
you become
stone, the perpetual
lavèd god.

The desire to achieve centredness, to unite the natural with the human, animates Lowther's poetry. The need for centredness causes her to relish sensuality however and wherever it manifests itself—in childbirth, in carnality, in nature. It also impels her to expose those forces that deny it through domestic violence ("Kitchen Murder" or "To a woman who died of 34 stab wounds") or through abuses of power so absolute that entire peoples are oppressed ("Chacabuco: The Pit" or "The Age of the Bird"). Lowther aims to engage the heart and mind intellectually as well as sensually, which she explains so eloquently in "Poetry" (from *Final Instructions*):

Firebombs are in the mind
but so is love,
its soft flowering explosion
scattering violent seed
sweet, sweet.

Such violence is
my work's intent.
Come walk with me.

• • •

So, for the reader, is *Time Capsule* worth the walk? For me, it must be clear by now that my answer is affirmative. The strongest poems are drawn from *A Stone Diary*, and the best work from the three previous books published in her lifetime convincingly foreshadows them. All these poems together trace her growing technical abilities: the deft use of line breaks to counterbalance and further the agendas of syntax; the careful, if irregular, use of punctuation; the haunting imagery; and the pure sinuous language "grow[ing] smoother and smoother"—until the poems cease to be structured linguistic entities, but rise off the page, beguiling as holograms.

Had Lowther lived, I suspect she may have combined the poems in *Final Instructions* with the best work found in "Time Capsule" to create an impressive fifth collection. Who can know what further nuances her revisions could have teased out of the poems she'd have chosen to include? Lowther cannot be held accountable for the quality of any of the new poems brought to light here since it was not her decision to publish them in their discovered state. Nor should be the hand that saw them bound into the present volume more than twenty years after her death. Lowther is past accountability, but not judgement. The intention of the "Time Capsule" section is to give the reader a sense of Lowther's unrealized possibilities. Some of the newly discovered poems, such as "Words for My Son: II" and "Random Interview" are one-dimensional, even bland. Others like "Elegy for the South Valley," "The Animals Per Se" and "Ion" exhibit her signature confidence. The achievement that *A Stone Diary* represents, further substantiated by the regular flashes of brilliance in the poems that come after, leads me to believe she would have further broadened her enviable skills and thematic appetite.

I seem to talk about poetry of interest to me with anyone who will listen, and what's said in reply often resonates. While I was reading *Time Capsule*, a friend mentioned a colleague whose son is studying with a scientist who'd taught the Apollo program's astronauts how to ascertain which lunar rocks to bring back to Earth. The scientist believes his young protégé may possess the acuity needed to develop rockhound skills in the astronauts who shall someday voyage to Mars. In light of how sparingly Lowther had mined the metaphoric materiality of humanity's time on Earth, I like to imagine what she might have written in response to our expanding knowledge about the universe through which we spin. Poems like "The Comet" from *Final Instructions* and "Magellan" from "Time Capsule" suggest a growing interest in cosmology. Like that young man who may one day help reshape our understanding of Mars, Lowther might have found material for her poetry in what could be learned from that understanding, perhaps even limning the geomorphic features Earth might share with distant heavenly bodies. Like Neruda's poetry, which Lowther equates with a "bloodstone" (the "dark jewel of history"), hers is "a seed patient as time" that Canadian literature is entrusted to carry into the future. Had she lived, Lowther may have expressed a human geology not just of the Earth, but of the universe.

1997

Diana Brebner: Snow Angel

DIANA BREBNER DIED YOUNG from breast cancer on April 29, 2001. A memorial was held in Ottawa on May 20, the day she would have turned forty-five. It was a beautiful spring evening, with the windows behind the altar of the Unitarian Church allowing those in attendance to meditate on the sweep of the Ottawa River while celebrating her life. Though I had met Diana fourteen years before, the memorial would remind me that I had not known her well. Over the years, we had struck up the sort of easy familiarity and habit of association that exists between poets, which I believe sometimes causes us to feel closer to each other than we are. Though Diana and I saw each other irregularly, especially in the last years of her nine-year struggle with cancer, we still followed each other's poetry, read each other's books, and both ornamented and fueled each other's pursuit of what passes for the writing life.

While as co-editor of *Arc* I have had the opportunity to publish poems of Diana's that appeared in her first two books, *Radiant Life Forms* and *The Golden Lotus*, winners respectively of the Gerald Lampert and Pat Lowther Memorial Awards, it is not the distant paper relationship of author and editor that I will carry forward as my chief memory of her serious, sometimes eccentric concept of our common vocation. In the late 80s, when I had more youthful energy, I selected the featured guests for Ottawa's Tree Reading Series. Diana's first appearance at Tree, which I believe was also her first public reading, stands apart. After the open set, Diana had the lights switched off in the tiny upstairs room where the series then met in the Glebe Community Centre. In the glow of the candles she brought with her and lit on the scarred table that doubled as lectern, Diana seemed to summon up her poems from the impassioned depths that forged them, intoning each line with the magnificence of a brooding Russian mystic. Through her imagination, she drew her audience into the heightened space that she believed poets and poetry must inhabit. It was quite a debut. Who in that room will ever forget the force of epiphany that powered her that night and would continue to transform her into the wise, articulate poet we now mourn?

Another memory: late one night in the autumn of 1990, just after the publication of my fourth book, I answered the door to find Diana on the steps with a bottle of Moët & Chandon champagne, in apology for not attending my launch earlier that month. She explained she could not stop since she had her two small daughters in the back seat of her car. She left as quickly as she had come, and I might have thought her dropping off a bottle of champagne nothing more than a hallucination or a dream had I not moved the physical evidence from apartment to apartment. It was to be the only champagne I would ever receive to mark the publication of any of my books, and sadly no event in my life would seem of sufficient import to open it in the years to follow.

After a decade, I began to worry that my lack of genius for occasions, especially in comparison to Diana's, was letting the bottle go flat. Finally, in absence of a day any more appropriate, on New Year's Day 2000 I shared it with a friend who thought me crazy for putting off such a simple pleasure for as long I had. The bubbly was still remarkably effervescent, I am happy to say, but I have wondered since if my fecklessness or talent for quiet privation had allowed it to mellow and mature. Another bottle of Moët & Chandon has been chilling in my fridge for several months now. While my appetite for indecisiveness is insatiable, the bottle shall not linger there for quite as long. I will think of Diana— and her long-ago gesture of friendship—when I finally open it.

Someone else's memory of Diana, reported to me by a third person, highlights her legendary aptitude for black humour. After she died, I talked on the phone with one of the many fine young Ottawa poets whom she had mentored. Her student related what she described as "another Diana story." Upon hearing that Diana's cancer had spread to her liver, a good friend had offered to bring supper by and spend the evening. When asked what she wanted to eat, Diana deadpanned "liver." The friend, stunned, was ready to take her at her word until she realized the silence that followed was nothing more than a well-placed pause she was expected to fill with laughter. After Diana's student had hung up, I weighed the possibility that Diana had also intended the undiscussed double-entendre. Her mind was far too subtle for her not to be aware, despite the bad news, that she'd implied she was still a liver, that she meant to live what remained of her life with signature brio.

One final memory, this one mine from the time before her cancer was diagnosed. Diana once sent me a card with a poem enclosed that she had dedicated to me. The epigraph it bore, "in camouflage like Finnish marksmen," is a line from a poem by Joseph Brodsky. She had written "Snow Angels" after finishing the Russian poet's collection, To Urania, recalling also that I had studied with

him at Columbia University in New York several years before—a detail of my
biography that had long impressed her. The poem mystified me, however, not
because it was not moving or well written, but because I could not settle on
what message, if any, she had intended for me in particular:

> They come across snow, white & camouflaged,
> and, from our point of disadvantage,
>
> who can tell what they mean? Or even,
> what colour they are, beneath snow
>
> robes, wings, feathers, the primitive
> coverings, weighing their light bodies down.

Normally, when any one of us reads a poem, we hope to find something in it
that speaks to us, but when one is dedicated to us, we feel more personally addressed: the poem must contain a blessing or a warning that the poet had de-
vised for us specially, perhaps thinking we needed guidance:

> Friend, I hope you have seen:
> at least one, up close; no more terror
>
> in that than in white marauding bears
> with their fanged cavities, black and
>
> blood, red, naturally seeking
> you, food, never victims. Snow angels
>
> come. Across darkness you see them
> at their best, holy ghosts of their kind.

I never asked Diana for clarification, embarrassed to betray my failure of imagination or simple thick-headedness:

> Maybe they are as lost as we
> can be in snow. Something,

deep and hungry, swallows them.
And in the shaped holes we find: remains,

some celestial parts, and a last message,
desperate, marked in the snow.

Perhaps her message was no more than that she and I belonged to a community of poets that included Brodsky, that perhaps through me she felt a link to him, a poet whose conviction she admired because his genius was to write poetry of the highest order. A year later, in 1990, "Snow Angels" won the League of Canadian Poets' National Poetry Contest, an accomplishment that may have been the first indication to the wider world that Diana's own star was destined to rise. And rise its "celestial parts" did, and because of the quality of her poetry, may its ascent, through the "shaped holes" it has left, continue higher and higher.

2001

INSIDE THE BLIND

Where Have All the Poets Gone?

AT FIRST BLUSH, SUCH a question seems disingenuous—if not misguided. Today we seem so overrun by poets, ranging from the kitchen-table variety to the most Parnassian, that we could consider drafting them all into a hastily organized equivalent of Katimavik. Before lights out each evening, after picking apples or fighting wildfires in some poetry-deprived purlieu, they can concentrate at last on enjambments rather than on their reputations. With a little mutual distance, we might obtain a little shared peace. Yet, if I fantasize about their sickly, narcissistic eyes staring at me above a face mask, fearful of contagion through my meddlesome editorial suggestions, why do I also find myself speculating about their whereabouts? Why am I not happy with the easy, impatient answer that, sequestered in airless garrets, tens of thousands of paddle-dipping, armchair E. Pauline Johnsons and orchidaceous Frank Oliver Calls are hiding their faint light in their overstuffed desk drawers while harbouring delusions of fame and rejection? Or is it that I am looking for "real poets," as one fellow literary-magazine editor recently suggested?

I don't think so, though many of the "real poets" in this country appear to be less zealous in their publishing habits than the pretenders are. Many seem to have relaxed the self-discipline that might otherwise motivate them to send their *finished* poems to literary magazines. In other words, they appear to have put aside aspects of the professionalism required in other fields not only to realize ability, but to tap opportunity. As a literary-magazine editor, I am puzzled by Canada's known and unknown poets alike. I have no idea what they are doing with their beaux—and not so beaux—mots. Fiction submissions outnumber poetry submissions at the *Malahat* by at least three to one. The flood of the former in comparison to the trickle of the latter sometimes forces me to revise the traditional equal representation of the two genres in each issue to an imbalance that allows the quarterly to continue to live up to its decades-long reputation for publishing "the best" that the country has to offer. Canada's poets, whom I have always thought of as being starved for the kind of recognition that is sated only through frequent publication, do not seem to be beating down my door en masse. Why, then, am I constantly told by both the "established" and the "emerging" (ugly terms espoused by the granting agencies) that to publish between the *Malahat's* covers remains a high moment in any poet's life?

So, if our poets have not all started writing novels, what are they up to? A perusal of new books of Canadian poetry sent as review copies to the *Malahat* reveals that few magazines are listed as publication credits. Compare this to books by American poets and you will see our peers south of the border have cultivated very different strategies for realizing their ambitions and delusions, for they have often already published most, if not the entire contents of their books in magazines. Some even go so far as to indicate which poems have appeared where, as if to provide further testament to their poems' complex public lives. An acknowledgements page acts as an alternate to the contents page, a skeleton key to the literary world in which a poet aspires, even succeeds, to function. As I read any collection by an American, I find myself checking where each poem first saw light; I muse about what more this might tell me about the poem, the magazine, and the poet. My reading pleasure is increased.

Why do American poets appear so zealous in their submission habits when compared with their Canadian colleagues? A partial answer might be found in the National Endowment for the Arts' requirement that poets must have a demonstrated publication record in order to be eligible to apply. Recent NEA guidelines indicate "between January 1, 1999, and March 1, 2006, an applicant must have published a volume of forty-eight or more pages of poetry; or twenty or more different poems or pages of poetry in five or more literary journals, anthologies, or publications which regularly include poetry as a portion of their format. Up to sixteen poems may be in a single volume of poetry of fewer than forty-eight pages. This volume, however, may count as only one of the required five places of publication. Applicants may use online publications to establish up to fifty percent of their eligibility, provided that such publications have competitive selection processes and stated editorial policies."

While Canadian granting agencies at all levels of government also use publication as a base criterion for eligibility, to my knowledge none sets it within the context of a time frame. The NEA's range of seven years and two months from which support material must be drawn may at first seem generous, but given how competitive it is to publish in the United States, maintaining a sufficient number of credits can be arduous even for poets of high accomplishment. While guaranteeing that they remain eligible for NEA funding cannot be the only reason why American poets send submissions to magazines by the mailbag—a U.S. magazine of the *Malahat's* reputation typically receives ten times (or more) as many unsolicited submissions—I cannot help but feel envious of such a simple synergy between policy and practice.

In their own defense, Canadian poets could counter that, as a magazine editor, I already have too much to choose from and should therefore be happy with the degree of support shown by those among them ready enough to submit. And besides, how would the *Malahat* cope with ten times as many submissions to read per year? In other words, I should be content. And to an extent, they are right, for on occasion, I do discover a poet previously unknown to me whose work is refreshing, even awe-inspiring. And, yes, I have to admit that many fine household names, if any poet can be such a phenomenon, do indeed send their work—thank God!

Nevertheless, when I have quizzed some already well-known Canadian poets, many plead submission burnout. I would have thought that sending their work out regularly would have hardened them, but the inverse seems to be the case. I can only conclude that they have increasingly become more sensitive to the possibility of rejection instead of less, as if submitting were akin to the persistent picking of a scab or being exposed repeatedly to lead. They say that they no longer can tolerate the humiliation of waiting for a reply that may not arrive for months, especially if the outcome ends up being wholesale rejection. Magazines are for the aspiring, they rationalize, are for unproven poets with more stamina and stores of patience (*Yeah, right...*). This attitude rankles, for when I was new on the scene eons back, it was a thrill to publish in a magazine alongside Richard Outram, say, or Phyllis Webb. Whatever happened to mentorship or even peermanship? To my mind, apprentice and seasoned poets should strike a symbiotic relationship between the pages of a magazine for the reader's benefit: the pleasurable shock of the new balanced by a regularly fed awe for the avidly followed.

Though any literary magazine endeavours to recruit the best writing available, publishing in one should be viewed by poets as less a litmus test for quality than a testing ground, a laboratory where they may try out new work, often below the radar of unappeasable reviewers who seem more interested in books anyway. While granting agencies more and more attempt to impose commercial values upon literary magazines, true editors are not moved by them—who on earth is going to make millions publishing poems and stories? The real risk that they take in selecting and publishing poetry (and fiction) is aesthetic, one more often about seeing potential and possibility in the work itself. Who knows whose writing will define a generation? And if some experiment is in retrospect a bust, well, it will soon disappear into the comforting oblivion of the backlist.

A literary magazine creates a place where writers can meet their readers and casually converse one on one, however briefly, with the editor as moderator. While publishing a poem in a magazine can provide no guarantee that the eventual book into which it might be collected will be any good, a magazine appearance does offer "feedback"—starting with the acceptance itself, which at minimum says the poem reads well and convinces. In 1912, when Harriet Monroe founded *Poetry* (Chicago), the English-speaking world's quintessential literary magazine, she described it as "a chance [for poets] to be heard in their own place, without the limitations imposed by the popular magazine. In other words, while the ordinary magazines must minister to a large public little interested in poetry, this magazine will appeal to, and it may be hoped, will develop, a public primarily interested in poetry as an art, as the highest most complete expression of truth and beauty." While not every literary magazine can be *Poetry* and define (for some) what the genre will be for nearly a century, they each can be a "place of their own" for the poets who publish in them, a place where, page to page, they can debate with one another and with their readers about important things—"beauty is truth, truth beauty" being among them. The late Ralph Gustafson, editor of several editions of the *Penguin Book of Canadian Verse* as well as a Governor General's Award-winning poet, used to say that a poem does not exist—does not enter into the conversation—if it is left in a drawer. All I am saying is that our poets should open their drawers more often.

By no means do I want to cast aspersions on the work that is sent in for consideration to the *Malahat*, especially on those poems that it does accept. Still, how can I not help but wonder as to why the unsolicited submissions of poetry seem so thin these days? While our "established" poets nurse their wounds and embroider their scars, have our "emerging" poets found new, more immediate, and satisfying ways to converse with their audience through e-zines, blogs, listservs, and social-media sites that have a breadth of reach unimaginable in Monroe's time, let alone fifteen—or even five—years ago? For readers, is the proliferation of such unmediated access sufficient?

I don't suppose literary magazines like the *Malahat* are on their way out quite yet—it would be a sad prospect to consider just months before marking its fortieth anniversary this fall, especially when I so ardently believe in the intimate tête-à-tête that literary magazines create between writers and readers. Or is Canada's poetry simply at a moment of feckless transition while its fiction—at least based on the startling work we get to choose from at the *Malahat*—moves from strength to strength?

These are fighting words, I know, but all I ask is to be proven wrong. I urge our poets to send out their work—poems they have charged with real passion and wit—and participate in the lively forum that our literary magazines are able to create when at their best. In the December 2006 issue of *Poetry*, editor Christian Wiman speaks to the appropriate rarity of true poetry in any age. In Canada, rarity may apply not only to quality but to availability as well.

2007

Aspiration, Devotion, and Community:
A Short Introduction to the Long Life
of a Little Magazine

WITH THE PUBLICATION OF *We All Begin in a Little Magazine: Arc and the Promise of Canada's Poets, 1978–1998,*[1] *Arc's* editors celebrate the magazine's twentieth anniversary. Founded in 1978 at Carleton University, it is part of a Canadian literary-magazine movement that rode the wave of vibrant, sometimes profligate literary production that Canada's now legendary Centennial year had spurred. In the mid- to late 1970s, many magazines were founded to document, shape, provide a forum and cultivate an audience for contemporary writing. After several issues, *Arc* left the shelter of Carleton's financial umbrella, receiving funding from various levels of government as well as the support of its subscribers, faithful and fickle. Associate editors came and went, as did editors. Without the volunteerism and support of many poets and readers in the Ottawa literary community, *Arc* would have long ago gone the way of lead type.

In "We All Begin in a Little Magazine,"[2] the short story by Ottawa-born writer Norman Levine that lends its title to this anthology, an established, expatriate Canadian novelist rents the house of a London doctor for three weeks one summer. It turns out that in his spare time Dr. Jones, the house's owner, publishes *ABC*, a small literary magazine whose potential contributors in his absence telephone or drop by the house at all hours to check on the status of their submissions, to seek advice and encouragement, or even to request a bed for the night. The chaos their interruptions create provokes the novelist to recall

---

1   The Arc Poetry Society co-published Arc's twentieth-anniversary issue with Carleton University Press, an arrangement that I negotiated with CUP's editor-in-chief, John Flood. Just over a decade before, as owner of Penumbra Editions, he had released the first edition of my collection of poems about Emily Carr, *West of Darkness*.
2   Norman Levine's widely anthologized story, "We All Begin in a Little Magazine," originally appeared in his collection of short stories, *Thin Ice*, published in 1979 by Deneau and Greenberg Publishers Ltd., of Ottawa.

his own beginnings as a writer when, having arrived in England immediately after the Second World War, he and his colleagues first began trying to get their own early work published and have "careers." The little magazines of their apprenticeships, like *ABC* (and *Arc*), were indispensable to their nascent sense of literary selfhood. "We used to send our stories, optimistically, to *The New Yorker* and *The Atlantic*. But that was like taking a ticket in a lottery. It was the little magazines who published us, who gave us encouragement and kept us going."

Even today, any editor of a "little magazine" who reads Levine's story cannot fail to recognize something of themselves in Levine's description of Dr. Jones's office: "The floor was cluttered with papers and magazines and manuscripts with letters and envelopes attached. On a wooden table, a large snap file had correspondence. A box had cheques for small amounts. There were also several pound notes, loose change, a sheet of stamps, and two packages of cigarettes.... There was typing paper, large envelopes, a typewriter, a phone, telephone directories, and some galleys hanging on a nail in the wall. A smaller table had an in-and-out tray to do with his medical work, more letters, and copies of the *Lancet*. The neatest part of the room was the area where unsold copies of *ABC* were on the floor against the far wall." Despite a glassy-eyed but forward-looking migration to computers, email, electronic artwork, and websites, this passage well illustrates how close to a cottage industry the business of running of a literary magazine was and has stayed. To keep going demands constant, sometimes solitary, anonymous acts of devotion. Before lavishing attention on the fine details of style and craft, literary-magazine editors must often first push above the suffocating tenacity of scheduling design and printing, monitoring renewal rates, and paying invoices. In Canada, increasingly more insecure granting agencies persist in re-engineering the management of a literary magazine into an exhausting trapeze act of accountability that pertains less to literature and more to unpleasurable appeasement.

To subscribers and casual newsstand browsers, the sleight-of-hand mechanics of editing, production, and financial spreadsheets are invisible and secondary. Any literary magazine is primarily about the new work of the authors it publishes and the recent books it reviews. In *We All Begin in a Little Magazine*, readers will rediscover poems that appeared in *Arc* over the last twenty years by some of Canada's best writers who began and have sometimes continued to publish in *Arc* and its peers. These poems show their authors to advantage, turning the spotlight back to an initial brush with publication or else showing them in full maturity, or, more likely, somewhere in between. Their combined presence in *We All Begin in a Little Magazine* suggests how the promise illustrated early in a poet's writing life evolves toward a confidence that is earned through years of commitment to craft, the promise kept.

Levine's narrator recalls the sense of community that the little magazines fostered in his time, and how the little bits of money paid to contributors like himself for a poem, a book review, or a short story momentarily helped make ends meet by covering a meal or two, or perhaps by paying for a packet of cigarettes. Levine's is inarguably a nostalgic view of the down-and-out life of the novice, but it is difficult to dismiss his description of the timeless satisfactions of publication itself. Like the hackneyed cigarette smoked after sex, appearing in print remains almost as good as, and sometimes better than, the act of writing itself. And like all other impulsive acts, making one's deathless writings available in editions of two hundred or three hundred has unanticipated, long-term effects: "I had complete faith then in those little magazines. What I didn't know was that what they bred was infectious. They infected a lot of young people with the notion that to be involved with literature was somehow to be involved with the good life. And by the time you learned differently, it was usually too late."

The faith, ill-advised or not, that Norman Levine celebrates goes both ways. The editors of small magazines like *Arc* also become "infected" by the unshakeable, idealistic belief that what their contributors have to say and how they say it, not to mention the act of publishing them, matters and is even *ennobling*. On good days, they believe that by publishing work their authors and readers may one day view as juvenilia, works-in-progress or, worse, candidates for burning, they are in some small and speculative way helping to nurture a national literature. Poor dears, we won't break the bad news to them, will we?

The current editors of *Arc* would nevertheless argue that the poets represented in this anthology have become or are in the process of becoming significant voices in Canadian writing. Certainly they are important to the history of *Arc*. That the magazine's changing corps of editors and associate editors have had the opportunity since 1978 to "encourage" such poets and to "keep [them] going" is as it should be and is without doubt our most important reason to exist. We are in complete empathy with the impetus of Norman Levine's short story, even if its narrator was eventually driven to complete distraction by the endless parade of Dr. Jones's and *ABC*'s literary hopefuls and proteges. By the time his three-week holiday was over, he was more than glad to vacate the selfless doctor's house in favour of the indifferent quiet of the seaside resort town he calls home. So much for the good life he dreamed of in his youth....

Despite the sometimes soul-destroying work, nothing is more satisfying for a literary-magazine editor than to take delivery of the latest issue or for its contributors to arrive home one day and discover a copy—with their poem printed *correctly* inside—awaiting them in the mail. After twenty years and forty issues in print, the editors of and contributors to *Arc* can only hope that our shared readership past, present, and future has, does, and will continue to feel exactly the same way.

1998

Getting on the Island: Literary Contests as Reality TV on The Aquarium Channel™

A NUMBER OF YEARS ago, a fellow poet recounted the dinner conversation that took place after a public reading he'd given. The first impulse of his host—a prize-winning poet of national distinction—was to ask him how many awards he had won. In the *Mouse-That-Roared* celebrity culture that is the sad lot of contemporary Canadian poetry, the Griffin Poetry Prize being a soul-bewildering aberration, such a conversation-killer strikes me as not only rude, but ludicrous. Who but a few poetry mavens and a handful of their hangers-on would care? I guess it's desirable to imagine oneself to be an angelfish cutting a swath through a fishbowl of guppies.

Such self-entitled one-upmanship points to the dogfish-in-the-manger pre-occupation with winning that for at least a decade has been overtaking Canadian writing with increasing appetite. More and more literary magazines across the country are launching contests to compete with such venerable leviathans as the re-branded CBC Literary Awards (once upon a time more humbly known as the CBC Literary Competition), with each magazine anxious to cast its net for a share of the contest dollar. Thanks to an exponential growth in society's interest in writing as recreation as well as a vocation—a plenitude that makes the logorrhoeic Confessional poets of the 50s and 60s, in retrospect, appear few in number—writers today are in such abundance you'd think, if they were cod, that the fishery had never been closed down and undersubscribed editors able, like fishers, to walk on water on the backs of those willing, yes teeming, even thronging to pay for the pleasure of being hooked, gaffed, and filleted. I have come to wonder, however, if there are not more contest winners and losers in Canada than readers of not only poetry, but of every genre—except those proliferating self-help guides, such as the late 1980s classic, *How to Get Ahead in Advertising*. Oops, that's a movie, but it helps me segue into my next point: contests are the literary world's answer to reality television.

Let's market the pilot for this particular show as *Getting on the Island*. And it does come with a few refreshing, if unchallenging handicaps:

- You don't know who your competitors are;
- You don't (necessarily) know who the judges are;
- You submit your hastily finished entry, without the requirement to improve your chance to win on the next episode;
- The number of episodes is mercifully finite: enter, wait, multiple-submit, win or lose;
- If you win, you get to appear in print, laughing all the way to the bank while secretly hoping that the magazine is not cash-flow-challenged or at least has overdraft protection;
- Being read is possible, not inevitable.

On the plus side,

- Unlike more typical reality-TV contestants, you are seldom subjected to humiliation before a viewing audience of millions;
- You're unaware of the ridicule—or worse, odium—with which your hastily finished entry may be held by the screeners and/or judge(s);
- You're unaware that for many magazines the success of a contest is largely determined by the number of Johnny-One-Note entries received in comparison to the few sent in by those aspiring to be Gertrude Stein or John Milton, an ever-shrinking minority of angelfish who stand out against a near-parthenogenetic majority of guppies (it's true, more than half of contest entrants are female) who happily pay for the joy of being assigned a number and summarily scanned, before being dispatched to the plant, where their viscera—their hearts and what passes for souls—is turned into cat food;
- You can only be voted *onto* the island by the judge(s), not off, since you were never on the island in the first place.

At worst,

- You get a one-year subscription to a magazine, which you need not read and may well throw, issue after issue until expiry (of the subscription, not you), into recycling;
- Should your hastily written piece win, *Getting on the Island*'s ratings are still low because magazines only run contests to plump up sagging circulation;

- The majority of said circulation is composed of other entrants who read your prize-winning piece with an admixture of envy and contempt.

At best,

- You pay a small amount of money for the opportunity to win a *slightly larger small amount of money*;
- Should your hastily finished piece win, it may "benefit" from a copy or substantive edit prior to publication—or maybe not;
- It gets tossed back because it's the undersized fingerling you fear it to be;
- You get more time to work on it before submitting it to another contest in the belief that it will now swim more capably, beyond the grasp of the undertow sniffing around the next island;
- Your hastily finished piece will be evolved enough to gain an insouciant, devilfish-may-care foothold (surprising, because until now it had no feet) on the remote beach of temporary acclaim and breathe with real-enough lungs, rather than gills, and maybe even walk erect, with head held high, like one of the few, like a normal, "human" poem.

In sum:

- However much you'd like it to be, winning a contest is not as iconic or career-capping as being one of the astronauts who will one day plant a flag on that microdot in the sky called Mars, while competing nations watch enviously from Earth, their servers so completely overloaded from playing *World of Warcraft* that NASA's streaming keeps cutting out;
- Here the parallel falls down, for in a literary contest your adversaries are not usually from competing nations, but are your fellow citizens who, like you, have thrown their names aspirationally into the hat. Sure, the veterans chosen already know how to pilot a fighter jet and can pump 300 kilos sans steroids, but, given a leg-up, so can you. Your competition is not the other side (those so wealthy they can fork over millions to bribe their way onto the rocket are a nation unto themselves), but the penniless hordes of stargazers (your fellow entrants), who all want to plant a flag on the red planet before you do (dream on, losers);

- Okay, maybe the parallel is not as off (the air) base as I had thought, *Top Gun* pun intended. Perhaps you've instead signed up to fight in a closer war on Earth, not dreaming to be another wealthy has-been who blasts off to build a mine on another planet or asteroid. You can't forget that the drones (the entered poems) that you operate remotely may neutralize an excess of hostile operatives—or perhaps you're counting on it—so that someone on the side of right (and taste) gets to claim a contested island somewhere between Vanuatu and Iceland with that bloody, elusive flag;

- Maybe an even more frightening contemporary metaphor would be to imagine that you're jobless and living in a basement in the suburbs. To make some fast money as a contest winner, you decide to wire yourself up as a suicide bomber who blows away the competition. So much for your trenchant turns of phrase. You never get to enjoy the fifteen minutes of going viral because, like all the great, you're still unread... I mean, dead.

However sit-on-the-edge-of-your-fishbowl-exciting I might be making The Aquarium Channel™ begin to sound, please note: it's still The Aquarium Channel™. Fellow watchers nationwide, aren't you bored yet? Are my metaphors overfishing? In the scenarios above, has anyone besides me noticed that there're no fish in the tank? And, wait a second: no tank?

Did someone change the channel?

Fish or no fish, the more news-breaking question is this: how did we get to this point where all we care about is starring in future seasons of *Getting on the Island*? But, before continuing, I should first concede the point you've been thinking amongst yourselves. As the former co-editor of *Arc Poetry Magazine* and the present editor of *The Malahat Review*, I have been responsible for inaugurating or managing eight contests that still run today, each one pitched to a different entrant demographic in order to maximize both magazines' share of the contest dollar, which at the rate it's appreciating could soon be a world currency equal in strength to the 人民币 (or Chinese renminbi).

In 1996, with the help of *Arc*'s board, I established the Poem of the Year Contest in response to what I perceived to be a changed funding environment that placed more emphasis on financial viability. The Canada Council for the Arts had overhauled its periodicals program and, as a victim of Mike Harris's Common Sense Revolution, a much-reduced Ontario Arts Council, once arguably the most enlightened arts agency in the country, came up with a funding formula that seemed more based on quantitative rather than qualitative measures—or a frightening merger of the two. If memory serves, one part of the OAC form asked applicants to quantify excellence. In order to maintain the support of these agencies—as well as from the Regional Municipality of Ottawa-Carleton and the former City of Ottawa prior to amalgamation into a national capital with more control over its suburbs, which is the equivalent of *Toronto Life* appropriating the ill-will of *Maclean's* 905 readers to use it for fashion-conscious evil—it became apparent that we had to increase circulation in order to survive, so that poets in Canada would have a national magazine available to them for the publication of their work.

In absence of a bottomless marketing budget to attract subscribers, starting a contest seemed the best strategy, especially in comparison to launching a direct-mail campaign, which would never pay for itself and sadly be treated by recipients not as a message in a bottle cast up at their feet by a fast-rising tide of financial angst, but as noisome, unopened junk mail. With a subscription offered for "free" upon the receipt of an entry fee, new subscribers are netted painlessly by contests (in comparison to other methods that, like a booty call after a binge of drinking, lead to less midnight sex and to more of a next-day administrative hangover), bringing in the fast money necessary not only to pay the winners, but also to cover a modest judge's fee, advertising, and increased production costs. What could be easier, what was there not to love? Up until this point, the waters around the island had been sparsely populated. Not only were we attracting fish in quantities we'd never enjoyed before, we were landing a few good ones.

However, my eyes slowly began to open. That first year, I was so disappointed in the poems that the final judge had selected for first, second, and third place from the fifty finalists that the board had screened in, I established Editor's Choice. Each member of the board involved in reading the entries was invited to choose a poem for publication from among the forty-seven remaining finalists. It was a way of drawing some of these overlooked poems into the magazine.

In retrospect, I think Editor's Choice was one of the best ideas I've had as a designer of contests. Now in its fifteenth year as part of the Poem of the Year Contest, it continues to shine light on other worthy poems and helps mitigate some dark aspects of the contest trade: those that pit poet against poet in a kind of competition that I have become less convinced is able to discern lasting quality, but has more to do with a poet's ability to write the kind of poem that gets noticed. Is an angelfish, however stylish or adept at marshalling its fins, really just a guppy with a boa? Are some guppies really more like stealth hammerhead sharks that it takes more than the time available (i.e., almost none) to detect?

For, without meaning to denigrate them, it has become apparent that certain kinds of poems win, an observation underscored by the small school of angelfish who with regularity win or place in contests. Now, in comparison to their deadbeat guppy peers, these writers may only be well-disciplined professionals who enter contests because, thankfully, they perceive them to be much-needed lures that keep them writing (WE LOVE YOU GUYS!). However, because these competent few do keep winning contests mounted by a growing and diverse cohort of magazines, I've begun to wonder if the legitimate virtues of their work are also more amenable to a harried, quick-and-easy, permanent-press kind of taste that contest screeners and judges tend to share. Perhaps these more graspable poems inadvertently echo what I have before characterized as a prevailing trend in Canadian poetry: bland eloquence. Invoke a landscape or a cityscape, mimic a few plangent EMO guitar riffs, apply the back of your hand to any one of a number of well-mapped conjugal, extra-curricular, or familial acupressure points, and *blah, blah, blah* . . . you're on the island. Put it this way, I doubt a L=A=N=G=U=A=G=E poet would win many, if any, of today's contests. Erín Moure and Christian Bök, independent-minded barracudas that they are, would likely be fish food. It's worthy of note that *West Coast Line* does not have a contest of its own. Are most other literary magazines collectively and unconsciously celebrating the same kind of poem, almost as if, in a shared plot to take over the world, they are collectively auditioning for clones of the *Führer* for an angelfish remake—*"Sieg heil,. swish!"*—of *The Boys from Brazil*? Hardly, but after three decades of contests, literary magazines are still caught up in the regimens of survival.

And speaking of survival regimens, another early observation that circulation data have yet to refute: very few contest entrants are ever converted into regular subscribers. In their defense, many writers say that entering contests is their way of supporting magazines, and it's a defense I accept. However, the vast majority of contest entrants do not seem to evince such values. Comparing contest-subscription lists year upon year brings to light a smaller number of repeat contestants than I, as an editor and contest designer, would like to see. As much as I like guppies, and by these I don't mean gay urban professionals, though I like them too and am also on the lookout for a GPS (gay-positioning system) good enough to work on land and underwater (to hell with gaydar), and like shooting fish in barrels, I want to feel confident that they represent a growing readership for the authors the magazines do publish. Increasingly, I have my doubts.

During my seven years at *The Malahat Review*, I have increased the number of annual contests from one to four, one for each annual issue of the magazine. These contests cover almost every permutation of the genres that the magazine publishes and are tailored to attract the writers who typically work in them. Almost every aspect of the *Malahat*'s operations is geared to increasing the aggregate number of entrants we receive through all the contests. For one reason only, I've made *Malahat* a lean, mean contest machine not unlike the great white shark terrorizing the lemming-like inhabitants of Amity in Steven Spielberg's *Jaws*: to ensure its circulation surpasses the 5,000 paid copies we need per annum to be re-admissible for support from the newly tweaked and renamed Canada Periodical Fund, a program foisted upon the magazine world in 2010 by the Department of Canadian Heritage under the Harper government. While I do relish pointing my finger at the present hegemony, the ancien régime was hardly better, for it was during the Chrétien era, when Paul Martin was finance minister, that everything began to change.[1]

Nothing in the CPF's three basic eligibility criteria focuses on quality, by which I mean excellence. Magazines need only be Canadian-owned (a kind of quality that does make sense); feature content that is 80% Canadian-authored (though so much for providing Canadian readers with the occasional substantial introduction to writing from other parts of the world edited by Canadians knowledgeable about the needs of Canadian readers); and have the above-mentioned minimum circulation (which is much easier for consumer magazines to achieve and even surpass, though even they cannot do so in their sleep). Many in the Canadian cultural community feel that the new benchmark for circulation was set purposely to exclude literary and scholarly periodicals. The only argument the Department of Canadian Heritage has ever proffered to justify this change and its effect on the literary-magazine community was to allege that these particular grants, given their small size, "consumed" far more

---

1   In 2017, the Department of Canadian Heritage of the Justin Trudeau government lowered the minimum annual circulation required to be eligible to apply for support to 3500 paid copies, which will mean that many more small-circulation literary journals can potentially obtain funding.

departmental resources to administer than was deemed justifiable to taxpayers. This is always the first pro-forma line of defense, one made without ever acknowledging that the poets of this country pay their share of not-so-ill-gotten gains, a share inevitably accrued from other income sources, to the Canada Revenue Agency. Even guppies (and the occasional angelfish or barracuda) deserve to swim through the castle in the Department of Canadian Heritage's fishbowl, knowing it has every appointment they need to disappear into its imaginative corners from dungeon to turret—especially since, despite their aversion to fat cats, they too have ponied up for the kitty.

Most of Canada's literary magazines, with few other quick fixes available to them, have started their first contests, or have expanded the number of contests they run, in order to meet criteria that Canadian Heritage knows are onerous for them to attain. To make their contests effective, they must commit ever higher percentages of their scant human and financial resources to them, which is ironic since the Department excluded these magazines from their program precisely because they burned up too much staff time, and we all know time is money in this fish-eat-fish world. The Canada Periodical Fund would argue that it has other programs, such as Business Innovations, to which these magazines may apply. That may be true, but these are for one-time projects that provide little long-term stability for small magazines. The real question is: where do Canadian Heritage's values really fall? Is it truly interested in fostering the slow evolution of a culture that includes literary accomplishment, which literary magazines are suited to cultivating, or is it more concerned with bums in seats at any cost? Does it even care if those bums read?

This year, as I completed *The Malahat Review*'s grant applications, I noticed something telling: while the number of subscriptions tied to contests is increasing at a healthy, reassuring rate, the number of "non-contest" subscriptions has gone down. In other words, the number of subscribers unmotivated by the need to get on the island is smaller, percentage-wise. While this trend attests to the enviable resolve that *Malahat* staff has found to secure a growing share of the contest dollar, I find it troubling. Is appealing to the competitive instinct the only reliable strategy left to us to grow our circulation? Instead of converting contest subscribers, out of a love of literature, into regular ones, which is the long-term goal of any marketing plan, perhaps the reverse is true. Maybe *Malahat* is converting its small following of regular subscribers into contest-aholics. What happened to curating the best content possible in order to maintain and expand a faithful readership?

Last year, the British Columbia Arts Council revamped its grant application form, introducing, without warning, a new emphasis on "creating community." Thinking on the fly, I argued that contests help build a more broad-based readership for our contributors while exposing entrants of diverse abilities to our contributors' work in order to give them a sense of where to set the bar to hone and test their mettle: "self-improvement" as a "group activity," like a pottery class or yoga, being a laudable community value. The letter spelling out the results of our otherwise successful application revealed that the jury disagreed with me without offering further explanation. Perhaps the elephant overcrowding the jury room is that no true "community-creating" endeavour should ever be tainted by the self-interested intake of filthy lucre. Tell that to the national charities, many of which attempt to hook donors with proffered gifts of calendars and self-adhesive address labels. It's easy to be high-minded when divvying up an increasingly miniscule grant sinkhole (the gutting of arts support in British Columbia is a fish tale for another fish-fry), but how can any jury or government now be myopic enough to deny that the "community" of readers magazines like *The Malahat Review* or *Arc* serve is largely composed of contest entrants? It's time the granting agencies come up for air and smell the stink they're helping to create.

I have wandered very far in tone from the beginning of this article, which is part of an *Arc Poetry Annual* with the possibly tongue-in-cheek theme of Poet vs. Poet (or maybe it should be Angelfish vs. Angelfish, Angelfish vs. Guppy, or Guppy vs. Guppy?). All kidding aside, despite the fact I have been joking around while acknowledging my very deep reservations about how contests and awards are shaping literary magazines and literary culture in the age of reality TV, I can't see any way forward at present without them. Apart from selling back issues at everything-must-go prices—a legitimate ploy, I might add—there are few other Band-Aid solutions that, without taking too much of a bath financially, will allow us to "earn back" the capital and grudging respect of the current ilk of culture politicos. With their used-car-salesmen aesthetics, it must be hard for them to appreciate the real merit of everything else we are doing besides running contests and encouraging their winners to climb up to the next rung in the fish ladder, the National Magazine Awards. *The Malahat Review*'s contest winners have had remarkable success, especially in the NMA's poetry category—and such wins are no doubt noted with checkmarks in our file. As much as I enjoy watching the magazine snag golds and silvers and am extremely happy for the talented authors who are awarded them, I have come to wonder if even these wins help to perpetuate what I fear has become no more than a fishy and desperate cycle of fleeting but addictive recognition in a culture that values consensus only.

Maybe my real message is not about poet vs. poet at all, but poet vs. an unwelcome new kind of fish in the sea, a garbage fish with no literary values of its own. Or maybe it's not about the fish itself, but about the introduction of a new kind of fishing. After all, even garbage fish are worth writing about and should not be shunned. Are literary magazines no longer the islands of excellence visited by those of discerning or idiosyncratic tastes? Are they instead being turned into roving, industrial-scale, shark-like fishing trollers launched to ply the seas in order to catch as much unwitting prey as possible—without discrimination or the time to drop anchor to think about the consequences—by dragging baited lines festooned with ever shinier hooks?

2012

Inside the Blind: On Editing Poetry

Is it ever possible to retrace, let alone imagine, the sleights of "unseen hands" behind the editing of poetry, "that most personal and mysterious of literary art forms"? Journalist Sameer Rahim ponders this conundrum in the *Telegraph* after Scottish poet John Burnside won Britain's T. S. Eliot Prize in 2012. What manner of succor and support does a poet need or even ask for? Rahim attempts to "lay bare" the koans of poetry-editing esteemed by the major publishers of the genre in the U.K.—Faber, Picador, Jonathan Cape, Carcanet, and Bloodaxe—and as experienced by some of the most successful British poets. Most of their in-house editors are poets too, no surprise. The stakes are high, Rahim contends, as he seeks to understand "the effects and risks of this little-understood practice." What the reputation of that nation's verse relies upon apparently comes down to something very subtle. At Picador, according to Scottish poet Don Paterson, the editing of poetry "depends upon tiny shifts of sense and emphasis, context and connection." Matthew Hollis, an English poet and editor at Faber, captures the job best when he says "an editor listens to an author tuning into their poems."

In "The mystery of poetry editing: from T. S. Eliot to John Burnside," Rahim expends a judicious amount of copy tendering an answer to a single question: can only poets edit poets? However simply put this question may appear, the mere posing of it surely affirms most poetry skeptics' worst suspicion that poets constitute a gnomic cult only accountable to its members. Yet, if poets hope to have a readership even larger than their own increasing numbers, they should include among their readers adept editors who have never sprung a rhythm. To be a good poetry editor, it's more important to be an insightful reader, I'd argue, than a practitioner. Many poets are so unable to back out of their own aesthetic culs-de-sac, they are of no use to their fellow sufferers.

When those of us who do edit poetry admit that we engage in this strange activity, non-poetry readers typically ask, "How can you edit poetry? It's so personal!" Our puzzled interrogators must envision the composition of poetry to be a solipsistic pursuit, and any attempt to contain a poet's ennui or to map better ways in or out of the inward-looking, labyrinthine results of such artistic folly to be itself folly. A shadow of a shadow of a mirror on the wall. Who is the most agonized of them all? How is an editor supposed to know?

Because I believe that poetry is not a form of "self-expression" but of "expression," and therefore something to be shared as well as grasped, albeit on its own terms, it makes room for the editor to act as a mediator of sober or not-so-sober second thought between poets and their readers by advancing the latter's understanding of what the former means. While poets have developed the discipline to anticipate how readers will experience their poems and revise them accordingly, they can benefit from an adroit editor's awareness of how poems work.

I have assisted poets with their labours for over thirty years. In addition to editing many book-length manuscripts, I co-edited *Arc* for thirteen years, from 1990 to 2003, and edited *The Malahat Review* for fourteen, from 2004 to 2018. As well, I did my time as the editor of student journals in my undergraduate years. Being attentive to what Paterson calls "tiny shifts" is how I'd describe editing poetry at the micro level. I enjoyed this close work as a literary-magazine editor, but though time happily disappeared while I'd edit someone's poem, I never had enough of it in a workday to lose myself for long stretches. Perhaps there never can be sufficient time available because, when held before the mirror of the mind's eye, a poem can inspire infinite reflections. Still, before any such reflective work can begin, "larger shifts" must be addressed at the macro level first, not in a single poem but between many poets and many poems. Though I never had adequate time in my schedule for these shifts either, it's at this stage that manuscripts are identified and recruited for publication. The macro and the micro are symbiotic: you can't edit a poem without first acquiring it.

In 2014, the *Malahat* received around 1200 submissions of poetry, each comprising up to six poems. This means that the magazine's poetry board and I considered up to 7200 poems, however cursorily. That year, we published only ninety-nine poems by fifty-five poets, with every poem sent to the *Malahat* only having a 1.4 percent chance of being accepted. Anyone who assumes that submitting to literary magazines doesn't involve being at the mercy of very tough peer review is mistaken. Overall, I found that the number of accepted poems in comparison to the number of poems submitted never changed substantially from year to year, and the poems needed to have weight-bearing bones in order to survive the selection process. Usually the poetry appearing in the *Malahat* and in *Arc* was sufficiently polished when accepted, though there were always exceptions where suggestions of a substantive nature were required. It took trial and error to know how and when to provide feedback, and while I refined what I know about managing poets at the *Malahat*, I cut my teeth on and broke a few limbs over the editor/poet relationship at *Arc*. I learned more from missteps than from any sly sleights of hand. The following example was my Rubicon.

Sometime during my tenure at *Arc*, a young poet submitted a very promising, multi-part poem that I felt was not yet ready for publication. I provided her with detailed comments and encouraged her to resubmit. We went through three rounds of this until a third party made me realize I had gone too far. This third party, a friend of the poet, took it upon himself to write me in order to chastise me. Apparently, my encouraging intransigence had pushed his friend close to, if not past, the brink of despair and certainly to the end of her patience because she had come to feel that whatever she tried in response to my comments never satisfied me. I was torturing her, he said, by always dangling the carrot of publication teasingly just beyond her grasp. I immediately felt remorseful, but I never heard from the poet again, so could not apologize or offer any redress. I had not kept her address on file. This was before email, when we communicated with writers through sometimes handwritten letters and sases—and mercifully before Twitter. God knows what she or her friend might have tweeted about me! After my gaffe, I made the following rules for myself about giving comments:

- Never make suggestions about poems that I don't want to see again or would never publish in revised form.
- A cold shoulder can be the editor's best friend. Providing comments on unpromising work—often motivated by feeling empathy more with the poet's intentions than with their skills, or by feeling pity because their themes are born out of trauma or, worse, heartache—only leads poets on and encourages them to resubmit, which only makes more work for the magazine. Show love to stray kittens and they definitely follow you home, hoping you will take them in unconditionally. Drown them at the outset by saying absolutely nothing.
- Editing is like fly-fishing. It involves shrewd baitings of the hook, arch castings, and deft reelings in. If I did make editorial comments on a poem I was about to return, I already estimated it highly enough to be willing to publish it should it be submitted again. The problems to be addressed must be few because a close-to-publishable poem should not need major rewriting. Comments should be expressed neutrally, be concrete, and practical-sounding

without seeming intrusive or running counter to the poet's intentions. They must appear to elucidate those intentions instead. This approach will make most poets feel that an editor has "read" them and truly "got" them, and they are likely to entertain an editor's "intelligent" ideas about their work—which means the effort to formulate them will not have been wasted, even if the "appreciated" poets don't agree with everything the editor has had to say. I always indicated in my accompanying letter or email that while my ideas might be phrased ineptly, I hoped their inexactitudes pointed to better solutions of the poets' own. I'd let them know that following my advice to the letter was not the sole way to guarantee publication; rather I was more interested in seeing the poem or poems in question made strong enough to see print by whatever means. In my experience, after receiving comments of this nature, poets invariably sent their poems back, having applied most, if not all of my suggestions. Whether this is a measure of my ability or the poets' desire to be published is for book reviewers to decide.

- Always endeavour to remain indifferent to the outcome. The poems that I'd comment on in a rejection letter, or later in an email, were ones I could take or leave. After all, they were being rejected. It was never much of a loss if they were not returned in revised form because poems of whatever calibre always came in faster than could be read. However, if I really liked a poem, one in which I saw real potential, I would make it clear that if it came back *moderately* stronger, even if the changes made were not ones I'd proposed, I would publish the revised version. This was always a very risky commitment to make, and I would only do so concerning poems that were extremely close to final form and that I was very sure of. Such an offer would show that I trusted the poet to know best. I am happy to say that I can think of no instance where being so generous blew up in my face.

Turning to the editing of poetry at the micro level, I found that even the best poets need an editor's aesthetic, if not moral guidance. I have two examples of this that pertain to the same poet I published regularly in the *Malahat*. In the first instance, with regard to a poem articulating a response to a musical composition, I suggested the word "awesome" might not be the most precise descriptor of the moving effect being evoked. Observations like this, if delicately articulated, must always be straightforward and posed as questions like "Are you sure this is how you want to say what you mean in this manner?" Such a change seldom involves much work, either for the editor or the poet, and, as in this instance, is easily made, maybe saving the poet from later embarrassment, if "embarrassment" is the right word.

In the second instance, I was interviewing the poet for the *Malahat* website about a set of poems from an upcoming issue. The questions I asked were complicated, and it became apparent that a small if crucial detail was missing from one poem. My proposed revision was disarmingly simple, neither altering the poem's texture nor impinging upon the poet's voice or authority, and it was accepted with gratitude, if not delight. My point here is that sometimes getting to the nub of what is wrong, especially when the problem does not mar the surface enjoyment of a poem, is very hard and delicate work that requires the editor to read his or her own reactions carefully before sharing the resulting recommendations, equally carefully and clearly, with the poet. The energy involved makes me wonder how many problems of a subtle nature are missed by magazine editors in the rush to get poems into print. I guess I'll cede the adjudication of such subtleties to book publishers.

There do exist poets who continue to tinker with their poems long after they've been submitted. Truthfully, once magazines accept them, often months after they were received, most poems do vary slightly from their submitted versions—for example, an adjective or a line break changes. On occasion, the later versions deviate radically from what was accepted for publication, and not always for the better. It's therefore the editor's task to persuade the authors to return to versions closer to what they'd originally sent. Often the subsequent revisions between submission and acceptance are products of compulsive, anxious, or impatient overwriting, and it doesn't take much inducement to persuade poets that their earlier versions are stronger and can be made better by a supervised transfer of a select few changes that rose to the top of overheated later drafts to what will become the cool tempered steel of published text.

All the surgery an editor performs on a poet's work before or after acceptance must be based not only on a knowledge of the wide variety of bodies—from ectomorph to mesomorph—poems come in, but also on the diets they are fed and the ills afflicting them. It's perhaps best I now explain how I think a poem is written.

After years of writing poetry myself, I have come to recognize that each poem is a wild animal at liberty somewhere in nature, no matter how each poet conceives of nature. I may be sitting at my desk or with my laptop in Starbucks, but in my imagination, I am a zoologist out in the field. I may have insinuated myself up in a tree or hid among the rushes at the slough's edge, but in either case I am behind a blind of my own construction, trying not to be noticed while jotting down careful—dare I say, artful—impressions of the shy creature on the other side. As a poet-zoologist, I apply all my powers of observation, as if I were in the poetry Olympics. I keep adapting how to use my growing array of tools because the creature I am observing keeps changing or belongs to a mistakenly identified species. I am humble, if emboldened, before the enormity of the task I've set myself—which is to catch every verbal twitch the poem makes. It takes patience as well as skill to catch a true likeness, to put into words everything that I've learned through my careful watching; it may take many attempts back behind the blind, however long between visits, to get the poem down right. This patience can involve days, months, or years, with me climbing up into the same tree ever more limberly or arthritically countless times without scaring off the poem in order to see it in all its moods and habits. What's curious is that, however often I am up in the tree or up to my eyes in the slough, the poem is always going about its business. I may change, what I know about poetry may change, but the poem does not change, only my powers of observation and transcription. It's these changing powers that can make the poem seem different from when it was first seen. And these differences are worth noting too, for they are part of the experience of observing it as well. Most importantly, this kind of patience—and discipline—involves something I will call quietude. I am most successful when I am most still. My presence inside the blind must seem ever more tenuous in order to catch the subtlest and most telling qualities of the poem's comportment. It's almost as if I have to find a way to see how the poem would behave without my presence. The poem is the transcript of all modes of observation—thematic, prosodic, musical, and linguistic—whatever filters I drop before the lens of my field camera or call up on my iPhone. I am sure none of this sounds very spontaneous, that the poem will end up being a still life of some sort, but the key to my task as a poet is to instill into my final draft the poem's spontaneity and vitality, through my patient, selfless craft of observation and transcription. This selflessness is perhaps why I think of poetry, even the most personal of poetries, as expression, not self-expression.

So where exactly does the editor come in? The editor must find a way to step inside the blind as well, to look over the poet's shoulder without interrupting to see the poem as it actually is in order to determine if and where the poet's transcription falls a hare's breath—to keep with the animal theme, I've spelled "hair" as "h-a-r-e"—short. How does the editor do this? First, by having read a lot of poetry. In other words, by becoming familiar with the complexity of the poet's task and tools. Secondly, an editor of poetry must be a good reader of their own responses, for it's this self-awareness as a reader that will allow them to be of use to each poet with whom they work. They are up the poet's tree or in a slough not their own, and they therefore must be respectful of how the blind functions while taking note of how it's equipped. It may be reassuring to know that the blind remains in place long after the poet has stepped away from it, so it's there to be stepped into by the editor. It's through stepping inside the poet's blind in order to quietly and unselfconsciously note their own reactions to the poem still cavorting out in the savannah, *as unaware of them as they are of the poet,* that the editor can, to borrow from Faber's Edward Hollis, attend to "an author tuning into their poems" more effectively and most helpfully.

• • •

"Wing On," a poem by Toronto poet Maureen Hynes, appeared in the Spring 2015 issue of *The Malahat Review.* Maureen's and my exchanges by email clearly illustrate the strategies I deploy to help poets imagine their way into "tiny shifts" that may be needed for a potentially final "open" tuning of a poem. Sometimes the subtlest of shifts can make for the most dramatic of effects, for they affirm the poet's ability to capture and embody a poem's liveliness. Such shifts feel intrinsic, in the same way the unanticipated leaps a panther makes from branch to branch feel intrinsic, and they can offer the poet—and the poem—authority.

"Wing On" took about five months to insinuate its way through the *Malahat's* selection process. There were six members on the poetry board at that time and once a submission is flagged for consideration, it is next read by everyone before being discussed at a quarterly board meeting, where poems for upcoming issues are selected from between twenty to forty submissions screened in for final review. I'd arrange the submissions from the least likely to the best bets and, over the course of the meeting, they'd fall like dominos. After one such meeting, I wrote the following to Maureen in early February 2015:

Thank you for your submission of August 31, 2014.

I apologize for taking so long to get back to you about your poems. You submitted just around the time we were making a transition from paper submissions to using Submittable, which visited many logistical challenges upon us. Yours in fact was the last submission received by regular mail to have survived the screening process for discussion at the poetry board meeting last week. It's a distinction of sorts, I suppose! Let's say you are on the cusp.

On that note, I am pleased to say we'd like to accept "Wing On" for publication in our Spring or Summer 2015 issue. It is an exquisitely written poem.

Please confirm that it is still available.

Thanks for your patience. It will be lovely to publish your work once more.

Please note the tone of my email. It's professional, informative, and, I hope, warm. I acknowledge past connections by alluding to Maureen's previous appearances in the *Malahat*. I explain why it had taken the poetry board so long to come to a decision about her work; Submittable did indeed impose a steep learning curve on the *Malahat*. Though I don't say much about the substance of the poem at this point, I do say something—that it is "exquisitely written."
  Over the years I came to realize that when I contacted writers about their work, I should make a point of explaining why I had decided to accept it for publication and, in response, many later told me that I was the one of the few magazine editors in the country to do so—which is thought-provoking, since I may have only said one or two words. Are magazine publishers really so overworked that they have lost the ability to show appreciation? In her reply, Maureen writes the following:

Oh, John, what great news! Thanks so much. It's always a high honour to be published in *The Malahat*. This is just a quick note to let you know that "Wing On" is definitely still available & I will fill out the required form for you and send it within a day or two.

That said, I am in the process of revising lots of poems that will be in my upcoming poetry book from Pedlar and there have been a few revisions to the poem. Can I send you the two versions, the one you got and the new version, and you can decide if you want to publish it just the way you originally got it, or in the revised form. I don't want to burden you with editing too much, but you might prefer the choice between the two.

I compared the two versions. Maureen only partly falls into the category of poet who tinkers with her poem after sending it to the *Malahat*. Because I was now taking possession of one of the oars from Beth Follett—the editor at Pedlar Press—in that leaky rowboat called *Revision*, Maureen was stuck in the prow, answerable to the two of us, conducting a form of poetic, on-board shuttle diplomacy. This is what I said in reply:

> I prefer the version you submitted to us; it's more unruly, but fresher, I think. That said, I have made some comments on the revision, which I attach. What do you think? I hope I haven't made things worse.

In the remarks I made to Maureen about "Wing On," as written at the time of acceptance, I did not say that I felt the dedication to the late James Schuyler, a New York School poet and a contemporary of John Ashbery and Frank O'Hara's, was key to readers' appreciation of the poem. While I can't claim to be wholly conversant with Schuyler's writing, I do know that many of his poems work in an associative, collagist way that eschews the more obvious conventions of rhetoric, with images piling up in a sometimes chaotic syntax. While Maureen's poem doesn't in any way slavishly parallel the construction of a Schuyler poem, it does pay tribute, which is one reason why I was very tied to preserving her question-like opening, which I proposed in my first set of comments:

> You could say something like this:

> What pebbles and beads to hold
> through your secular jazz memorial

> in the Wing On funeral home
> A row of bluets to stain the stone

Wing On

for James Schuyler

What pebbles to place on the poet's tombstone
Jiggle them in our pockets during a secular service

at Wing On, the old Chinese funeral home on Spadina
A row of bluets to stain the stone

Just one greasy lipstick kiss on his granite
in a ruby shade called *Willing*

not smeared all over like Oscar Wilde's marble stone
Set delphinium feathers and Noxzema jars

pill bottles filled with catalogue seeds
a tiny plastic boat to swim out to

It's pink-shirted teenagers day up the street
Honk for Equal Love they wave at truckers and me

Let's flashmob the grotto at Lourdes
Let's fishnet the legs of all the girls

Amaryllis, hyacinth, every shade of rosehip
a *cross-stitched border of spruce and juniper*

Let's scoop a few coins into the busker's cup
And buy the poet a meal

Why don't we take one yellow song, carefree
and refined, put it on a long stem and stand it

in a tall skinny crystal vase? Add a pair
of topsiders to wear on the little boat

VERSION AT TIME OF ACCEPTANCE IN FEBRUARY 2015

Wing On

for James Schuyler

Some pebbles and beads for your grave
to hold all through your jazz memorial

in the Wing On funeral home
A row of bluets to stain the stone

Just one greasy lipstick kiss on granite
in a ruby shade called *Willing*

not smeared like Oscar Wilde's tomb
Delphinium feathers and Noxzema jars

pill bottles filled with catalogue seeds
a plastic toy sailboat for windy days

It's pink-shirted teenagers' day up the street
Honk for Equal Love they wave

Let's flashmob the grotto at Lourdes
Let's fishnet the legs of all the girls

Amaryllis, hyacinth, every shade of rosehip
a *cross-stitched border of spruce and juniper*

Toss a few coins in the busker's cup
And buy the poet a meal

A brand new pair of running shoes
to wear on your little floating boat

Sing a silver song, carefree
and refined, stand it in a tall skinny vase

I like "secular" [which had been used in the submitted version of the poem, but not in the present one] because it changes the nature of the occasion's solemnity. Starting with a question is crucial.

Appreciating that there were reasons why the text had migrated in the direction it did and out of respect for Maureen's craft, I didn't encourage her to return to the slightly longer-lined, more descriptive, and more word-rich—or prolix—submitted version, which began:

> What pebbles to place on the poet's tombstone
> Jiggle them in our pockets during a secular service
>
> at Wing On, the old Chinese funeral home on Spadina
> A row of bluets to stain the stone

I did not want to advocate that Maureen entirely undo the work she may have already undertaken with Beth, so I focused only on those turns of phrase and details that still rang true to my ear. Note in the work sheets that I complimented Maureen on those changes that made the poem work more effectively ("your tomb" rather than "the poet's tombstone") and provided rationales for my suggestions ("I propose keeping marble as a contrast in substance to the pebbles" and "Scoop a few coins into" [rather than "toss a few"] is more original, more visual"). I recommended we "compromise" on how to phrase the closing two couplets, hoping to strike a balance between the submitted and current versions that would preserve elements I preferred in the former while respecting the direction revision had taken her:

> The original ending feels stronger. What about this is as a compromise:
>
> Why don't we add a pair of topsiders
> to wear on your little floating boat. Or take
>
> a yellow song, carefree and refined, put it on
> a long stem and stand it in a tall skinny vase.

I think you need the stem reference, otherwise it's hard to grasp that the song has become a flower or sprig of something. And yellow [to describe a song] is better than silver because it is a floral colour. It also suggests summer or spring. Silver song makes me think of silver bells and Christmas.

Upon receipt of my tinkering, Maureen replied:

Thanks so much, John. Unruly is appealing, I think. Will fiddle around a bit more & get back to you with, I guess, version 4.

If I recall, a weekend intervened, and early in the following week, Maureen sent me version 4, along with the following comments:

John, a thousand thanks for your edits. I now have 6 versions but I think that I will go with the attached, which is closer to the original one that you accepted.

My only regret is losing "secular jazz memorial" or "secular service." I just think the first phrase clunks, with "secular service" slightly better, but I am hoping that "jazz memorial" will give the same message, i.e., slightly undercutting the occasion's solemnity.

I'm really glad you like the "tiny plastic boat" and the topsiders and the original ending, not to mention the original beginning – I agree with you about the energy that starting with a question gives the poem.

Let me know if you still have concerns. Though I triple-checked, I may have gotten mixed up going back & forth between all the (unruly) versions.

Looking at Maureen's preferred revision, you will see that she observed the spirit of my edit without doggedly accepting every suggestion. She instead pushed the poem to positive effect, which was all I could really have hoped for, especially at its opening. Further, she made the two critical changes I had urged

FIRST SET OF COMMENTS

Wing On

for James Schuyler

Some pebbles and beads for your grave
to hold all through your jazz memorial

in the Wing On funeral home
A row of bluets to stain the stone

Just one greasy lipstick kiss on granite
in a ruby shade called *Willing*

not smeared like Oscar Wilde's marble tomb
Delphinium feathers and Noxzema jars

pill bottles filled with catalogue seeds
a plastic toy sailboat for windy days

It's pink-shirted teenagers' day up the street
Honk for Equal Love they wave

Let's flashmob the grotto at Lourdes
Let's fishnet the legs of all the girls

Amaryllis, hyacinth, every shade of rosehip
a cross-stitched border of spruce and juniper

Toss a few coins in the busker's cup
And buy the poet a meal

A brand new pair of running shoes
to wear on your little floating boat

Sing a silver song, carefree
and refined, stand it in a tall skinny vase

"What pebbles to place..." is better. Immediately we understand the narrator is struggling to comprehend and put this death into perspective.

You could say something like this:

What pebbles and beads to hold
through your secular jazz memorial

in the Wing On funeral home
A row of bluets to stain the stone

I like "secular" because it changes the nature of the occasion's solemnity

Starting with a question is crucial to the energy of this poem.

Much better than "the poet's"

I propose keeping marble as a contrast in substance to the pebbles.

"tiny plastic sailboat" says "toy" so I prefer what you had before.

You have "days" in the line before. "a tiny plastic sailboat to swim out to" Is a more interesting line.

"Scoop a few coins into" is more original, more visual.

The original ending feels stronger. What about this is as a compromise:

Why don't we add a pair of topsiders
to wear on your little floating boat. Or take

A yellow song, carefree and refined, put it on a long stem and stand it in a tall skinny vase.

I think you need the stem reference, otherwise, it's hard to grasp that the song has become a flower or sprig of something. And yellow is better than silver because it is a floral colour. It also suggests summer or spring. Silver song makes me think of silver bells and Christmas.

FIRST REVISION

Wing On

for James Schuyler

What pebbles to place on your tomb
hold all through your jazz memorial

in the Wing On funeral home
A row of bluets to stain the stone

Just one greasy lipstick kiss on your granite
in a ruby shade called *Willing*

not smeared like Oscar Wilde's marble tomb
Set delphinium feathers and Noxzema jars

pill bottles filled with catalogue seeds
a tiny plastic boat to swim out to

It's pink-shirted teenagers' day up the street
Honk for Equal Love they wave

Let's flashmob the grotto at Lourdes
Let's fishnet the legs of all the girls

Amaryllis, hyacinth, every shade of rosehip
a *cross-stitched border of spruce and juniper*

Let's scoop a few coins into the busker's cup
And buy the poet a meal

Why don't we take a yellow song, carefree
and refined, put it on a long stem and stand it

in a skinny crystal vase? Add a pair
of topsiders to wear on the little boat

her to incorporate into the closing two couplets—"yellow" rather than "silver" and the retention of " a long stem"—yet she reordered the details gathered in them in a way that had appeared in none of the previous drafts:

> Why don't we take a yellow song, carefree
> and refined, put it on a long stem and stand it
>
> in a skinny crystal vase? Add a pair
> of topsiders to wear on the little boat

I remember being entirely delighted and replied:

> This poem is now reading really well. I have two more sugges-
> tions for you (one involves "secular"!).

I purposely restricted myself to introducing only two additional changes, rather than challenging more details of less importance to me, choosing to avoid being unnecessarily intrusive. The first of my comments pertained to the line "Let's scoop a few coins into a busker's cup":

> For some reason, "let's" undercuts its use two couplets up ["Let's
> flashmob the grotto at Lourdes / Let's fishnet the legs of all the
> girls"]. It makes the line feel mechanical. Why not try something
> like this:
>
> A few coins scooped into the busker's cup
> to the poet a meal.

It amuses me now to note that "secular," emphasized in my accompanying email with an exclamation, carried forward through almost all of Maureen's and my exchange. I had attempted to reinsert it in my initial edit—"secular jazz me-morial" rather than the "secular service" of the originally submitted version, with the rationale that its presence undercut the "solemnity" of the occasion—but, as Maureen admitted in her remarks accompanying this latest draft, she could not, "with regret," find a place for it. I attempted one final time to shoehorn it in before "Wing On," in the third line, making it read as "in the secular Wing On funeral home." Its retention was not to be, as is seen in Maureen's response:

SECOND SET OF COMMENTS

Wing On

for James Schuyler

What pebbles to place on your tomb
hold all through your jazz memorial

in the secular Wing On funeral home
A row of bluets to stain the stone

> Here's a place where you could stick this word?

Just one greasy lipstick kiss on your granite
in a ruby shade called *Willing*

not smeared like Oscar Wilde's marble tomb
Set delphinium feathers and Noxzema jars

pill bottles filled with catalogue seeds
a tiny plastic boat to swim out to

It's pink-shirted teenagers' day up the street
Honk for Equal Love they wave

Let's flashmob the grotto at Lourdes
Let's fishnet the legs of all the girls

> For some reason, "let's" undercuts its use two couplets up. Makes the line feel mechanical. Why not try something like this:
>
> A few coins scooped into the busker's cup to the poet a meal

Amaryllis, hyacinth, every shade of rosehip
a *cross-stitched border of spruce and juniper*

Let's scoop a few coins into the busker's cup
And buy the poet a meal

Why don't we take a yellow song, carefree
and refined, put it on a long stem and stand it

in a skinny crystal vase? Add a pair
of topsiders to wear on the little boat

I really, really wish I could put "secular" in this poem, but I don't think it works in front of "Wing On," which was an old Chinese funeral home, no longer in existence. I don't think it was secular. I think you are absolutely right about the third use of "Let's," but I don't want to switch to the passive voice, so I am just leaving it as "Scoop a few coins…" and I think the reader can mentally carry the "Let's" over the intervening couplet to the new stanza. Hope so anyway.

Reflecting upon "secular" now, I wonder if Maureen had been humouring me from the start and never had any intention of re-introducing the word into her poem! Poets and editors alike keep their cards close to their chests, even when things are going well. We had one more exchange because she had one last concern:

One final teensy question: I am really tempted to take the apostrophe away from "teenagers'" because I think of "pink-shirted teenagers" [in the line "It's pink-shirted teenagers' day up the street"] as an adjectival phrase rather than a possessive one but… do you think it's egregiously ungrammatical without the apostrophe?

This was my take—

I think you should leave the apostrophe on "teenagers'"; it makes them flesh and blood, rather than a descriptor for a kind of day akin to "a summer day."

—And I then added,

No problem about "secular"; I was only suggesting placing it before Wing On as a way to keep it in. The poem reads beautifully without and no one will think anything's missing.

When the version of "Wing On" that Maureen and I agreed on saw print in *The Malahat Review*'s Spring 2015 issue, I was still satisfied that she had addressed all of my key concerns, if not exactly in the ways that I had proposed.

FINAL DRAFT, PUBLISHIED IN *THE MALAHAT REVIEW*, SPRING 2015

Wing On

for James Schuyler

What pebbles to place on your tomb
hold all through your jazz memorial

in the Wing On funeral home
A row of bluets to stain the stone

Just one greasy lipstick kiss on your granite
in a ruby shade called *Willing*

not smeared like Oscar Wilde's marble tomb
Set delphinium feathers and Noxzema jars

pill bottles filled with catalogue seeds
a tiny plastic boat to swim out to

It's pink-shirted teenagers' day up the street
Honk for Equal Love they wave

Let's flashmob the grotto at Lourdes
Let's fishnet the legs of all the girls

Amaryllis, hyacinth, every shade of rosehip
a *cross-stitched border of spruce and juniper*

Scoop a few coins into the busker's cup
And buy the poet a meal

Why don't we take a yellow song, carefree
and refined, put it on a long stem and stand it

in a skinny crystal vase? Add a pair
of topsiders to wear on the little boat

Now is the time to lay the last of my cards on the table: I often make my suggestions look and sound awkward in order to not to appear too hands-on while signaling the direction in which I feel the poet should go. I don't really care if I come across as having two left iambic feet as long as I get the results I want. And if I make a few misspellings in my comments, it allows me to present myself as someone less than omnipotent: John as Gomer not as Yahweh. I firmly believe it is the author who has most at stake with publication, not the magazine editor. For the latter, the edited poem, after it's seen print, is wiped from short-term memory by the countless poems by other poets to come, each with its unique challenges to parse. The poet must be able to live with the poem as it appears in print—the equivalent of blood—because it will carry forward, as is, into the future—until another opportunity for textual change presents itself and further refinements ease—or force—themselves into the light.

I have only recently read the version of "Wing On" in *The Poison Colour*, Maureen's fourth book of poems, which Pedlar published in the autumn of 2015. It turns out that the *Malahat* rendering of the poem survived intact with only one further subtle improvement. That tiny shift, finessed either by Maureen or Beth, pertains to the tokens left in tribute on James Schuyler's grave in the eighth line of the poem: "Place delphinium feathers and Noxzema jars" instead of "Set...." The more ambiguous "Set" in the *Malahat* version is open to misinterpretation, for as well as "set down," it can mean "fix" or "fix in place," or worse "harden," in the way concrete slowly sets. Behind "place" is the hand, or many hands, that over time had left the plant fronds and jars in private and anonymous recognition of the poet's importance; and "place" better evokes the reverence with which such gestures are made.

I would not have been surprised or alarmed, however, if my comparison of the *Malahat* and Pedlar iterations of "Wing On" had revealed evidence of greater editorial change or ended up being radically different from each other. After all, Beth could have come up with better edits than mine after climbing stealthily up inside her author's blind. Even the poem's placement in the book could have led to more significant differences between our two versions. How many uses of the word "yellow," for instance, can readers tolerate in short succession before they see red?

It shouldn't matter if multiple versions of the same poem exist in the public record. The probing and attentive reader may well end up studying them side by side, ideally in the order of their creation, and enjoy pondering what the author's decision process was in the course of the poem's evolution, migrating from manuscript to magazine to book. In every instance, the reader is offered a fresh opportunity to climb up into the blind and look over the poet's shoulder as, with or without the input of an editor, she notes down the poem's unique, changeable, and *unruly* behaviour.

2015/2018

Stepping Back: Listening to Indigenous Perspectives

"art for life's sake"

—attributed to Cherokee-Appalachian poet Marilou Awiakta
by Daniel Heath Justice

ONE AFTERNOON, IN JANUARY 2017, Kromar delivered "Indigenous Perspectives," *The Malahat Review*'s share of the print run arriving at its University of Victoria office by truck from Winnipeg. The aroma of ink, like the smell of fresh bread, wafted up the instant I slit the tape sealing the top box to pull out a copy. The cover—a detail from Coast Salish/Okanagan artist Lawrence Paul Yuxweluptun's *Christy Clark and the Kinder Morgan Go-Go Girls*—winked up at me. B.C.'s now former premier, recognizable in navy-blue-pantsuit drag, is depicted wearing an Indigenous mask; a snake-like tongue slips from between her rouged lips. The only detail missing from her power-suit ensemble was a strand of government-issue pearls. She met my eye, as if to dissuade me from going any further. "Too late, Christy." I cracked that baby open; in my hands spread a year's worth of deep listening, shared insight, and editorial trust, not to mention the courage of the writers inside. This issue-length, Indigenous-curated survey of contemporary Indigenous writing literally had weight and felt excitingly new.

The inspiration to publish "Indigenous Perspectives," which was guest-edited by WSÁNEĆ poet Philip Kevin Paul, Tlicho Dene novelist Richard Van Camp, and Michi Saagiig Nishnaabeg scholar, writer, and artist Leeanne Betasamosake Simpson, can be traced back to a letter that the British Columbia Arts Council sent to the *Malahat* and other grant applicants eighteen months earlier, in July 2015. After confirming that the Council had renewed the magazine's operating grant for another year, its executive director, Gillian Wood, "strongly encourage[d]" us to address a systemic lack of aboriginal content and engagement within this sectoral group [in plain-speak, the province's literary-magazine community?]. Future applications must address the client's efforts and strategies in these areas with regard to programming, editorial board, staffing and volunteer composition. Members noted that active recruitment of persons with aboriginal expertise is urgently required."[1]

The message was clear. If the *Malahat* didn't pull up its socks concerning not only Indigenous content but also Indigenous involvement, it could anticipate the Council being less beneficent or even downright cold-hearted in future years. I also knew the Council was right. I was well aware that the *Malahat* had published little Indigenous writing before and after I became editor in January 2004. In such a nationally prominent journal whose name the founding editors had appropriated without leave from the Malahat First Nation almost fifty years before, an appropriation that needed addressing as well[2], such a deficit was shameful.

In the early 1990s, when I was *Arc*'s co-editor, its entirely settler board had considered devoting an issue to Indigenous poetry, but the cultural-appropriation debate ensuing at the time intimidated us as much as it had inspired us. Because we knew almost nothing about Indigenous writing and didn't want to be accused of cultural insensitivity, the idea was shelved. That timidity and a lingering sense of a lost opportunity followed me to the *Malahat*. But fifteen years later, in response to the B.C. Art Council's letter, how to rise to its challenge and transform a scarcity into a surfeit? Solicitation had always been an obvious answer, but it had never been my habit to invite writers to submit their work, preferring instead to pursue an open-door policy. This must stem from my belief

---

1   Letter of July 24, 2015, to John Barton, Editor, *The Malahat Review*, from Gillian Wood, Executive Director, British Columbia Arts Council. *Malahat* file for the 2015/16 BCAC Aid to Periodicals grant application.

2   I wrote a letter to the Malahat First Nation in 2016 to open a conversation about how best to address the University of Victoria's use of its name in the magazine's title. UVic's Office of Indigenous Affairs warned me that I may not receive a response, which turned out to be the case. The appropriation of its name by a small-circulation literary magazine, the Office said, might be a low priority. Nor would such an appropriation be anything new. Everywhere you turn in Victoria, you encounter a business with "Malahat" shoehorned into its name.

that all writers should have an equal chance of being published, even though, as a queer writer, I know it's not true. I simply wanted it to be true for myself and for others, so made it the perhaps-too-discreetly advertised hallmark of my editorship. Professing that Indigenous authors should feel as welcome as any to submit their work to the *Malahat* was unsatisfactory because too few of them did so. Though I'd read new work by Indigenous writers in other magazines and would have loved to have featured some of it in the *Malahat*, I didn't want any Indigenous writer to believe the return of work we'd asked to see was motivated by anything more complicated than issues of craft. A policy of not soliciting protected me from being bruised by bruised feelings, especially in situations where the decision not to publish could be misinterpreted as an expression of prejudice.

You'd think after thirty years of editing, I'd have had a thicker skin. The *Malahat* suffered from many similar deficiencies in content that the overwhelming flow of unsolicited submissions papered over. Where were the writers of colour, the new Canadians who wrote in neither English nor French, and the writers who experimented more audaciously than the majority of the magazine's decorously talcumed authors were wont? What about queer writers? I never wanted to be accused of unfairly advancing the careers of writers from my own community. Looking back, I see that I'd confused advocacy with favouritism. As reconciliation took hold in Canada, the lack of an abiding Indigenous presence in the *Malahat* became more and more noticeable.

But how to change the *Malahat*'s editorial direction without walking off a cliff? Anxious in the past about putting my foot down wrong, I felt as unschooled and extemporizing as Wily Coyote. Any misstep I might make before the overhang underneath disintegrated could justify the doubts Indigenous writers may have held about working with an editor like me, someone who'd grown up in Calgary during the 1960s, when nothing meaningful was taught about their cultures in the city's publicly funded schools. My education from kindergarten onwards had patently not prepared me for challenges like this.

On the Gestetnered map Mrs. Wilson had handed out in Grade 3, I'd only been asked to plot the routes European explorers had drawn across an empty, not emptied-out, continent. I may have learned about the fur trade, but I learned nothing about the assimilationist agenda of the Indian Act and the residential schools. Annual pilgrimages to the Calgary Stampede may have furnished my family with our only opportunity to meet people from the nearby First Nations, but we'd make a quick, silent tour of the "Indian Village" before moving on to the Big Four building, where local businesses parted us from our money for questionable consumer products. The Glenbow Museum collected and displayed Indigenous artifacts from across North America, and one summer I was enrolled in a week-long day camp on how to make moccasins. As a small child I remember climbing the stairs leading up to the Horseman's Hall of Fame on the second floor of the Calgary Brewery Aquarium. The Hall's dioramas commemorated Indigenous/rancher relations, including the signing of Treaty 7, through which I now know Crowfoot and other chiefs ceded 130,000 square kilometres of Blackfoot territory to Canada in exchange for 2.59 km^2 of land for each family of five. Brown and white mannequins populated each display; the Siksika war bonnets and scarlet Northwest Mounted Police uniforms that they wore were what caught my attention. Meanwhile, sharks hundreds of miles from the ocean circled in a claustrophobic tank on the floor below.

The aquarium and the Hall of Fame closed in 1972, when I was fifteen years old and the latter's reconstructions of history turned hazier and hazier in my memory. All through my childhood, on family excursions to Banff, an hour's drive west on Highway 1, we'd traverse the Stoney Nakoda First Nation's land, which to me looked no different from the Crown lands surrounding it. Sometimes we took the old 1A highway fifteen minutes farther north instead, and pulled in at the McDougall Memorial United Church near Morley, by then an unstaffed historic site, but never stopped anywhere else before we left "Indian land." I don't recall if there were gas stations, restaurants, or other places to stop, though the reserve was inhabited. The people who lived there were thus there and not there. This may best define the relationship mid-twentieth-century settler society meant for me to have with Indigenous people. I wasn't told to think ill of them, I just wasn't encouraged to know them.

As I grew older, I began to follow the news reports of First Nations' Canada-wide struggles for the guardianship of their traditional lands. By disposition, I was inclined to take the underdog's side; today I would view it as the side of the oppressed. In 1977, the Berger Inquiry quashed pipeline development along the Mackenzie River; in June 1990, Oji-Cree MLA Elijah Harper stood up in the Manitoba legislature to deal the necessary fatal blow to the Meech Lake Accord[3]; less than a month later, the Mohawks at Kanehsatà:ke

---

3   The Meech Lake Accord, led by the federal government and negotiated by the ten
     provinces, attempted to make Quebec a signatory to the repatriated Constitution of 1982.
     Elijah Harper delayed the ratification vote in the Manitoba legislature long enough that the

staged a seventy-eight-day-long blockade of lands they considered sacred, onto which the town of Oka, Quebec, had wanted to expand its golf course. By then, I was living and working upriver in Ottawa as a federal-government librarian at the National Aviation Museum and volunteering my spare time to co-edit *Arc*. Only when Indigenous writers began the previously mentioned public conversation with settler writers about cultural appropriation did the seed about the need to change get firmly planted. In my case, the seed lay dormant for a long time before flowering.

I have a family connection to a key moment in history. J. A. V. Preston, one of my maternal great-grandfathers, volunteered for the Northwest Expeditionary Force that came from Ontario in 1885 to suppress what I was taught in high school to call the Northwest Rebellion, but later learned to call the Resistance. Commanding a sentry unit upriver from Batoche, my great-grandfather describes in his diary hearing gunfire echo down the bluffs of the South Saskatchewan River:

Monday, 11th May.

For three days we have been able to hear the guns at Batoche, about forty miles below us. The sound seems to follow the river banks. From couriers who pass occasionally we learn that our forces are attacking the rebel position at Batoche, but until now with little success. And tonight, Captain Bonnycastle in command of our two Companies received orders from the General to move forward at once and join the main body.[4]

I knew about my great-grandfather's involvement in the detention of Louis Riel from an early age and, in the spring of 1990, on a trip to Saskatchewan two months before the standoff at Kanehsatà:ke, my boyfriend and I followed his movements as best we could by car; he'd travelled by train, paddle wheeler, and on foot. I had wanted to get into his moment. When I was the writer-in-residence at the Saskatoon Public Library, I returned to Batoche one cold autumn day in 2008 and, standing on the steps of its restored church, I listened to a

---

June 23, 1990 deadline passed before all ten provinces and the federal government could approve the Accord.

4   "The Diary of Lieut. J. A. V. Preston, 1885," *Saskatchewan History*, 8(3), 1955, 100.

Métis interpreter recount how he'd only that year managed to track down descendants of one branch of his family, which had scattered far and wide in the aftermath of the battle. Like nothing else, his story made actual the loss he and Indigenous people like him had sustained for generations. I'd entered and, in some sense, have never left the interpreter's moment. At age fifty-one, I was hearing about the experience of an Indigenous person firsthand for the very first time. Because of my great-grandfather's involvement, I felt implicated. I continue to feel so.

Many non-Indigenous Canadians whose families originate in the British Isles, France, and the homelands of other colonizing powers fail to see a causal connection between ourselves and the present-day descendants of the peoples our ancestors displaced from their lands on a continent we now both consider home. The family bibles, yellowed land-grant titles, and bits of lace we ignore or take to Goodwill often came down to us unaccompanied by the stories of our ancestors' arrival in North America. I feel fortunate that my great-grandfather kept a diary, even though many entries are upsetting:

Sunday, 31st May.

Received news last night that General Strange had had a brush with Big Bear, and that our aid was required to hunt the redskin. Our Brigade accordingly boarded steamers early in the morning and are now on our way west to try conclusions with Big Bear. We hope to clean him out in quick order. Should we go into action (and we at any moment), I feel sure we will all be found at the post of duty to the last.[5]

It's conceivable the scattering of the Métis interpreter's family is tied to the actions of my own ancestor. However terrible it is to contemplate, many of us must own up to the blood ties we have with the forces that caused Indigenous people before and since Batoche to run for their lives.

Every direction I look in my past, I can find blood-soaked footprints. Because a paternal ancestor was a high-ranking British officer at the Battle of the Plains of Abraham outside Quebec City in September 1759, he played a role in negotiating the surrender of Montcalm's forces. I used to joke with

5   Ibid, 102.

my francophone boyfriends that if they truly wanted someone to blame for the Québeçois not being *maîtres chez nous*, they'd need only look to me. It's both satisfying and humbling to admit that my family tree of farmers, lawyers, university academics, and generals is now, like Sir John A. MacDonald, on the wrong side of history. How shocked they'd all be. For my Indigenous friends, I fear this turning of the tables of psychological advantage may only be a pyrrhic victory. Despite the concern for their welfare many non-Indigenous Canadians now feel, the powerful among us, who seem always to be crying the crocodile tears of contrition, still control the spoils. After slipping on the glove that the B.C. Arts Council had thrown down when it challenged grant recipients to make space for Indigenous people in everything we do, I began dwelling on the intergenerational trauma that my ancestors had caused them.

In late January 2016," Ktunaxa writer Troy Sebastian emailed the *Malahat* to thank us for including work by Tuscarora writer Alicia Elliott and Cree writer Jesse Rae Archibald-Barber in our Winter 2015 issue on creative nonfiction and for featuring the work of Suquamish/Duwamish artist Jeffery Veregge on its cover. Troy encouraged us to publish more of the same in future issues. Over coffee a few days later, I told him of my plan to devote the Winter 2016 issue to Indigenous writing and asked him for advice. It would be one of many excellent conversations we'd have. I recall him politely implying that Indigenous writers found Joseph Boyden to be a safe writer for non-Indigenous readers to like. And I did like Boyden's novels. I offered in exchange that I hoped my experience of being a queer writer gave me sympathy for, if not a full understanding of, how Indigenous writers approached the challenge of being heard and read. .

What was the plan I shared with Troy?

It was simple. I would meet the British Columbia Arts Council's expectations to the letter.

I knew asking the magazine's non-Indigenous editorial board to devote more pages to Indigenous writing, either by spreading these pages across the four annual issues or by collecting them into a single "special" issue, would only partly satisfy the Council's desire for change. Instead, I decided to transfer the editorial responsibility for the Winter 2016 issue to Indigenous writers. With input from the University of Victoria's Office of Indigenous Affairs, I chose as the issue's title the straightforward "Indigenous Perspectives" and crafted the following preamble to open the call for submissions the magazine posted on its website and advertised as widely as possible:

The Malahat Review invites writers who identify as Indigenous to submit their unpublished work to an issue on contemporary Indigenous writing in Canada.

To be published in December 2016, "Indigenous Perspectives" will celebrate the aesthetics, concerns, contributions, and achievements of Indigenous authors living in or from "Canada," recognizing their crucial role in providing a truly complete picture of what it is like to be alive in North America in the past, future, and especially today.

Submissions are welcome from all First Nations, Métis, and Inuit writers. Recognizing that the current international boundaries imposed on the continent are not necessarily compatible with Indigenous peoples' own sense of place, we invite "non-Canadian" Indigenous writers with close connections to Indigenous communities within "Canada" to submit their work or to query in advance.

I next approached Kevin, Richard, and Leanne to see if they would respectively be interested in editing the submissions of poetry, short fiction, and creative nonfiction that 133 Indigenous writers would ultimately send in for their consideration. All three of them instantly agreed to be guest editors—all within a day of my having contacted them, one within minutes. After requesting they review and, if necessary amend, the submission guidelines, I gave them the passwords to the email accounts I'd set up for each genre, advised them of approximately how many pages they each needed to fill, and provided them with a production timeline. Except for one request for editorial input, I did not hear from any of the guest editors until they had all chosen which writers they wanted to publish. Normally, I would have watched the content for an issue amass over several months and even lose sense of what had been accepted for publication through the combination of haste, distraction, and over-familiarity. Instead, I read what Kevin, Richard, and Leanne had spent months choosing over one week—and was knocked flat. To this day, I remain moved, amused, bemused, horrified, and impressed by the pathos evinced by the poems, short stories, and works of creative nonfiction that would shortly appear in the magazine. What the authors wrote was clearly heartfelt, and my heart clearly felt.

Now began the phase of the issue's development that for me became the most transformative. After Kevin, Richard, and Leanne had finished finetuning their contributions substantively, I worked with the authors to prepare their texts for publication. With the poets, this sometimes amounted to no more than confirming that the electronic files they'd originally submitted were still the most current. More often the exchanges were fuller. As best I could, I aimed to make the contributors' experience of publishing in the *Malahat* wholly positive, one where they'd feel their perspectives and approaches to their subject matter were respected by offering them exactly the same non-intrusive but honest editorial guidance I would tender to the contributors to any issue. For these contributors, I may have done so even more assiduously. Many authors had juxtaposed their experience of colonialism with resurgence, expressing indignation beside joy, grief next to wonder, and pain alongside strength. I hoped the contributors would perceive my editorial process as respectful, even concerning comma use and em-dashes. My role was to explain or suspend house style, and, as a careful and engaged reader, to be a useful set of eyes. I endeavoured to offer text-focused comments that elucidated, not clouded what they had to say. Never did I want them to feel I was blunting their messages to protect the easily bruised scruples of the magazine's mostly settler readership.

Preparing text for publication often inspires an unusual, if transitory, form of closeness between editor and author, one forged, surprisingly enough, through Track Changes in Word. The beauty of this function allows an editor to make or propose changes without expunging the author's original phraseology, in turn enabling the author in a few keystrokes to return their text to its original form or to accept a proposed change. I did my best never to edit hastily or to make assumptions. If I didn't understand a passage or a reference, I posed open-ended questions in comment fields that would, I trusted, create opportunities for authors to improve, to arrive at a deeper engagement with their own visions for the readers' benefit. I hoped they'd feel that the final, agreed-upon text was even more emphatically theirs than it was prior to submitting it to Kevin, Richard, or Leanne for consideration. The exchanges that revision occasions typically become warmer. Those with the contributors to "Indigenous Perspectives" often attained a rarely achieved level of candour, as if I were being more completely seen as well. At times, I felt so stirred, it was overwhelming.

Exchanges with two contributors stay with me. The first was with the last author to confirm his work's availability. He told me he'd hesitated to reply to my emailed acceptance because he wasn't sure if his work was truly Indigenous.

He feared his parentage—Mom was white, Dad was First Nations—and growing up middle-class made his candidacy dubious. Extolling the virtues of his piece, I assured him it belonged in "Indigenous Perspectives" because one of the guest editors had felt strongly enough to select it. I also told him he was not the sole contributor with a background similar to his. In fact, I had been struck by how precisely some contributors spelled out theirs to honour the bloodlines that made them who they are. He was in good company, I assured him. Cherokee writer, scholar and UBC professor Daniel Heath Justice acknowledges in *Why Indigenous Literatures Matter* that

> the specifics of identity are complex and contestable in nearly every [Indigenous] community as a result of diminishing resources and the intrusion of settler ethnicity logics...but Indigenous peoples continue to affirm the responsibilities, relationships, and rights that have connected us to our lands and one another since well before the arrival of Europeans and other peoples to our homelands.[6]

The same criteria that had determined the rest of the issue's contents had been applied to this young writer's work. It was not my place to confirm his fears, but to make him feel welcome. My exchange with the second contributor led me to a real understanding of what "Indigenous Perspectives" could mean to the *Malahat*'s readers. In her review of *In This Together, Fifteen Stories of Truth & Reconciliation*, Rachel Yacaaʔał George, an Ahousaht of the Nuu-chah-nulth First Nation and a PhD candidate in the University of Victoria's Indigenous Governance program, takes this anthology's mostly non-Indigenous contributors to task for not truly grasping what reconciliation is about. She chides them for their "silence on self-determination, and on the importance of our lands."[7] As I understood her review, George felt the anthology's authors each evinced a settler preponderance for wanting to find and hold an "appropriate" position on the injustices our society had visited upon Indigenous people in order to add weight to their claim to moral rectitude without giving

---

6 Daniel Heath Justice. *Why Indigenous Literatures Matter.* Waterloo: Wilfrid Laurier University Press, 2018, 7–8.

7 Rachel Yacaaʔał George, [Review of *In This Together, Fifteen Stories of Truth & Reconciliation*] *The Malahat Review* 197, Winter 2016, 155.

anything substantive up. A tangible expression of reparation, George explains, involves not only the ceding of high-moral ground, but also the actual return of land and authority over its bounty, and the agency to care for and protect its sacred sites.

For me, the penny dropped. For the first time, I understood what my role as the editor of *The Malahat Review* was when it came to this issue. I'd long compared the magazine's pages to real estate; as in a game of Monopoly, aspiring writers aimed to tender winning bids, whether through the rickety edifice of a thirty-line poem or the sprawl of a many-roomed, 10,000-word-long short story. To make what I hope won't come across as a trivializing metaphor of George's just, eye-opening criticisms, I immediately realized that each page of "Indigenous Perspectives" could be construed as land, as psychic territory from which settler worldviews had been withdrawn, there to be filled by Indigenous points of view. Land seen as Indigenous writers see it, readers given the chance to glimpse it as they do.

Philip Kevin Paul, in his introduction to the poetry he chose for "Indigenous Perspectives," recounts how, having weeded out "the overwhelming, but unpublishable, didactic verses and rants[….] the anger's still in me too":

> Even at this point in my development as a poet, I find myself having to resist the temptation of just "putting it out there." I've struggled for years with a poem tentatively titled "Waterfront Mansion." This started after visiting the house and garden my girlfriend tends in North Saanich. As the day progressed, I grew increasingly angry. No Saanich person, here in our own territory, could afford such a house in such a location. If we were to land on the beach, where we used to harvest crabs and sea cucumbers, we'd likely be treated with suspicion, even hostility.[8]

I'll never forget the first time I read this passage in manuscript while preparing to send "Indigenous Perspectives" to the *Malahat*'s designer for layout. Kevin's words cut through me as deeply and unexpectedly as the Métis interpreter's words had when I'd visited Batoche eight years before. One moment, I am lightly copy-editing Kevin's prefatory remarks; the next I am standing shoulder to shoulder with him on the lawns of this house overlooking the

---

8   Philip Kevin Paul, "A Quiet Matter," *The Malahat Review* 197, Winter 2016, 3.

Saanich Inlet, a finger of the Salish Sea that jabs into the ribs of an island now named after Captain George Vancouver. I had never experienced the kind of displacement Kevin describes, even vicariously, until this moment. Nor had I considered how frequent this experience must be in the daily lives of the WSÁNEĆ people and other Indigenous peoples in Canada and around the world. The more I listen to and consider stories like Kevin's, of which there are many in "Indigenous Perspectives," the less abstract colonialism becomes. As Ojibway author Drew Hayden Taylor says, "the issues that people in a dominant culture might consider social issues, were everyday."[9] The awful normalcy of what Kevin describes entered my body and I re-experience it each time it comes to mind with sudden, increasing understanding. If I had literally stood beside him on that lawn and he had shared his thoughts aloud, I would have wanted to put my arm around him while together we looked across the Inlet in silence. Nothing in my own life has ever been equivalent. But I can keep listening, aware that what Indigenous people feel and recount in stories like Kevin's is constant, especially when life brings them face to face with the truths a complicit, colonizing culture still imposes. Nor are such stories the whole of their everyday, as "Indigenous Perspectives" amply illustrates. Its poems, stories, and essays are as suffused with grief as they are abundant with joy.

Like ink, that joy seems to have permeated the paper stock upon which "Indigenous Perspectives" is printed. The evening after Kromar delivered it to the *Malahat* office, Leanne Betasamosake Simpson read at Open Space, an artist-run centre in downtown Victoria. The week before, the gallery had kindly invited me to join Leanne and their staff for the dinner beforehand. She was consequently one of the first people to hold a finished copy of the issue in her hands. I'll never forget watching her turn to the table of contents and browse the names of so many writers whose work she said she already knew. For me, on the other hand, the issue had been the skeleton key to a new world. I'd had the privilege of meeting writers on the page whom no earlier opportunity had brought to my attention.

Over the months Leanne, Kevin, Richard, and the contributors worked on "Indigenous Perspectives," I'd not once taken into consideration the impact stepping back from the editorial process would have on me. Rising to the challenge the B.C. Arts Council had set now seemed a secondary accomplishment in comparison to what I was learning. Daniel Heath Justice points out:

9   "Writing Wrongs: A Panel Discussion," *Write*, 45(1), 2017, 37.

while Indigenous writers have confronted that oppressive context [imposed by settlers] and created a richly expansive literary tradition that engages with colonialism, these traditions are
in no way determined by colonialism. Indigenous texts are by
and large responsive, not reactive. They are at least as concerned
with developing or articulating relationships with, among, and
between Indigenous readers as they are with communicating
our humanity to colonial society, if not more so.[10]

When I think back, this is what watching Leanne browse "Indigenous Perspectives" brought home to me in an instant. All through the issue's compilation, I'd
never lost sight of the possibility that the Indigenous readers would appreciate
the contents differently than I would and that this difference was appropriate
and crucial. It never mattered to me whether or not I would be made privy to
the conversations that the issue might inspire them to have. The guest editors
and contributors made me feel that the issue was truly consequential and this
in itself was both enough and humbling.

Within two weeks of "Indigenous Perspectives" seeing the light of day,
Troy Sebastian came by the office to pick up contributor copies with Mohawk/
Tuscarora poet Janet Rogers, a past City of Victoria Poet Laureate and the
now-former host of *Native Waves Radio*, a weekly show that aired on CFUV,
UVic's student-run station. Two years before, in March 2015, Janet had spoken
on a *Malahat* panel called "Has It Got Better: Minor Voices or Major Talents,"
which took place on the last afternoon of WordsThaw, the magazine's s annual
writers' festival. Also invited to present their perspectives on the panel were
Hanna Leavitt, a writer with vision challenges from Victoria, and Daniel Zom-
parelli, a Vancouver-based gay-male writer and editor. Aaron Devor, now the
University of Victoria's founding Chair of Transgender Studies, moderated.
The idea for the panel had emerged from conversations I'd had with another
queer writer about the frustrations we'd faced when our queer-themed poems
weren't read properly, if read at all. In arranging the panel, we'd decided to include non-queer writers who may or may not have experienced similar challenges and hoped that through a mix of perspectives commonalities might emerge
alongside differences, with audience members obtaining a deeper appreciation
of the different terrains Janet, Daniel, and Hanna inhabit as writers.

---

10 Justice, xix.

Janet spoke first and made it unambiguously clear she found the panel's major/minor premise to be inappropriate. As an Indigenous writer, she was not going to play ball by engaging with a topic mired in faulty assumptions and expressed surprise she had been invited to participate. She said, as a writer, she didn't feel marginal or subordinate to anyone. By placing her on a panel with this particular lens in a festival featuring only one other writer of colour, the *Malahat* was de facto stigmatizing them both. Janet's response dumbfounded me, for casting any sort of aspersion had never been our intention. In retrospect, I can understand why she had construed our intentions, as we'd framed them, the way she did. However, while I listened to her opening remarks, which she expanded further during the discussion Aaron led between the panelists and with the audience, I remember thinking she was answering in full the question the *Malahat* had hoped she'd address: labels like "minor" or "major" were trivializing and should never be used; to do so is a slur, even if not deliberate, and the *Malahat*'s decision to hold this panel illustrated that "it" had not "gotten any better," at least not on that March day in Victoria. I now wish I had contacted Janet after WordsThaw to discuss the panel's failings and apologize for any misunderstandings caused. A missed opening. Who knows what fruitful conversation might have resulted? Her remarks nevertheless deepened my resolve to do better. "Indigenous Perspectives" offered me a chance to make another attempt.

When I handed Janet a copy of the issue that afternoon in January 2017, she dumbfounded me yet again. Watching her hug it to herself, I thought she would rise to the ceiling and even pass through it. She appeared more than ecstatic, expressing her delight with an exuberance I can still hardly account for. What a difference an issue makes. Seldom have I witnessed such a spontaneous expression of joy from anyone, let alone a contributor. Troy, she, and I were joined in the awareness that we were part of something of true importance. Each of us proudly holding a copy, we posed for a picture I look at regularly and will always treasure.

Two months later, in March, the *Malahat* staged the fifth-annual edition of WordsThaw, with "Indigenous Perspectives" as its focus. To guarantee we'd have a sufficient number of copies on hand, I ordered a reprint, even though the initial press run had been considerably longer than the number of copies I would ordinarily request. Never in my thirty years as a literary-magazine editor had an issue been as popular; never before had I needed to go back to press. The Office of Indigenous Affairs purchased copies for its elders and staff; online orders came in daily. WordsThaw coincided with the announcement of a new UVic certificate program in Indigenous Nationhood, and the organizers of the celebration marking its creation graciously adjusted their schedule, inviting the *Malahat* to host on two consecutive nights a lecture by Richard Van Camp and a literary showcase of Indigenous and non-Indigenous readers in the Great Hall of the First Peoples House, the social, cultural, and academic home for Indigenous students at the university. All three guest editors participated in the reading, which attracted one of the *Malahat's* largest audiences. Leanne, who presented last, thanked me for "handing over the keys" to the three of them and the Indigenous literary community. In reply, I explained that I only had ever held them in trust. By handing them over, I realized in the months ahead, I had hoped to affirm the magazine had always been and would always be a safe place for Indigenous writers and for any writer who had not previously felt welcome. Broadening the creative base of *The Malahat Review* had long been my greatest aspiration and challenge.

Change is the word that best explains the importance of "Indigenous Perspectives." In "Construction of the Imaginary Indian," Tsimshian-Haida scholar Marcia Crosby criticizes settler culture for holding onto stereotypes of Indigenous peoples, perceiving them to be either without history or inheritors of a great tradition in danger of rapidly dying out, as Emily Carr had feared when she travelled B.C.'s northwest coast to paint what she perceived to be abandoned villages and totem poles. Crosby admonishes artist Bill Reid[11] for perpetuating this cliché, when, in 1957, he narrated a CBC documentary, *The Silent Ones*, about an expedition to the then-called Queen Charlotte Islands to "repatriate" totem poles for UBC's Museum of Anthropology, thereby "support[ing] the illusion of a people who have come to an end, rather than a people who are changing."[12] In other words, a people who live in the present, whatever and whenever that present is, and who possess the agency to transform and be transformed by it, and to have a role in determining what transformation is. The assumption, Crosby argues, that the Indigenous peoples are soon to be no more

---

11   Bill Reid (1920–1986) was of mixed heritage: his father was an American of Scottish-German descent and his mother was from the Kaadaas gaah Kiiguwaay, Raven/Wolf Clan of T'anuu, more commonly known as the Haida. Through the power of his work as a carver and jewellery maker, he is credited for helping to make Indigenous art of the Northwest Coast nationally and internationally known.

12   Marcia Crosby, "The Construction of the Imaginary Indian," *Vancouver Anthology*, Stan Douglas, ed. Vancouver: Talonbooks, 1991, 292.

explains and justifies the removal of the poles to a provincial institution…that the poles…exist…in a forest by themselves, connected to a geographical location rather than a people; it is an idea that lends itself to the smooth transference of our land and heritage to public institutions, corporations, private enterprise and individuals.[13]

The same can be said, sadly and ashamedly, about the appropriation of story. How and why "Indigenous Perspectives" came into being was an attempt to step past a legacy of displacement and to give its contributors the space to share their stories as they experienced them in the present of 2016. To the best of my ability, the settler-run *Malahat* was as uninvolved as possible in the definition, nurture, and transformation of that space.

Space is both temporal and digital, factors determining the degree to which readers may enter it. Siku Allooloo, an Inuit/Haitian Taino writer who had contributed a marvellous piece on the grief the Inuit feel in response to the decline of the caribou, suggested the *Malahat* post the issue's contents online to make it available to Indigenous readers either living in remote regions or unable to afford a copy. I saw the logic and justice of Siku's proposal. We contacted all the contributors to obtain their permission.

It was in the wording of the *Malahat*'s request that I made what I hope was my only significant misstep in bringing "Indigenous Perspectives" into print. I'd indicated that if any contributor did not respond within a set period of time, their permission would be assumed. Troy Sebastian quickly pointed out my error. Assumptions of automatic permission, he reminded me, were all too familiar to Indigenous peoples in the routine violation of their rights. What I'd considered to be a minor efficiency lay at the heart of the experience of being colonized. I was so grateful Troy had called me on my thoughtlessness. I immediately emailed an apology to the contributors and the *Malahat* began posting poems and stories only as they gave permission. Only a handful did not want their work made available online. Some gave reasons, though no justification was necessary or ever sought.

Space, of course, is emotional and intimate. In an exchange by email after her essay, "A Mind Spread Out on the Ground," had been nominated for a 2016 National Magazine Award she later won, Alicia Elliott told me having

---

13   Ibid.

"Indigenous Perspectives" guest-edited by Indigenous writers had made all the difference: "I never worried that I needed to censor myself or explain why certain cultural elements were necessary for the piece. I really think you can feel that love and comfort permeate the entire issue."[14] The creation of an editorial space at one remove from, if not to the exclusion of, colonialism's legacy, may not have motivated my decision to ask Leanne, Richard, and Kevin to be guest editors but, in hindsight, it's a consequence that entirely makes sense. Had I been the editor offering suggestions of a substantive nature, I'm sure the published result would have been appreciably, if subtly, different. Editing creates a space where authors can test their truths on editors prior to sharing them with readers. Trust is the indispensable prerequisite. Editing creates a lasting bond that becomes part of the words.

Alicia, in "On Being and Being Seen: Writing with Empathy," from the Spring 2017 issue of *Write*, describes the conditions under which it might be possible to write believably about experiences outside one's own: "To truly write from another experience in an authentic way, you need more than empathy. You need to write with love."[15] The same rule applies to the responsibilities of an editor. I have always felt my role is not to question the substance of any author's experience, whether they claim it as their own in a work of nonfiction or translate it into the imaginative realm of fiction or poetry. Nor is it up to me to challenge the authority with which they speak. Rather, my duty is to assist them in making the bones of their substance more visible while giving them flesh by nurturing the leanest, most stylistically becoming writing possible. It's not my job to pare away the viscera that I don't follow but, instead to patiently pose questions and make suggestions so that what was not clear can, with time and effort, transform into something readers feel in their own guts. I have always tried to give authors the courage to present the particularities of their points of view, however awe-inspiring, amusing, or disturbing they may be. If I've gone to the trouble of selecting a poem or story for publication, I have already begun to fall in love with it. Careful editing with the author lets me to get know the work more deeply and to fall in love more completely. With "Indigenous Perspectives," the *Malahat*'s editorial boards and I invited Richard, Kevin, and Leanne to fall in love on our behalf and on behalf of the *Malahat*'s readers.

---

14   Email of April 21, 2017, from Alicia Elliott to John Barton. Quoted with permission.
15   Alicia Elliott, "On Seeing and Being Seen: Writing with Empathy," *Write* 45(1) 2017, 23.

Love is what I feel to this day. Never could I have guessed, before the issue's publication, how great its many lessons would be, the virtue of "absenting myself" being the most significant. By stepping back, I was treated to the most transformative editorial experience of my career as a literary-magazine editor. I marvel still. I gained so much more than I would have expected by giving up what most would consider to be the best part of an editor's job: the exercise of taste. It's as if I'd suddenly understood I was a magician. With a wave of my red pen, I edited myself out. When it became time for me to return to the stage, it wasn't so I could pull another rabbit from my hat, but to hold a printed issue in my hands. Instead of being on stage alone, I was surrounded by the voices of contributors whose work I might have already known had I listened more attentively in the past.

Of course, the publication of "Indigenous Perspectives" was never that simple, though it may have felt to me as if it were. While I was off in the wings, the guest editors shouldered the work that healing is, the kind of healing only they should do. What Daniel Heath Justice asserts so eloquently in *Why Indigenous Literatures Matter* I hope also applies to the months of combined labour that led to "Indigenous Perspectives": that for the editors, contributors, and readers, it "fundamentally... affirm[s] Indigenous presence."[16] Billy-Rae Belcourt, Darrel J. McLeod, and Joshua Whitehead each later received a nomination for a 2018 Governor General's Literary Award for poetry, nonfiction, and fiction respectively. Though their contributions to the issue appeared in their nominated books, it was exhilarating when Darrel's memoir, *Mamaskatch: A Cree Coming of Age*, won the nonfiction award.

It will take me years to understand why ceding editorial control was so revelatory, but I have come up with some provisional answers. First, as I've said earlier, I knew that creating space in the *Malahat* for Indigenous writing curated by Indigenous writers, as an initial gesture of reconciliation, felt right. Second, I became a reader of my own journal. The work in "Indigenous Perspective" reads as alive, multifaceted, and *changing* (to echo Marcia Crosby); in response, I felt more alive, and changed. The contributors amazed me many times over with how they and other Indigenous peoples had found the resilience to express, sustain, and rise above what history had so unjustly served them. They spurred me to ask new questions of myself. I felt the weight of their pain as I was lifted up by their bliss.

---

16 Justice, xix,

Third, the issue inspired me to take the measure of my own family history. In the afterword to "Indigenous Perspectives," I said:

> If today's Indigenous peoples carry the burden of what their ancestors suffered in face of more than half a millennium of colonial displacement, I'm willing to assume responsibility for what [my ancestors] imposed. Awareness of their actions sits on my shoulders. Along with supporting the redress of historic injustices, I'm certain of one step to take: engaged empathy.[17]

While the society my ancestors helped create did cause Indigenous peoples suffering that must be atoned for in moral and material ways, Alicia Elliot urges us not to turn redress into another form of objectification. "Look at us as we are now and feel your pupils go wide, taking in what we've survived and what we've accomplished."[18] In the same spirit that Alicia asserts we should write with love—"If you can't do that, then why are you writing about us at all?"—it is my firm belief we must edit with love. Love involves many qualities, here it must include creating conditions for trust, curiosity, and attentiveness. Its expression must acknowledge our part in the perpetuation of some of this country's most bitter truths. It sometimes involves walking off the stage and returning only when invited.

As a Canadian writer and editor whose origins trace back to present-day Northern Ireland, the English Midlands, Norfolk, and the Nordic countries, whose ancestors played a key role in the colonial, Dominion, and federal government's displacement of Indigenous peoples from their lands, "Indigenous Perspectives" has caused me to see Canada very differently from what I had esteemed it to be since grade school and had celebrated at Expo 67 when I was ten years old. I am glad of the long-overdue reality check. I look forward to a time when how Indigenous peoples see, live in, and love the land has absolutely transformed our national dialogue into a conversation among nations. Such a deep spiritual change will allow for a far better country, one as inclusive as what we continue to purport our current state to be. I don't feel in any way diminished by what I have come to understand as my culpability. Everything I have learned helps me come to terms with it. Through my exchanges with the

---

17 John Barton, "Long Overdue," *The Malahat Review* 197, Winter 2016, 160.
18 Elliott, ibid.

guest editors, the contributors and the readers and presenters at WordsThaw, I discovered that I live in a country much *bigger* than the one I occupied before. It manifests a history offering more possibilities and traditions than I'd ever known it to possess, a history not only about conquest, that starts earlier and still includes my own, however less firmly established its thread. That it's taken most of my life to arrive at this fuller awareness saddens me, but I'm more than affirmed by the rootedness I feel. Taking ownership has permitted me to start a healing process of my own. As a long-time visitor on the unceded lands of the Lukwungen-speaking peoples and of the Songhees, Esquimalt, and W̱SÁNEĆ peoples, I am honoured to be able to sit at my desk on a warm autumn day two blocks from the ocean and articulate something of the experience of being on and off stage as "Indigenous Perspectives" took shape, honoured to recognize that the first inhabitants' historic relationship with these lands shall continue into the future and, with their blessing, to believe that our shared love for this place will sustain it.

2019

Vulnerability, Embarrassment, and the Final Draft

HOW DO POETS EVER know when poems are finished?

Some revise obsessively, continuing to annotate the typeset versions long after they have appeared in books. Others seldom change a word or line break, the published poems barely departing from the first drafts. Are revisers forever preoccupied with apprehending in words the flux that their poems continue to drown-proof in, no matter how far they may drift from where they surfaced and took a first breath?

Do non-revisers believe poems to be only as authentic as their original inspiration? Do revisers believe in perfectibility while their alter egos see perfection residing exclusively in the spontaneous capture of gesture? Do the former not trust their readers while the latter enjoy their unquestioned faith?

I am on the side of the revisers, I have to admit, however envious I may sometimes be of extemporaneous poets who write a poem in a single sitting. My first attempts are incoherent agony, but afterwards I sit obsessed at my computer recasting prosody, shifting line breaks, exploring the nuances of initially image-perfect, now suspect metaphors. Poems may take me months, years, decades to finish. I rescue them from the welter of words I keyboard into memory.

But, unlike many, I seldom consult or even save earlier drafts and instead move forward with the poem, unrepentantly indifferent, even ignorant and amnesiac, to its past as it evolves from incarnation to incarnation, never looking back. I don't believe in false steps or mistakes. My favourite commands are "Cut" and "Delete." I love "Backspace," "Block," and "Insert."

And thank god for "Save."

．　．　．

Robert Creeley, as quoted by Charles Olson in his 1950 essay, "Projective Verse," famously said "Form is never more than the extension of content." Later, in 1964, Denise Levertov in an essay called "An Admonition," revised this to "Form is never more than the revelation of content."

It is revelation I am after.

As a gay poet.

As a writer.

I want to know what the poem is really about, what fires it. I need to find out. For me, not every possibility a poem may hold can be disclosed in a single draft or in a single read. Even reading is a kind of revision. Who steps into the same poem twice? Even the most simple of poems is visceral; it has depths to be repeatedly plumbed by reader and writer alike.

However, as I zero in on the final draft, I find I pull away, tamp my ardour for the poem, and begin to consider how it might be understood and experienced by its readers.

I never expect a sympathetic reading, though up to this point I have only written in order to be heard and understood. I finetune the poem's optics, street-proofing it for what I know to be a cruel, sadly negligent world. I begin to write more defensively, find myself attempting to balance honesty with plausibility. I have discovered this balance hinges exclusively on the compromise to be struck between embarrassment and vulnerability.

. . .

The poet is always the first reader of his own work. He—and, in my case, the poet is "male" but what I am about to say may apply, if anyone wishes, to poets of whatever gender, orientation, race, quirk, or chosen subjectivity—must learn to separate himself from the experience of the poem (though I often think "he" in syntactical ploys like this one is general, generic, neuter, gay—the lacuna where the subversive is possible) and read it from outside. He must train himself to be ruthless, to be sensitive to every social and aesthetic nuance and valence of language. He must be paranoid and alert to the bathetic. He must also endeavour to preserve his innocence.

Embarrassment has everything to do with technique, with how well language is deployed; vulnerability is tied entirely to what the poem is about, to what language expresses.

I write against embarrassment and cultivate vulnerability.

Form must never imperil content—except on purpose.

I aim to write myself free of the poorly executed, but I resist the avoidance of any discomfort I might feel about the poem's subject experience that might otherwise inhibit my deeper expression of it. I ignore anyone looking over my shoulder. I know I am getting somewhere, wherever somewhere may be, when I feel exposed by what I am revealing. Not exposed personally—vulnerability is not a trope for confession or for confessional poetry—but by the specifics the poem enunciates, renders into being.

Outs.

Makes known.

Poetry is emphatically a mimetic aesthetic experience that transcribes not reality but a sensibility. The challenge any writer faces involves distinguishing oxbows of language from the backwaters of theme.

The avoidance of one over the other is never a rapid capitulation towards the decorous.

To be decorous is to fail.

I am not a laureate hired to write apostrophe.

• • •

Creeley and Levertov may not have anticipated an aesthetics of embarrassment and vulnerability when they coined what would become signature directives to later poets who, like me, have baroquely layered on their own gilt and feathers.

• • •

Would Frank O'Hara, more than forty years after his death, despair of the twenty-first century? In "Personism: A Manifesto," he said, "The recent propagandists for technique on the one hand, and for content on the other, had better watch out." If he could, would he look me up and down, shrug his shoulders while leaving the Museum of Modern Art after his brilliant day of getting it so right about Jackson Pollock, assume everyone is watching, and think me a charlatan?

Talk about public shame!

Earlier in "Personism," which he wrote in September 1959, two-and-half years after I was born, he said: "Pain always produces logic, which is very bad for you."

Don't ask me to write essays; it hurts.

• • •

(Maybe only Canadian poets feel embarrassed and vulnerable.)

· · ·

Olson's typewriter sits on the curb of history, waiting to be recycled.

A computer sits in its place on my desk. How intrinsically it captures the ways in which the imagination moves forwards to satiation—despite (and because of) every random turn, any subtle shift, each unexpected aside—so intuitively rendering itself in language.

Words registered in ever increasing memory by keystrokes—or erased.

Vulnerability registered, embarrassment erased.

With intimations of finality.

By touch-typing.

By fingertips.

· · ·

What flirts!

Perhaps Creeley and Levertov saw their aphorisms as invocations to be spontaneous, to be like lovers in tune with language's sensuality and intellectual pulse. Form and content seductively leading one another on, endeavouring, hoping to be as one.

Interchangeably.

Not to exhort us to painstaking revision.

Not to tip the pornographic, for example, towards the erotic.

Or perhaps I indulge in conjecture.

Remember that I said I was ignorant.

Remember that I say true revision by (my) definition is intuitive and results in poems that appear effortless. Poems that look as if they could be written in no other way, that could take shape through no other combination of words. All final drafts thus become first drafts, so assured are they that they stand as intense approximations of the immediate.

· · ·

Form and content are not indifferent to each other.

• • •

They mutually affirm.

• • •

Technique is never less than the articulation of what makes us vulnerable.

• • •

What makes us human.

2006

WORKS CITED

Denise Levertov. *The Poet in the World*. New York: New Directions, 1973.

Frank O'Hara. *The Selected Poems of Frank O'Hara*, Donald Allen, ed. New York: Vintage, 1974.

Charles, Olson. *Projective Verse*. New York: Totem Press, 1959.

Endings: On Closure

I SUPPOSE I DON'T have any single way to end poems, though I believe that they must be tied off in some way.

By this, I don't mean that an ending should pull all the meandering threads in a poem together by looping them into a unifying knot. Rather, an ending should incite readers to reflect upon what they have just read, even to the point that they might feel inspired to reread the poem in order to more closely shadow the way it had lured them toward the last line. The ending should come as a revelation, though I don't begin writing any poem by looking to get anywhere.

Or if I do, I resist being obliged to arrive.

Instead, I want to be surprised.

I believe readers will be surprised if I am surprised.

I let each poem unfold according to its own inner map (the map of my subconscious, for lack of any other template), allowing myself to engage with that unfolding, consciously adding pleats as form and content crescendo, so that all unfoldings ahead are spread by cascading details until, at last, by poem's end, its fan—and the scene painted upon it—is partially (or fully) disclosed.

My aim is to acknowledge the ending only when I come upon it, much as hikers do when they arrive at a hot springs they did not know they were climbing toward. I want the ending to be unexpected but satisfying. And by satisfying, I don't mean affirming or redemptive, but illuminating.

Even if darkly so.

2009

Acknowledgements

MOST ESSAYS IN THIS book were written in response to invitations. Several reappear here in radically different form. Thanks are due to the magazines that gave me cause to write the following: *Arc* ("Aspiration, Devotion and Community: A Short Introduction to the Long Life of a Little Magazine," "Diana Brebner: Snow Angel," "Fluid Epiphanies: Margaret Avison's 'The Swimmer's Moment,'" "Getting on the Island: Literary Contests as Reality TV on The Aquarium Channel™," "Inside the Blind: On Editing Poetry," "Men of Honour: Prototypes of the Heroic in the Poetry of Douglas LePan," and "The Message Inside: *Time Capsule*: Pat Lowther's Legacy"); *Books in Canada* ("Where Have All the Poets Gone?"); *Hamilton Arts & Letters* ("'It Will Be Me': Stayin' Alive, AIDS as Part of Life, and Life Writing" and "The Pain Closet: Outtakes from a Phantom Diary"); *Influency Salon* ("Time at a Standstill: Ruth Roach Pierson, Ekphrasis, and the Museum of Memories"); *Plenitude* ("We Are Not Avatars: How the Universal Disembodies Us"); *poetics.ca* ("Vulnerability, Embarrassment, and the Final Draft"); *Prairie Fire* ("Angels and Pilgrims"); and *Queen's Quarterly* ("Conditions Attached to the Driving of Motor Vehicles by the Holder of a Provisional Licence").

I delivered "Poetics of Orienting: Some Remarks on Sexual Disorientations" during "Sexual Disorientations," at the League of Canadian Poets' 1997 annual general meeting and it was collected into the panel proceedings. The introduction to *Seminal: Canada's Gay Male Poets*, an anthology I coedited with Billeh Nickerson, was published by Arsenal Pulp Press in 2007. "Adding Nothing to the Flow: Greening the Pregnant Man" appeared in *Nobody's Father: Life Without Kids*, coedited by Lynne Van Luven and Bruce Gillespie and published by TouchWood Editions in 2008. "We Are Not Avatars: How the Universal Disembodies Us" was delivered as a lecture at the Sage Hill Writing Experience in May 2009. "Time at a Standstill: Ruth Roach Pierson, Ekphrasis, and the Museum of Memories" was presented in June 2010 during Influency, a course that Margaret Christakos taught for the University of Toronto School of Continuing Education. At the invitation of NL Editors, I delivered "Inside the Blind:

On Editing Poetry" as a talk at Memorial University of Newfoundland in November 2015; thanks are due to Maureen Hynes for allowing the manuscript and published versions of her poem, "Wing On," to appear alongside my discussion of them and to quote from our email exchange prior to the poem's publication in *The Malahat Review*. "My Emily Carr" expands the 1987 and 1999 afterwords to the first and second editions of *West of Darkness: Emily Carr, A Self-Portrait* and combines them with "An Expansive Sense of Place: Emily Carr's Victoria," which appeared in the Spring 2006 issue of *Vernissage: The Magazine of the National Gallery of Canada*. I also combined "The Word Alberta: Here/There, the Poetics of Elsewhere" with "Queer Rose Country" to create an expanded version of the latter; the original texts appeared in the program and were presented at "de:scribing Albertas," a conference hosted by the University of Alberta in September 1996. "The Word Alberta: Here/There, the Poetics of Elsewhere" appeared in the Summer 1998 issue of *Open Letter*. "Visible But Not Seen: Queer Expression in the Age of Equity" was published in 2018 as an Anstruther Press chapbook in its Manifesto Series; an excerpt was published online by *The Walrus* in October 2018.

Thanks are due to friends and colleagues who supported me in the composition of these essays: Rita Donovan, David Eso, Robert Finley, Eric Folsom, Alisa Gordaneer, Neile Graham, R. W. Grey, James Gurley, Helen Humphreys, Chris Johnson, Ben Ladouceur, Brian Lam, Samantha MacFarlane, rob mclennan, Blaine Marchand, Kyeren Regehr, Philip Robert, Jan Ross, Andrea Routley, Doug Schmidt, Carmine Starnino, Andris Taskans, Janice Williamson, and Jan Zwicky. In particular, Siku Allooloo, Yvonne Blomer, Alicia Elliott, Jim Johnstone, Anita Lahey, Philip Kevin Paul, Janet Rogers, and Lynne Van Luven provided me with invaluable feedback.

I would especially like to thank Shane Neilson, who encouraged me to write many of these essays. Without his interest, this book would not have been published; his months of challenging, perceptive comment helped me hone it into the whole it was meant to become. Thanks also to Aimee Parent Dunn, Shaun Dunn, and Abigail Roelens at Palimpsest Press for their support, to Ginger Pharand for her careful copy editing, to Carleton Wilson for his design, and Derk Wynand for the pass of his shrewd eye over the proofs.

The epigrams are drawn from: "Pain" by Phyllis Webb, from *Selected Poems: 1954–1965* (Vancouver: Talonbooks, 1971); Leonard Cohen, *Beautiful Losers* (Toronto: McClelland & Stewart, 1966); "Song of the Answerer" by Walt Whitman from *The Complete Poems* (Markham: Penguin, 1975); "Avalanche" by Leonard Cohen, from *Stranger Music: Selected Poems and Songs* (Toronto: McClelland & Stewart, 1993), and Daniel Heath Justice, *Why Indigenous Literatures Matter* (Waterloo: Wilfrid Laurier, 2018).

"Visible But Not Seen: Queer Expression in the Age of Equity" is dedicated to Neile Graham and James Gurley; "'It Will Be Me': Stayin' Alive, AIDS as Part of Life, and Life Writing," to the memory of Scott Wilson; "My Emily Carr," to the memory of my mother, Nancy Barton; "The Pain Closet: Outtakes from a Phantom Diary," to the memory of my sister, Pam Barton; and "Aspiration, Devotion, and Community: A Short Introduction to the Long Life of a Little Magazine," to Rita Donovan.

About the Author

JOHN BARTON'S ELEVEN BOOKS of poetry and nine chapbooks include *For the Boy with the Eyes of the Virgin: Selected Poems*, *Polari*, and *Windsock*. His critical works include *Seminal: The Anthology of Canada's Gay-Male Poets* and *The Essential Douglas LePan*. Between 1989 and 2018, he edited *Arc Poetry Magazine*, *Vernissage: The Magazine of the National Gallery of Canada*, and *The Malahat Review*. He lives in Victoria, where he is the city's fifth poet laureate.

PHOTO CREDIT: JOHN PRESTON